U.S.D.A. Zones of Plant Hardiness

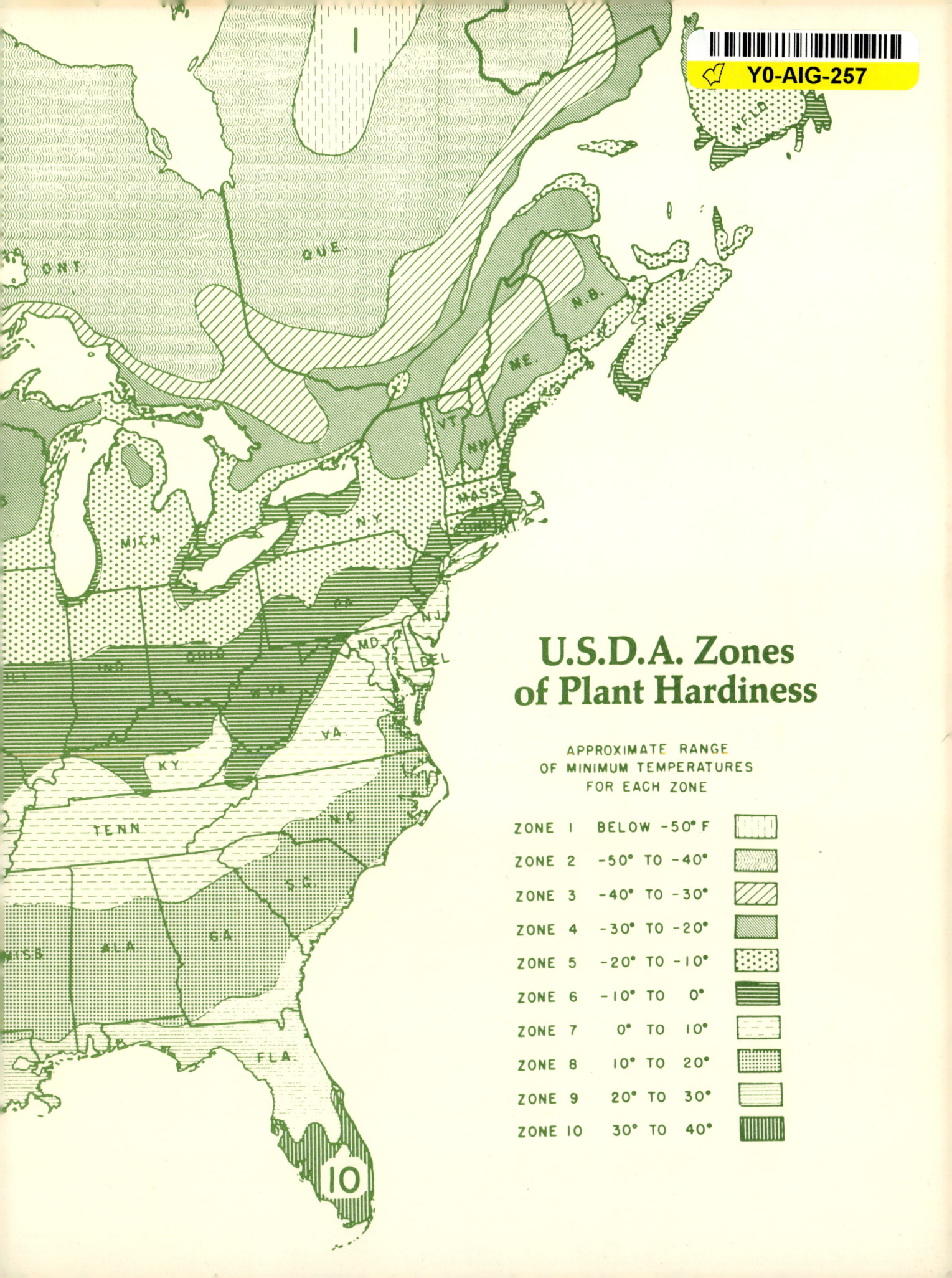

APPROXIMATE RANGE
OF MINIMUM TEMPERATURES
FOR EACH ZONE

ZONE 1	BELOW −50° F	
ZONE 2	−50° TO −40°	
ZONE 3	−40° TO −30°	
ZONE 4	−30° TO −20°	
ZONE 5	−20° TO −10°	
ZONE 6	−10° TO 0°	
ZONE 7	0° TO 10°	
ZONE 8	10° TO 20°	
ZONE 9	20° TO 30°	
ZONE 10	30° TO 40°	

The Good Housekeeping Illustrated Encyclopedia of Gardening

in sixteen volumes

Volume Three
blue vitriol to cambium

Ralph Bailey
EDITOR-IN-CHIEF

Elvin McDonald
EXECUTIVE EDITOR

Compiled under the auspices
of the Editors of Good Housekeeping

© MCMLXXII, The Hearst Corporation

BOOK DIVISION, HEARST MAGAZINES, NEW YORK

blue vitriol. See copper sulfate.

Blue wood aster. See *Aster cordifolius*.

Blunt-leaved plantain-lily. See *Hosta decorata*.

Blushwort. See AESCHYNANTHUS.

Bocconia. See *Macleaya cordata*.

BOEA (*boh*-ee-uh). Gesneriad Family (*Gesneriaceae*). Of the 15 species known in eastern Asia, the Malay peninsula and Borneo, only one is commonly grown. **B. hygroscopica** (hy-gro-*scope*-ih-kuh) resembles a small African violet (*Saintpaulia*) and needs similar care, except less fertilizer. It has clusters of pale blue flowers held above quilted leaves.

BOENNINGHAUSENIA (ben-ning-how-*seen*-ee-uh). Rue Family (*Rutaceae*). Pungent perennial herbs from the Mediterranean region and the Middle East. Propagate by seeds in a greenhouse or frame in spring.
B. albiflora (al-bif-*floh*-ruh). Known also as Ruta albiflora, this species grows to about 2 ft., and has dense clusters of small white nodding flowers in July and Aug.

Bog-asphodel. See NARTHECIUM.

Bogbean. See *Menyanthes trifoliata*.

bog garden. As a horticultural term, a bog garden lies somewhere between a wild-flower garden and a water garden. The soil is constantly moist or wet but does not necessarily have standing or running water. If there is such a spot naturally located in the garden it will provide a home for some lovely and unusual plantings without too much effort.

The first step is to clear away plants that are unwanted. Before weeds are cleared wholesale, however, it is worthwhile to wait through a twelve-month period to see what the "weeds" in the area are: some may turn out to be highly desirable native plants that flower or color, or add texture to the overall look at some point in the season. Also worthwhile is a study of the existing growth with a wild-flower guide in hand.

OPPOSITE: Tulips, daffodils, forget-me-nots, golden doronicum naturalized in a meadow display breathtaking spring color. Bulbs are among the easiest and most rewarding of all plants to grow. A comprehensive discussion of spring-, summer-, and fall-flowering bulbs begins on page 410.

When undesirables have been removed, add bushels of leafmold or other humus, preferably on the acid side, to pockets where plantings will be installed, and fork into the existing muck or soil. If the garden is large, steppingstones to give easy and dry access to planting areas should be placed: each may require an anchor stone beneath to keep it from sinking to ground level or beneath. A liberal addition of sand or gravel will help raise steppingstones in wetter spots.

The preferred site for a bog garden will have a small stream or spring to provide year-round water supply. Since water usually runs through any bog area to lower ground, it may be possible, and certainly would be desirable, to clear a pocket on the spill side and line it with stones or light-colored gravel to create a small naturalistic pool.

It is possible to create a bog garden in a dry area, but the maintenance demands will be extreme. The gardener will have to supply running water all year round and must arrange for an overflow pipe covering with a coarse screen to keep debris from blocking it. The in-between situation, where an area is boggy for part of the spring and fall, and dry the rest of the year, offers greater possibilities with fewer maintenance demands as the soil will be better suited to the requirements of plants that naturally occur in bogs. In such a situation, a small supply of water piped into the bog garden during the dry weather will be enough to maintain conditions suitable for the plantings.

The bright marsh-marigold, *Caltha palustris*, is one of the plants suited to culture in the bog garden. It is a native of North America where it grows wild in marshes and bogs. Double varieties are offered by some nurseries.

BOG GARDEN

The best plants for the bog garden are native plants whose habitats are wet areas. They require moist, rich, acid soil, so add lots of humus as the area is worked, and if necessary after a soil test, increase acidity with the addition of powdered sulfur. Among the better flowering plants for the bog garden are any of the calopogons, which are small orchids found in bogs; marsh-marigolds (*Caltha palustris*), fringed orchids (*Habenaria*), swamp pinks (*Helonias*), cardinal flowers (*Lobelia cardinalis*), all of which tolerate shade; yellow flag (*Iris pseudacorus*), Grass-of-Parnassus (*Parnassia*), bog-rose (*Pogonia ophioglossoides*). Bog plants grown for their foliage include giant reed (*Arundo donax*) and California pitcher-plant (*Darlingtonia*) (not hardy).

In the Plant Finder section of Volume 16 are complete lists of flowering and foliage plants suitable for the bog garden, including ferns that tolerate or grow best in damp ground.

Bog-myrtle. See *Myrica gale;* also known as sweet-gale.

Bog pimpernel. See *Anagallis tenella.*

Bog-rosemary. See *Andromeda polifolia.*

Bog violet. See PINGUICULA.

Yellow *Ligularia clivorum*, rose-red primroses, ferns and variegated hostas are featured in this bog surrounding a water-lily pool, where exotic blooms open all summer. Azaleas and rhododendrons color the background.

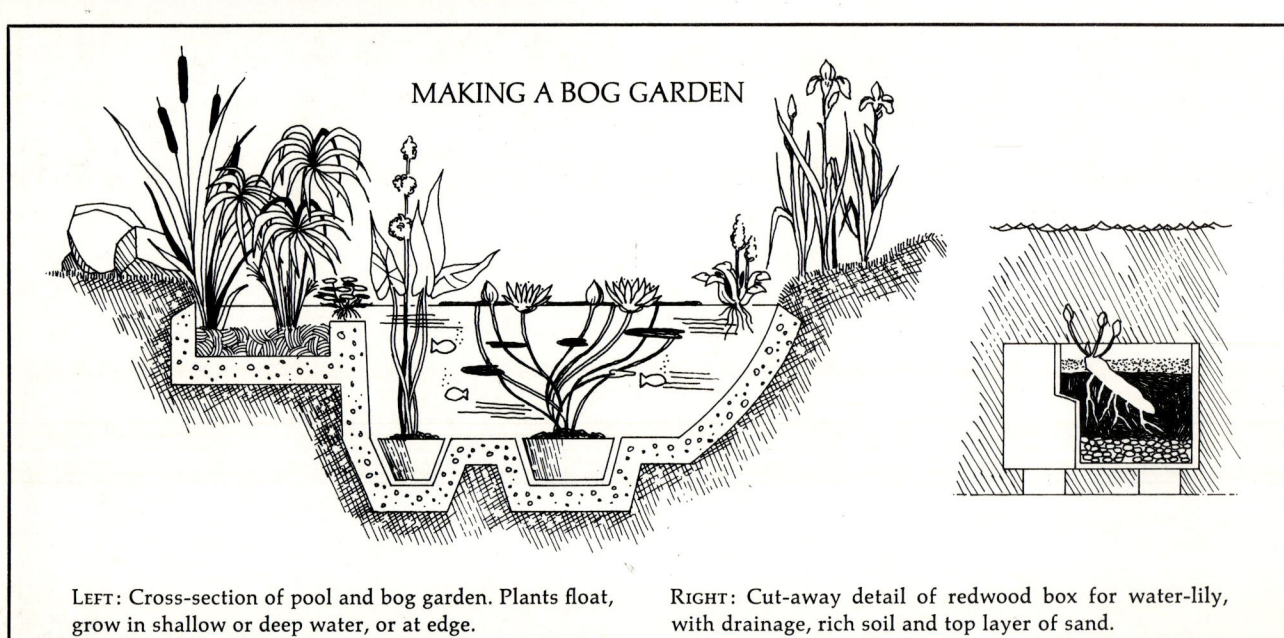

MAKING A BOG GARDEN

LEFT: Cross-section of pool and bog garden. Plants float, grow in shallow or deep water, or at edge.

RIGHT: Cut-away detail of redwood box for water-lily, with drainage, rich soil and top layer of sand.

Bokhara iris. See *Iris bucharica*.

bole. The stem or trunk of a tree.

bolt. To set seed suddenly, rapidly and prematurely. It is especially troublesome with lettuce and other leafy crops, and happens mostly during hot or wet weather, when plants shoot up inches, almost overnight.

BOLTONIA (bolt-*toh*-nee-uh). FALSE STARWORT. Composite Family (*Compositae*). Sturdy and easily grown perennials, native to our Midwestern prairies. Small, asterlike flowers of white, lavender or purple bloom profusely in July, Aug. and Sept., adding an airy, feathery effect to the back of the perennial border. Good for naturalizing and useful for cutting. These plants like full sun and ordinary garden soil, well turned to a spade's depth. Propagate by seeds or root division. Zone 3.

B. asteroides (ass-ter-*roy*-deez). A tall, well-branched plant, 3 to 5 ft. high, with abundant starlike flowers,

UPPER LEFT: White fringed orchid, the *Habenaria*, is one of many plants that will bloom in bog gardens. This is the species *blephariglottis*, native from Canada to Mississippi.
LOWER LEFT: The bog rose, *Pogonia ophioglossoides*, is scented. It is suitable only for the shady bog garden and is found in swamps all over the continent. It blooms in spring in the South, summer in the North.
BELOW: Boltonia is a sturdy and easy-to-grow daisylike perennial native to the Midwest. Small flowers are white, lavender or purple. An excellent plant for naturalizing, it thrives in ordinary garden soil in either sun or a slightly shaded place.

BOLTONIA

¾ in. across, much like those of the wild aster. The flowers are white and shades of purple.

B. latisquama (lat-iss-*kway*-muh). Blossoms are 1 in. across, in great profusion. The pink-to-purple flowers begin to bloom in late July. Otherwise it is much like *B. asteroides*. The variety *nana* (*nay*-nuh) is shorter, only 2 ft. tall, and has pink flowers.

BOMAREA (boh-*may*-ree-uh). Amaryllis Family (*Amaryllidaceae*). Tender vines from S. America suited to a cool greenhouse. Their attractive funnel-shaped flowers grow in drooping clusters. Oval leaves have twisted leaf stalks. They resent being moved, so indoors they should be grown in large tubs and trained on wires. Propagate by division, offsets or seeds; the latter over heat. Zone 9.

B. caldasiana (cal-daze-ee-*ay*-nuh). A native of Guatemala with leaves to 6 in. The flowers are reddish brown with longer bright yellow inner segments.

B. patacocensis (pat-ah-ko-*sen*-siss). The bright red blooms appear in Aug. and the inner segments are yellow ridged.

bone. Crushed bone is a fertilizer available from meat packers in three forms—ground bone, bone meal and bone flour. All are slow-acting, but the ground bone is slower than the bone meal, which is slower than the flour. Bone meal is most common.

Raw bone meal contains 2 to 4 per cent nitrogen and 22 to 25 per cent phosphoric acid. Steamed bone meal, slightly faster-acting, may contain 1 to 2 per cent nitrogen and 22 to 30 per cent phosphoric acid.

Although it is not a complete fertilizer (lacking potash), bone meal is a good but rather expensive food source for all plants, especially bulbs. It does not burn, and it has little if any effect on the pH of the soil. It is also a useful, long-range fertilizer in preparing seed beds for turf, although other sources of nitrogen and superphosphate will do a comparable service at lower cost.

Application is usually made in early spring at a rate of 3 to 6 lb. per 10 sq. ft. On lawns it should be incorporated in the seed bed if the phosphoric acid is to do much good. In beds, it should be worked in to a depth of 3 to 5 in. As a supplement to potting mixtures, from 1 to 2 cups per bushel may prove beneficial. For further information on soil modification, see entry under *soils*.

bone meal. See *bone*.

Boneset. See *Eupatorium perfoliatum*.

bonsai. Dwarf potted plants—usually trees and often in strange or even grotesque shapes—cultivated for centuries by the Japanese and Chinese.

Bomarea cantabrigensis, whose funnel-shaped flowers resemble the Peruvian lily, is a climbing plant from tropical America where it grows out of doors. In the North bomarea is grown in the cool greenhouse. The slender, climbing plants reach 6 to 8 feet. They dislike root disturbance and generally are planted in tubs and trained to wires fixed to the walls.

Development of a bonsai is a time-consuming process requiring care and patience and considerable artistic skill. There is more to it than the nurture and training of a plant, for a successful bonsai might well be described as the marriage of a plant and a container to create a delightful picture of nature in miniature.

Although the true bonsai is a hardy tree or shrub that is grown outdoors (in a pot) the year round, woody tropical plants may also be developed as bonsai. Only fairly small-leaved species should be used (otherwise the foliage will be out of scale with the rest of the plant). Zelkova, ginkgo, some of the pines and maples can become outstanding bonsai. As a rule, the most interesting bonsai are developed out of already runty plants with substantial, tapering trunks and naturally twisted or gnarled branches, or from young but otherwise normal plants. These may be found in the wild or in a nursery.

Bonsai pots—an important part of a bonsai—come in many designs. They range from 2 to about 25 in. in diameter; from 1 to 10 in. deep. Some are made of porous red clay; others are glazed. All should have drainage holes.

Soil mixtures vary, but in all cases should be capable of holding moisture and food while providing excellent drainage and aeration. Bonsai experts normally arrange the soil in layers, starting with a fairly coarse mixture at the bottom of the pot, generally working up to a fine mixture. The soil is topped off with moss, small ground-cover plants such as *Helxine soleirolii* or fine pebbles.

In potting up a bonsai for the first time, you should pick the soil away from the outside of the rootball and shear the roots rather severely. Then cut the top of the plant back to the same degree. (That is, if you reduce the rootball one-third in size, the top of the plant should also be reduced a third.) Then place the plant in the pot and pack the soil in firmly around it. Water well and set in light shade outdoors for two or three weeks. Then gradually move the plant into full sun.

The best time to start developing a bonsai is in the spring.

Repotting will be required as the plant becomes established and starts to grow. Some bonsai need repotting twice a year; others only every few years. The average is once a year. The process followed is the same as for the original potting.

No simple set of directions can be given for training bonsai. In general, it is a process of hard, selective pruning and thinning and of pinching out new growths. To control the direction of growth and to give the plant interesting warped lines, you may wrap fairly stiff copper or steel wire around the trunk and branches and then bend; or you may tie the stems to stiff, preshaped wires and rods.

To keep bonsai healthy, give them fresh soil every year. Feed often. Water regularly. Keep the plant outdoors and in the sun (except in midsummer and immediately after potting or repotting). However, in winter, in cold climates, store true bonsai on a cool (about 40°), bright sun porch or the equivalent. Never bring a true bonsai into a warm house except in moderate weather—and then only for a day or two. (Tropical bonsai plants, of course, are handled like house plants.)

A small pine trained to the windswept shape of a traditional bonsai rises from rock, soil and moss formed to resemble a cliffside. A Japanese art, bonsai is a living sculpture shaped from dwarfed trees and shrubs and grown in containers, pots or on stones. It is generally believed that the first bonsai were plants dwarfed and stunted by cruel weather conditions in Japanese mountains and brought to cities as a reminder of nature in its wilder state. Professional growers began to develop bonsai from native and nursery material, and learned to create the ancient-seeming twisted and unusual shapes we now associate with this art form. Bonsai lends itself to both outdoor and indoor culture, depending on the plant material. Woody tropicals are suitable as well as the needled evergreens and deciduous trees most often associated with bonsai. Bonsai pieces demand considerable attention and care, but don't require as long to create as most gardeners suppose. Given suitable materials and knowledge of the techniques, attractive bonsai can be created in a few seasons. By the bonsai here are the tools of the art—a rake, a dibbler, clippers of various sizes that allow the removal of small twigs and branches without damaging those around, and a small pointed saw. Bonsai are planted in three potting mixtures and topped with moss.

A Horticultural Art Form

By JERALD P. STOWELL

A bonsai is a living work of art shaped from woody trees and shrubs. Part agriculture, part art, bonsai are grown in containers, pots or on stones. The woody material is subject to three easily understood horticultural phenomena—pruning, shaping and containerization—to produce small, three-dimensional forms of pleasing lines and aspects; they are carefully planned and framed in attractive containers. In size they may range from a few inches to over six feet in height. Bonsai is pronounced "bone-sye," spoken without slurring the syllables and accenting each equally. It is two Chinese words: *bon*, meaning container, tray or pot; *sai*, meaning to plant.

Design and artistic style define bonsai—not a particular species of pine, azalea, cherry or plant genus, no matter how unusual or exotic.

(It is interesting to note that many contemporary Japanese are learning this art form in Japan. There has been a renewed interest in the traditional arts and crafts of that country since the Second World War. The average Japanese is as unfamiliar with the traditional principles of design and basic styles as are Americans.)

Many amateur growers of bonsai in America are using the technical information developed by the Japanese, but are adapting the rules of design and horticultural requirements to meet their own individual experience with nature. American styles are based on traditional Japanese styles, but are gradually being changed to reflect our own view of art and more particularly of nature.

Traditional Styles

After many years of refinement, certain styles have crystalized in Japan, and most growers use these styles as patterns for training their trees.

The *formal upright style* consists of a straight upright trunk with lateral branches arranged radially around the trunk at different levels to reflect what one might call a Christmas-tree shape.

The *informal upright style* is identical to the formal upright style except the trunk is not usually straight but irregular in form at the top; the top is bent toward the viewer.

The *slanting style* consists of a main trunk that slants either to the left or right of the viewer and the first major branch or trunk must slant in the opposite direction away from the main trunk.

In the *semicascading style* the whole tree slants sharply to one side, almost horizontally, one branch or trunk dips below the edge of the container, the effect of a tree growing on the edge of a hillside or cliff reaching down and out toward the sunshine.

The *full cascade style* is the same as the semicascade. However, a major branch or trunk must reach below the foot of the container. The slanting style, semicascade and cascade styles are centered in their containers regardless of the number of sides or the style of the container.

There are numerous other styles such as driftwood, root-over-rock, rock plantings and forest plantings as well as variations and combinations of styles based upon the basic five.

Bonsai is a form of gardening that lends itself to both outdoors and indoors, depending upon the plant material selected. Woody tropicals are just as good for bonsai as are native materials available anywhere. No matter what you choose, the art of training is the same. Technical horticultural details for use in a particular area differ since geographical and climatic conditions differ, especially in the United States. Anyone with the interest, time and a little space can build and enjoy a bonsai collection. It takes considerable care and attention but the results are rewarding and it does not take a lifetime to obtain. Respectable bonsai can be developed in a few seasons, given the proper materials and techniques.

Finding Materials

Probably the first bonsai were naturally formed dwarfs. Some time ago the Japanese began to collect picturesque trees stunted by cruel weather in the uplands and brought them back to their cities as a reminder of nature's wilds. Professional growers began to develop bonsai from native or nursery material, shaping the trees to give them the look of age and naturalness. Over the years they devised standards for shapes and forms which have become the classic styles, but the art of bonsai was born and had its origin in nature. Some of the most famous bonsai

A flowering bonsai developed from a bougainvillea, a plant generally seen only as a large vine. This specimen is obviously some years old, judging by the gnarled trunk. Although evergreens are most often seen in bonsai form, many tender and hardy deciduous plants are suitable for training. Design and artistic style are what ultimately define a bonsai.

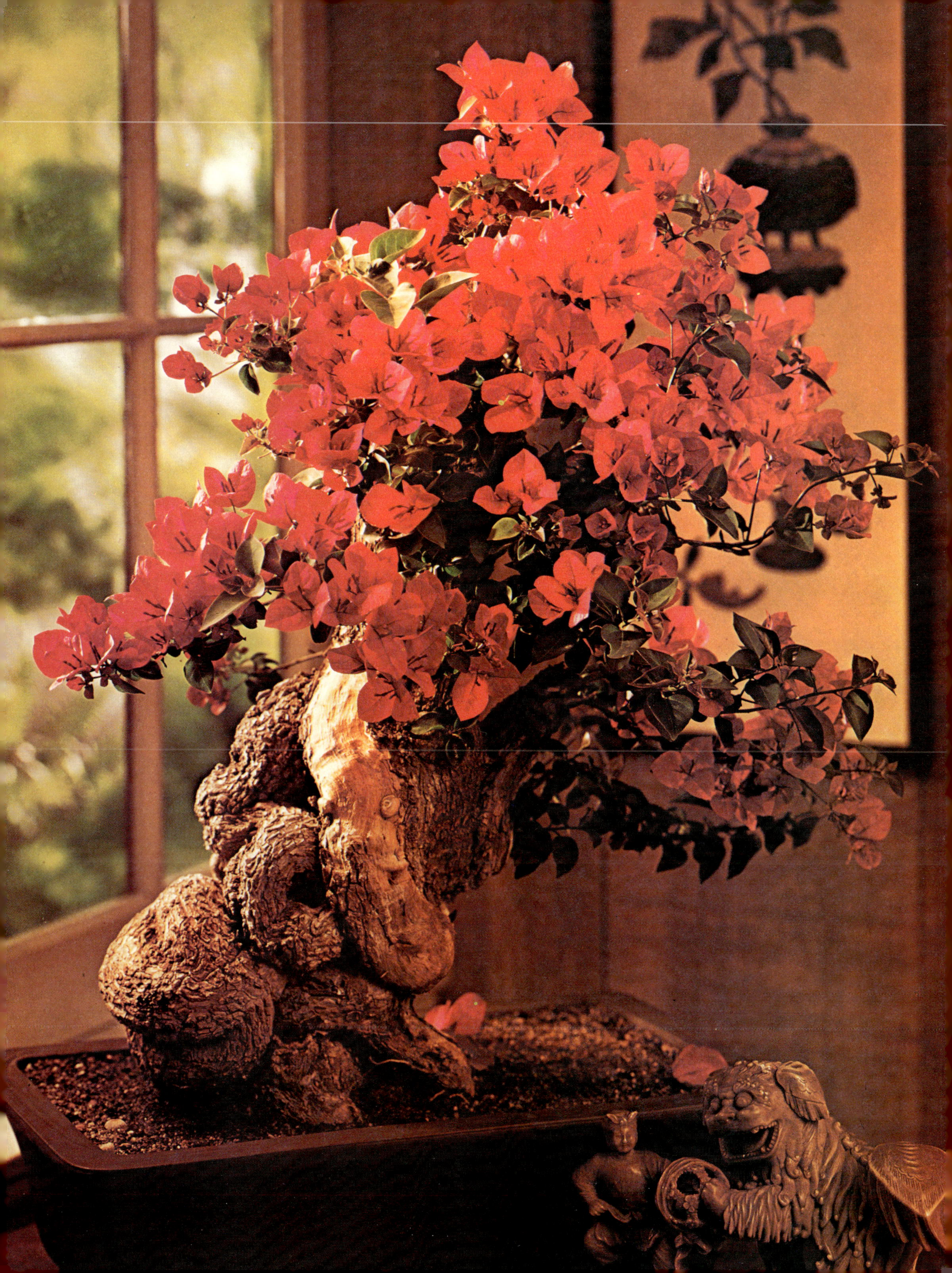

were once wild plants growing on a mountain, in a field or somebody's back yard.

Nature has a way of forming trees into shapes more beautiful than even the most skilled hands can create. The best places to look for raw bonsai materials are wilderness areas, but have a look at your own back yard and along roadsides. Shrubs and small trees growing in fields and on ocean dunes are usually well shaped. Since bonsai is a relatively new form of horticulture in the United States, there is a lack of suitable material from commercial growers. However, if materials are not available from the field, then ordinary nursery stock or can-grown material can be developed into finished bonsai. Most nursery plants are too symmetrical and must be changed by pruning or shaping with copper wire for bonsai use.

OPPOSITE: This old bonsai of Chinese juniper is in the informal upright style with driftwood effect. Bonsai containers are selected to harmonize in color and to balance the proportions of the plant.
ABOVE: Alberta spruce trained five years as a formal upright bonsai shows the required straight upright trunk with lateral branches arranged radially around the trunk at different levels to reflect a shape rather like that of a traditional Christmas tree.

In selecting nursery stock keep your eye open for slow growers and small foliage or needles; the healthy tree that branches close and low, with a beautiful texture and thick, shapely trunk. The pattern of main branches should be irregular and uneven and they should be well twigged. Try to visualize the tree as it will look in its finished condition. If you find a tree with these features and also find a good surface root system all around the trunk you will have first-rate material for bonsai. The root system is often too deep to inspect, but don't turn down a tree on that account if the other features are suitable.

Can-grown stock has one great advantage over field-grown stock. The root system is usually full and well contained. Shapes are interesting and easily viewed, and they are transportable any time. Even a bit of dwarfing of growth is seen when plants have been in cans too long.

The wild shrubs and trees found in fields or on dunes are more difficult to transplant with any sort of root system unless the roots are fibrous, like red-cedar (*Juniperus virginiana*) and some viburnums. Shrubs and trees growing in loam, peaty or leafmold-type soils are much easier to move. In stony mountain soil, roots are often wide and deep-spreading. In digging out all wild plants, make an effort to get as many roots as possible. This is imperative since the more roots the plants have the better are their chances for survival. Just after rain is often the best time for digging. Keep the tree cool, out of sun, and the roots wrapped in plastic on the way home. Transplant the field material to open ground and leave it there for one year, keeping it well watered.

Soil Requirements

There are three basic ingredients that make up bonsai potting soil—clay, sand and garden loam. The texture of the mix is important. Dry the ingredients, then combine and sieve into three grades—coarse, medium and fine. These will be used in layers, with coarse at the bottom. Bonsai soils are sieved to take out the fine powdery dust that would clog air spaces between soil granules. Fine rootlets absorb gases as well as moisture and nutrients. Therefore, it is vital that bonsai soils have good drainage qualities and yet retain moisture. Moisture evaporates more quickly from a bonsai container than it does from the same plant in the ground.

There are many soil substitutes for bonsai which have good drainage and the ability to retain moisture. I use Terra green or Turface, a commercial product, (a fired claylike pot shard) as a clay substitute. It retains one and a half times its own weight in water. Peat moss will also retain moisture. Sand and perlite are used for drainage and aeration.

Garden loam is used in bonsai potting to provide nutrients. Throughout the country, soil mixtures are different owing to the differences in climate and terrain. By varying the soil textures in the potting medium and offering the bonsai some protection from late afternoon sun, it is possible to avoid the need to water two and three times daily, excepting during the summer months when humidity is low, heat is excessive and prevailing winds dry out the plants. The point is that you will have to experiment until you find the right soil mixture. Texts giving general information are never, and cannot be, specific enough because conditions vary so greatly in the country's various gardening regions.

Container Selection

Bonsai containers are like frames on pictures or bases for sculpture. They must harmonize, complement the color and mood of the planting and be proportionate to the bonsai. The most appropriate containers now available are the traditional ones from Japan. They are made in numerous shapes, sizes, colors and textures. Selection depends upon the individual planting. Color, glazes and textures should be considered in order to harmonize with the bonsai planned. White or off-white is often used for red- or yellow-flowered, or fruiting plants, and for bonsai with lyrical moods as cherry, azalea, pomegranate, pyracantha and persimmon. Blue and green containers look well with plants of yellow-, red- and orange-contrasting flowers or fruits, and with plants that have fall foliage colors, such as maples and cotoneasters. Dark colors or black complement white berries or flowers, such as shadbush, white azalea, pear, crab apple and variegated foliage plants.

Shape of the container is a consideration, too, and is dictated by the individual bonsai. Plants with airy shapes are often planted in glazed pots that have ornamental designs. The very formal, dignified, upright bonsai looks well in flat rectangular or oval pots of muted color. Heavy, thick trunks and thick-foliaged trees need sturdy, bulky, unglazed containers to give proper anchorage and a look of permanency. Round and rectangular or square pots that are deep look well with a cascading bonsai. Shallow, round or oval pots are best for windswept styles and trees of an informal nature.

In bonsai as in other artistic forms it is possible to vary from tradition but classical bonsai adhere to fairly clear-cut rules governing the use of containers.

Developing a Bonsai

For the uninitiated, thoughts of developing a bonsai can be discouraging and almost frightening. The art of bonsai in the past was surrounded with mystery. The idea that a bonsai takes endless years of patience before it can mature into a beautiful tree is not true. Fine bonsai can be developed in a few hours following these simple procedures.

1. Trim out all dead wood, shorten long branches and eliminate branches growing at the same levels around the trunk. Leave clean cuts, no stumps.

2. Trees with excess branches should have a few removed leaving three at the lowest level of the trunk. An ideal bonsai reveals the trunk line for two-thirds of the distance up the trunk. The first third is completely bare of branches; the next third is bare of branches in front and framed by branches at the sides and back; the top third has branches all around. The side that displays the trunk is the front.

The main terminal of certain of the informal styles always bends to the front. Other branches toward the top should be left closer together.

The first three branches are No. 1, No. 2 and No. 3. No. 1 is the lowest, No. 2 is a little higher up on the opposite side of the trunk and No. 3 is at the back and a bit higher than No. 2 or between 1 and 2.

3. Root structure is part of overall design and should be allowed to show. Pull away soil and expose main large surface roots. Pointed chopsticks are best for this chore.

4. Start wiring with heaviest wire at base of trunk, inserting end in soil behind the base of the trunk and spacing spirals evenly. For the beginner, it's better to use two wires of medium gauge than one very heavy one.

LEFT: Arrow-wood (*Viburnum dentatum*) is well suited to training in this informal style. The plant shown resulted from collected material trained ten years.
OPPOSITE, TOP: This pitch pine (*Pinus rigida*) is in the semiwindswept version of an informal bonsai. It has been trained for ten years from collected material.
OPPOSITE, LEFT: The Mugho pine, especially *Pinus mugo pumilio* shown here, is a popular subject for training in the slanting style. This specimen is the result of training for 15 years what began as nursery stock.
OPPOSITE, RIGHT: *Malus sylvestris*, the common apple, is anything but common when adapted to the art of bonsai. This handsome dwarf tree with all the attributes of a gnarled old apple, in an informal style, was trained for three years as a bonsai, beginning with natural collected material that had already been dwarfed by cattle and deer in the open. Hummocks of moss cover the soil and rise to meet the trunk. These four bonsai represent hardy plants not suited to spending winter in a warm house; they need coolness.

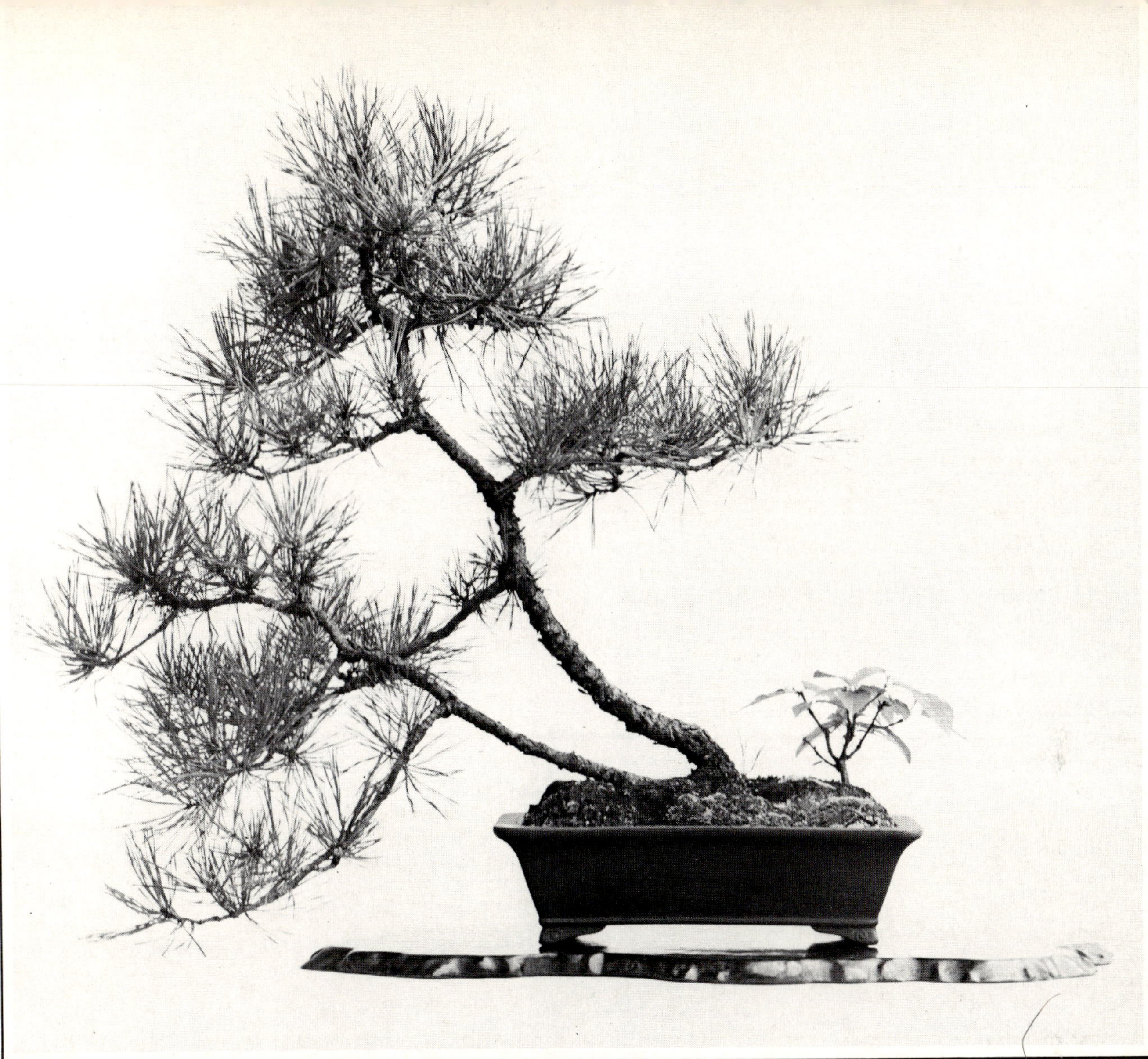

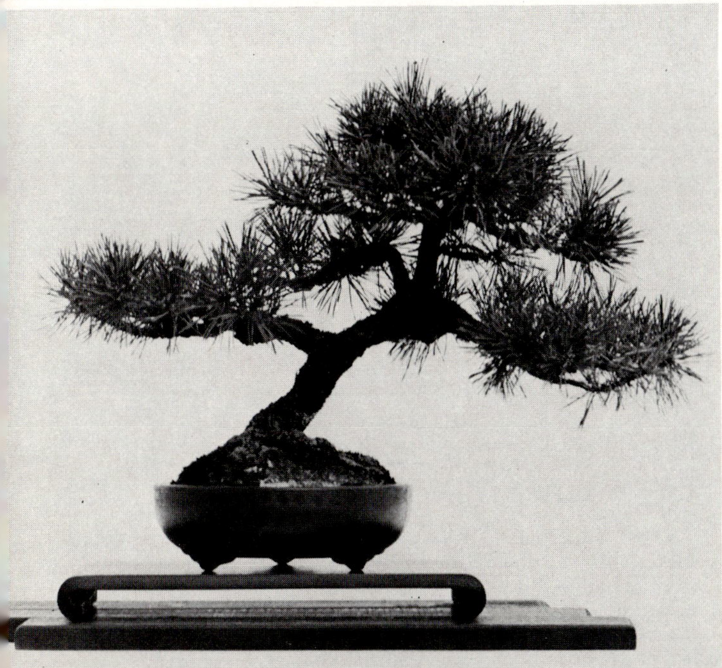

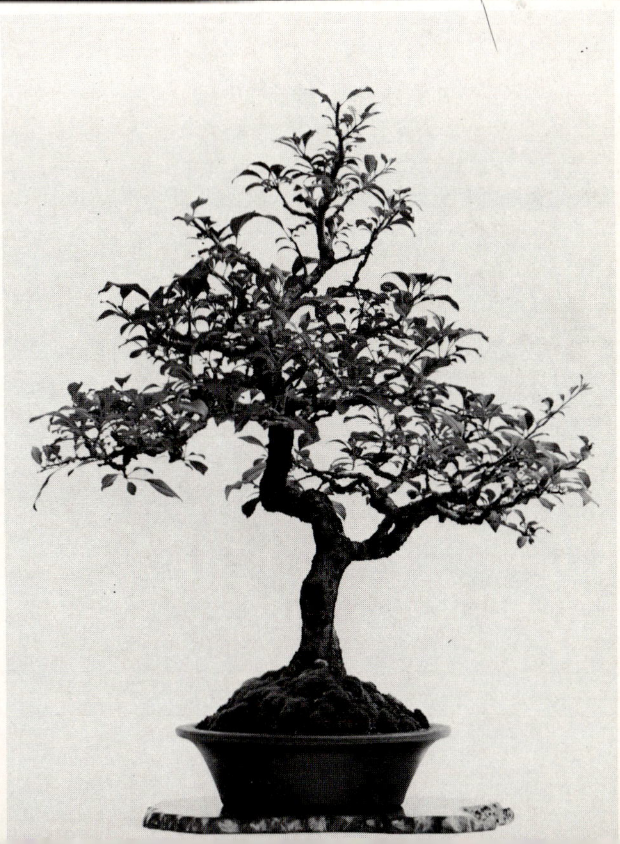

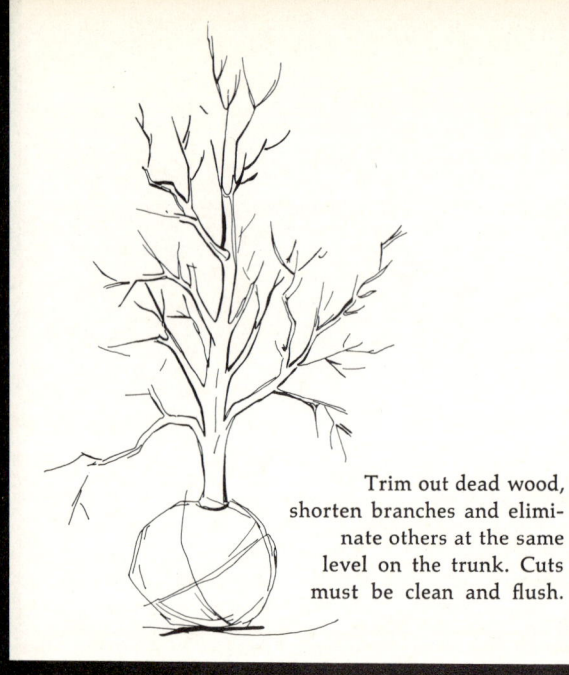

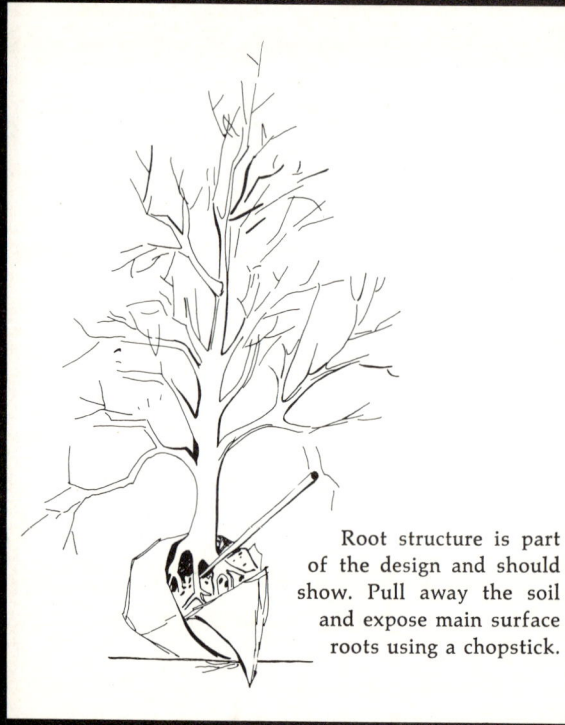

HOW TO START A BONSAI

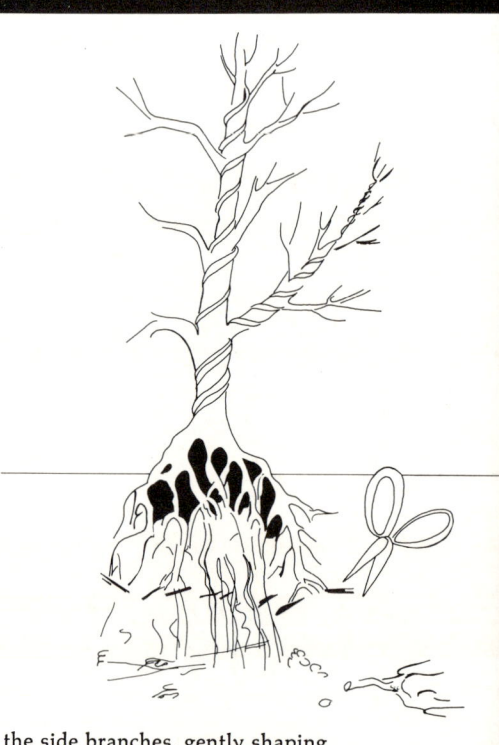

Trim out dead wood, shorten branches and eliminate others at the same level on the trunk. Cuts must be clean and flush.

Root structure is part of the design and should show. Pull away the soil and expose main surface roots using a chopstick.

Lower third of tree must be bare; the next third should have only side and back limbs; the top third, limbs all around.

Insert wire in soil behind base of trunk, wrapping wire in even spirals. Use one heavy- or two medium-gauge wires.

Wire the side branches, gently shaping them to the desired style before potting. Use a lighter wire to strengthen the natural direction of small branches. Expose the roots and prune them to fit the shape of the container you are using.

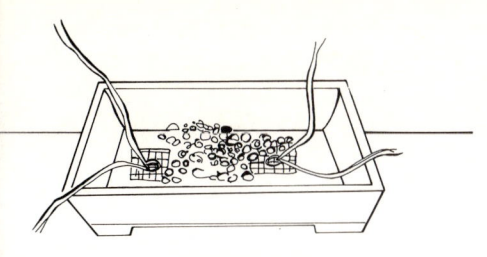

Cover the drain holes in the container with plastic mesh and thread and anchor wires through both holes and mesh. Put in the first layer of coarse soil.

Settle the tree roots in the soil by giving it a gentle twist. Cross the anchor wires over the roots, twist ends together and hide them in the root mass.

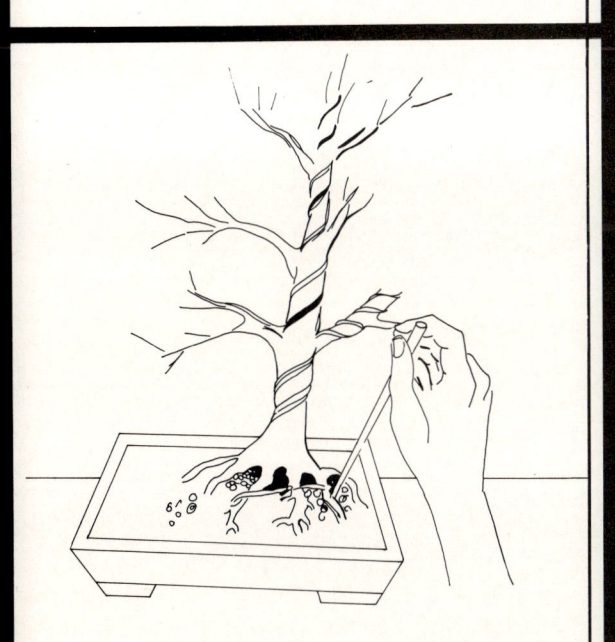

Add a less coarse grade of soil to the pot, working it in carefully around the roots with a chopstick. Care must be taken to firm the soil well, tamping it to fill the air holes. Finish filling with a third layer of still finer soil.

In all, three grades of granular soil have been used to complete the potting. Now finish off by placing wet moss over the dry soil surface. Perhaps the placement of a stone might be a suitable touch to complete the artistic composition.

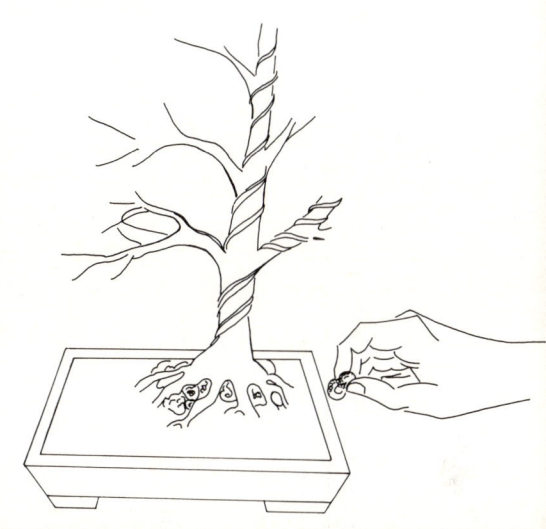

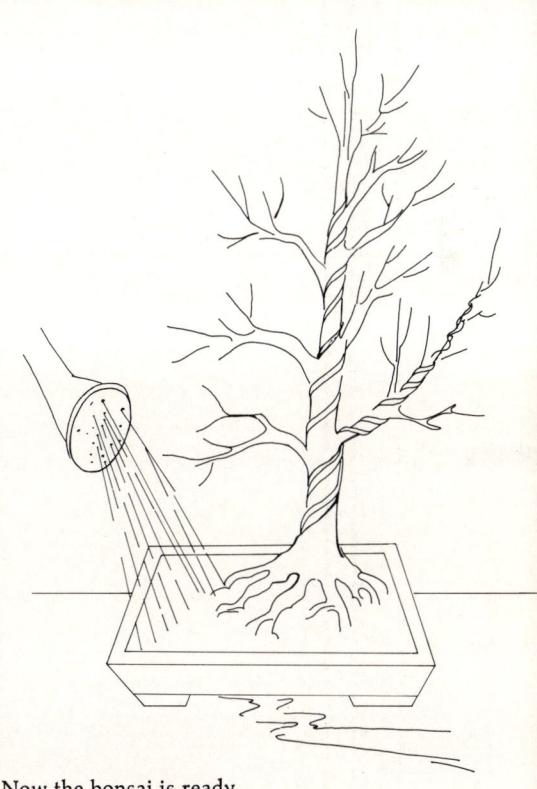

Now the bonsai is ready for watering. Plunge the pot in a basin full of water to reach just below its rim. Water from above with the fine rosette on a watering can. Display your handwork on a table in good light and enjoy it. In hot dry climates, shade it.

BONSAI

5. Neat wiring is essential to the appearance of the tree. Bend branches with opposed fingers and thumbs. Use lighter-gauge wires to shape or strengthen natural direction of lesser branches and twigs. After wiring the tree, gently shape the branches to the desired style before placing in the container.

6. In a container of the correct size for the tree, with drain holes covered with plastic mesh, thread anchor wires through holes and mesh. Put a layer of the coarsest soil into the bottom of the pot.

7. Expose roots of the tree by breaking the earth away with chopsticks. Shorten the roots to the general shape of the container. Settle the tree into the soil with a gentle twisting motion to eliminate air pockets.

8. Cross the anchor wires over the surface of the roots, twist the opposite ends together to tie them and tuck the ends back into the main root mass.

9. Put more soil of a less coarse texture into the pot. Work the soil into and around the roots with a jabbing motion of the chopsticks to fill all the air holes, and top with the finest soil mix. Then place moss (wet first in water) as desired on the dry surface of the soil. Add a stone if it seems to improve the composition, then place the whole bonsai into a basin full of water that will reach to just below the rim of the

OPPOSITE: This prostrate juniper (*Juniperus squamata* variety *wilsonii*) has been trained in the cascade style for ten years, originating from nursery stock.
BELOW, TOP: Leafy Boston-ivy (*Parthenocissus tricuspidata*) and grassy sweet flag (*Acorus gramineus pusillus*) in the manner of Mame bonsai.
BELOW, BOTTOM: *Serissa foetida* grown 13 years from a cutting with grasslike species of *Juncus*.

BONSAI

This grove-style bonsai has been trained for ten years from collected seedlings of the pitch pine (*Pinus rigida*). By careful placement, the bamboo stake and wiring on the largest is noticeable only from one angle.

pot. Water from above with a fine spray from a watering can. Be sure you have watered the plant on all four sides and thoroughly.

Routine Care

Bonsai is a form of gardening that lends itself to both indoors and outdoors, depending on the plant selected. In the North, tropicals do well inside and respond to a summer out of doors when possible. Native trees need to be out of doors all year round. Whichever you choose, the art of training will be the same.

Bonsai are grown outdoors on tables to facilitate watering, viewing, inspection for insects and periodic pruning. Provide a free flow of air and full light. In hot or dry climates, shade the bonsai with a lath roof. Avoid overhanging trees as shade.

Technical horticultural details for use in any given area differ since geographical and climatic conditions vary all over the continent. This demands revision of the Japanese techniques for each gardener as most of the standard texts refer to methods of handling bonsai in Tokyo's climate.

Watering is probably the most important factor in a bonsai's life. Throughout the growing season it cannot be neglected without injury or loss. Many books advocate watering at least once a day, and in warm weather sometimes as many as three times daily. Learning how to water is an exacting task, but experience will make it routine. Since granular soils are used for bonsai, the watering must be constant. If plants are in full sun until one or two in the afternoon and shaded the rest of the day, water only once daily unless the weather is extremely dry and windy.

The fine-nozzle watering can is recommended, but is really for the purist with time and love. To handle any good-sized bonsai, the garden hose is much easier, and quite satisfactory providing every plant in a collection is watered, and none is missed. The force of this kind of water spray directed up into the foliage of thickly growing trees such as Alberta spruce discourages pests and so serves a dual purpose. Be sure that the trees watered are hosed from all four sides. One side missed can mean dead branches and a spoiled shape.

A properly fed bonsai has good foliage color and well-formed flowers and fruits and an intricate, healthy network of branches. The easiest fertilizers to use are those which are water-soluble and contain trace elements, such as Hyponex and Ra-pid-gro. Do not use these at full strength, however, but in a solution that is half-strength. Never apply fertilizer to the leaves of a bonsai as this increases their size and is not desirable. Small leaves on well-branched trunks are bonsai ideals.

Pruning and Trimming

Pruning is extremely important, for without constant attention a bonsai quickly loses its shape and the intricate network of branches that makes it beautiful will not develop. If there is a secret to the art of bonsai, this is it.

Drastic pruning, a term that means the cutting back of a tree to a smaller size, is generally only for deciduous trees and is done only in spring. Trimming new growth is a constant need. Deciduous trees have their new growth shortened; leaves are sometimes cut off if the tree is healthy to promote branching and smaller leaves. Evergreens have new shoots pinched back leaving only four or five clusters of needles at the base.

ABOVE: An arrangement of benches with lath shade provides an attractive and convenient place for the daily care of a bonsai collection during the growing season. In cold climates even the hardy bonsai need protection in a cold frame or cold greenhouse. Tender kinds grow well outdoors in the summer, but need a moderately warm, sunny, moist atmosphere indoors through the winter months.

RIGHT: Fine-nozzle watering is best for bonsai, but slow if a large group of plants is to be watered twice daily in hot, dry weather. A hoze nozzle that delivers a large but gentle spray is also suitable. Hose trees on all four sides.

BONSAI

LEFT: Bonsai with new summer growth, ready for pruning. BELOW, TOP: Long shoots of new growth are shortened with small shears, leaving two or three new leaves. Drastic pruning is required only for deciduous trees and is done in the spring. BELOW, BOTTOM: Crab apple in semi-cascade style shows simple, natural branch shaping that makes a bonsai beautiful. OPPOSITE: Rock formation holds dwarfed balsam fir and zelkova with sedum and mosses.

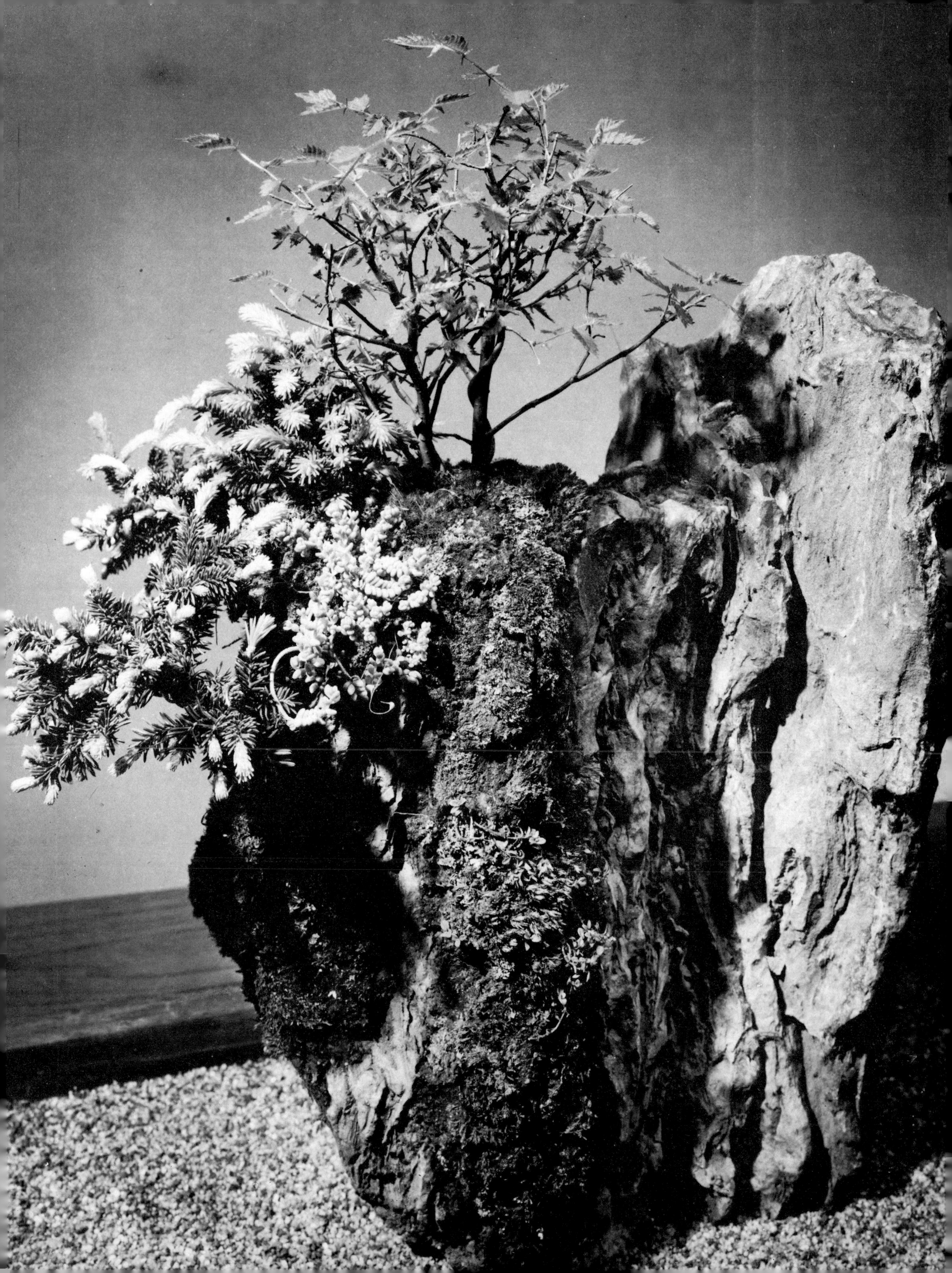

BONSAI

Winter Care

Winter care must be tailored to the needs of the plants selected and to local climatic conditions, no matter what the Japanese texts say. Bonsai require protection from severe drying winds during the winter months. In the Northeast and Midwest, December through March are the hardest times, as the plants may freeze and desiccate; the problem is lack of water in the soil when it becomes frozen. Evaporation draws the moisture from the plants, particularly from the needles of evergreens, and water must be replaced through the root system. If the soil remains frozen for several months, water cannot be replaced until too late and the plant will die.

A simple protective device is a packing case placed over bonsai in pots sunken into the soil up to the rim of the container, or, if possible, place the bonsai in a cold frame facing north, away from the warmth of the sun. It will keep plants frozen and dormant, and eliminate the need to water. Check plants periodically for possible dryness.

Bonsai will also winter safely in frost-free structures adjacent to a heated building or dwelling, such as porches protected enough so that temperatures do not go much below freezing, in bay windows, a lean-to facing north, plastic greenhouse heated by an open window or a cold frame placed over an open basement window. Watering must be tended to if such facilities are used since the ground will not be frozen and the plant will still be functioning.

Displaying Bonsai

Displaying bonsai in a western-style home or garden is a challenge each must work out for himself since our homes do not have the traditional *tokonoma*. Built into the living room of the Japanese home is the *tokonoma*, a low, wide recessed area where art objects are arranged against a background of a plain, soft, subtle color, all to be viewed at eye level from low cushions on the floor. Grouped in the *tokonoma* are flower arrangements or a small planting of grass or herbs, lacquer or bronze boxes, a handsome stone, books in decorative bindings and bonsai. The bonsai is not on permanent display but is brought in for special occasions. Usually the *tokonoma* holds three objects and, when one of them is a bonsai, it is given the most prominent position. The effect can be formal or informal. A scroll may be hung to one side at the back but never directly behind the tree; accent pieces are chosen for suitability.

The bonsai and any accessory pieces are placed on separate bases or stands, which are often of wood, frequently cross-cut slabs stained to emphasize the pattern of the grain. Or perhaps a small lacquered table with gracefully curved legs is used, or a polished stand fashioned from tree roots.

There are degrees of ornateness. Bases are always selected to match the mood of the bonsai. The base for a formal upright tree is also formal and extends a little beyond the feet of the container to give a solid, settled appearance. A dark-finished base increases the feeling of stability. Informal trees are displayed on simple bases of lighter aspect. If the bonsai is semicascading or cascading, it is placed on a tall stand to suggest a tree growing on a steep hill with branches hanging down the side. There are no rules; each display reflects the individual's taste in decoration. But again, emphasis is always on the bonsai; other objects must not detract from its importance.

In western-style living rooms, it is difficult to find at eye level a space with a clear background where a bonsai can be featured. Room dividers or sectional bookshelf structures where the distance between the

ABOVE: Winter care of bonsai depends on the climate and the needs of individual plants. In cold climates, bonsai set outdoors can draw no moisture from the frozen earth but lose moisture from needles through evaporation. Smaller plants winter-over safely in a cold frame facing north, away from the warmth of the sun.
OPPOSITE: A plastic greenhouse protects a large collection of bonsai in a cold climate. Snow banked on the sides insulates the interior and retains warmth. A ventilation grill set over the door allows air circulation on sunny days.

shelves can be varied may be used. These nicely accommodate bonsai of small to medium size. A gray, off-white, gray-green or beige background color is good. Coffee tables permit trees to be displayed in the round, but since there is then no particular background, the bonsai is not displayed to its best advantage. The Japanese would probably frown on such a place of display where other household objects become part of the bonsai picture, but our American sense of decoration is not violated so long as the character of the tree remains intact. In other words, individual taste has a part in the bonsai setting.

In summer, bonsai can be displayed in various ways in the garden or on the patio. They are most decorative when attractively placed in a setting and not simply massed on tables to facilitate their care. Since they are forms of living sculpture, they can be used as other pieces of garden sculpture are used. Sometimes individual bonsai are placed in the garden on tree stumps and stones. The beauty of each is clearly seen, yet all blend into the harmonious garden composition. Such an arrangement depends upon site and also upon suitable stands to support and display the plants.

Bonsai Societies

Bonsai has been known in this country for many years owing to Japanese immigration to the West Coast. Wherever the Japanese settled, bonsai were grown. But in the past the technical skills were not taught in the formal fashion in which they are offered today. In the East, collections of bonsai have long been on display at the Arnold Arboretum and the Brooklyn Botanic Garden. The spread of this horticultural art form was not from any active campaigning on the part of the Japanese but rather from our own interest in Oriental culture. In the late 1950's the Brooklyn Botanic Garden began to include the teaching of bonsai techniques in its educational program. Japanese masters were brought to this country and classes in bonsai became popular. Another reason for the spread of bonsai in North America has been its appeal as a combination of both art and horticulture and the increasing number of books available on the subject.

A number of excellent books by both Japanese and American authors have been published for those interested in this specialized form of gardening. Below is a list of just a few that are easy to obtain. The techniques and rules must be adapted to the individual gardener's local conditions.

Evergreen bonsai with grassy *Juncus* in smaller container displayed in a western-style home. A modern poster has been used in place of the traditional scroll used in Japan. Kept moist and the leaves misted frequently with water, even cold-loving bonsai can be enjoyed indoors for brief periods while the heat is on in winter.

Bonsai for Americans, Hull, George F.; Doubleday & Co., Inc. 1964.
Bonsai: Indoors and Out, Stowell, Jerald P.; D. Van Nostrand Co., Inc. 1966.
Bonsai: Miniature Potted Trees, Murata, Kyuzo; Shufunotomo Co. Ltd. 1964.
Bonsai for Pleasure, Murata, Keiji and Takema, Takeuchi; Japan Publications, Inc. 1969.
Bonsai: Trees and Shrubs, Perry, Lynn R.; Ronald Press Co. 1964.
The Master's Book of Bonsai, Koide, Nobukichi, Kato, Saburo, Takeyama, Fusazo; Kodansha International Ltd. 1967.
The Japanese Art of Miniature Trees and Landscapes, Yashimura, Yuji and Halford, Giovanna M.; Charles E. Tuttle Co. 1957.

The interest in bonsai has promoted clubs and societies across the nation as well as in several foreign countries. Organized clubs have sprung up in Switzerland, France, England, Australia, Brazil, India, South Africa and almost every state in the United States. Many major cities have clubs, such as: Atlanta, Boston, Cleveland, Philadelphia, Pittsburgh, Phoenix, Denver, Rochester, San Francisco, Seattle, Portland (Oregon), New York, Miami, Fort Lauderdale, Dallas, Cincinnati, Indianapolis, Buffalo and Honolulu, and additional clubs in suburban areas too numerous to mention.

On March 8, 1967, a group of 17 Americans flew to Japan to attend the first Bonsai Seminar and tour of Japan, which was sponsored by the Bonsai Society of Greater New York. The group spent one week studying the techniques of bonsai with Japan's leading authority and master of Kyuka-en Bonsai Garden, Kyuzo Murata. As a result of that trip, the American Bonsai Society was founded during the summer of 1967.

The American Bonsai Society is a nonprofit organization of individuals interested in bonsai. It has no subsidiary chapters and recommends membership in the local clubs and societies. To fill the need for communication and to promote bonsai in general, the Society devotes much of its time to three activities: *The Bonsai Journal*, the annual meeting and symposium and the Bonsai Appreciation and Judging School run by the Society.

The Bonsai Journal is published quarterly and contains well-illustrated articles of interest to beginners and experienced growers alike. It contains information on horticulture, history and esthetics, newsworthy items, announcements and book reviews. *The Journal* is sent to all members.

The *Annual Symposium* is held for two days during late spring, each year in a different city across the

United States and Canada. A varied program is presented: lectures and demonstrations on bonsai techniques, the annual business meeting, a banquet, exhibits and visits to local collections or nurseries.

The *Bonsai Appreciation and Judging School* is not intended to train judges but rather it is an all-day program designed to help those who wish to know more precisely how to understand and appreciate bonsai.

Membership in the American Bonsai Society can be obtained by writing the Membership Secretary, Mr. Herbert T. Brawner, 229 North Shore Drive—Lake Waukomis, Parkville, Missouri 64151.

Classes of membership are as follows:

  Individual
  Couple
  International (address outside U.S.)
  Supporting
  Contributing
  Patron
  Life

There are many prominent bonsai societies that welcome new members. Among them are:

Bonsai Clubs International is an association of bonsai clubs and is run by member clubs. There are non-voting individual memberships. Its objectives are primarily educational for a greater appreciation of bonsai and related fine arts. Membership includes *Bonsai Magazine* (issued ten times a year), help for new clubs, color slides and a lending library, seed distribution and a speaker program. Write to Bonsai Clubs International, 2354 Lida Drive, Mountain View, Calif. 94040.

The California Bonsai Society, Inc., was founded in 1950 under the name of the Southern California Bonsai Club. A nonprofit organization, it meets once a month to exchange ideas and discuss cultural problems. Since 1957 the Society has sponsored an annual bonsai exhibition—the largest in this country—at the California Museum of Science and Industry in Los Angeles. A beautiful color magazine, *Bonsai in California,* is published annually. For further information write to the English Secretary, California Bonsai Society, Inc., P.O. Box 78211, Los Angeles, Calif. 90016.

Mr. Stowell is an expert on bonsai and the author of Bonsai, Indoors and Out. *Past President of the Bonsai Society of Greater New York and of the American Bonsai Society, he is also a member of the Garden Writers Association of America, the American Horticultural Society and the Pennsylvania Horticultural Society.*

TREES AND SHRUBS FOR BONSAI

Deciduous trees

Abelia	
Acer buergerianum	Trident maple
campestre	Hedge maple
circinatum	Vine maple
ginnala	Amur maple
palmatum	Japanese maple
rubrum	Red maple
Amelanchier arborea	Shadbush, Shadblow,
asiatica	Serviceberry
Aronia	Chokeberry
Berberis	Barberry
Betula lenta	Cherry birch, Sweet birch
nigra	River birch, Black birch
papyrifera	Paper birch, Canoe birch, White birch
populifolia	Gray birch, Wire birch
Carpinus betulus	European hornbeam
caroliniana	American hornbeam, Blue-beech, Ironwood
japonica	Japanese hornbeam
Celtis occidentalis	Hackberry
sinensis	
Cercis canadensis	Eastern redbud
chinensis	Chinese redbud
Chaenomeles japonica	Japanese quince
Cornus florida	Dogwood
kousa	Kousa dogwood
officinalis	
Corylopsis	Winter-hazel
Cotoneaster	
Crataegus	Hawthorn, Haw, Thorn, Thornapple, Red haw
Diospyros kaki	Kaki persimmon
virginiana	Persimmon
Euonymus	Spindle tree
Fagus grandifolia	American beech
sylvatica	European beech
Forsythia	Forsythia, Golden bells
Hamamelis virginiana	Witch-hazel
Ilex serrata	Japanese holly, English holly

BONSAI

Deciduous trees

Ilex verticillata	Winterberry, Black-alder
Jasminum nudiflorum	Winter jasmine
Lagerstroemia indica	Crape-myrtle
Liquidambar styraciflua	Sweet gum
Lonicera	Honeysuckle
Lyonia ligustrina	Maleberry, Hehuckleberry
Magnolia kobus	
liliflora	
stellata	Star magnolia, Starry magnolia
virginiana	Sweet bay, Swamp-bay
Malus	Apple, Crab apple
Morus alba	White mulberry
rubra	Red mulberry
Myrica pensylvanica	Bayberry
Nyssa sylvatica	Sour gum, Pepperidge, Tupelo
Ostrya virginiana	American hop-hornbeam, Hornbeam, Ironwood
Oxydendrum arboreum	Sour-wood, Sorrel tree
Photinia	
Potentilla	Potentilla, Cinquefoil
Prunus incisa	Flowering cherry
maritima	Beach plum
mume	Japanese apricot
persica	Peach
serrulata	Flowering cherry
Pyrus calleryana	Callery pear
communis	Pear
pyrifolia	Sand pear
Quercus dentata	Daimyo oak
glandulifera	Japanese oak
ilicifolia	Scrub oak, Bear oak
palustris	Pin oak, Spanish oak, Swamp oak
phellos	Willow oak, Peach oak
robur	English oak
Rhododendron canadense	Rhodora
nudiflorum	Pinxter, Pink azalea, Purple azalea, Election pink, Wild or Purple honeysuckle

Deciduous trees

Rosa banksiae	Bank's rose
multiflora	Multiflora rose
Salix babylonica	Weeping willow, Golden willow
discolor	Pussy willow
Sorbus americana	Mountain ash
Spiraea	Spirea
Syringa amurensis	Amur lilac
microphylla	Dwarf lilac
vulgaris	Common lilac
Trachelospermum asiaticum jasminoides	Star jasmine
Ulmus alata	Winged elm, Cork elm, Wahoo
crassifolia	Cedar elm, Basket elm, Red elm, Southern rock elm
parvifolia	Chinese elm
pumila	Siberian elm
Vaccinium	Blueberry
Viburnum dentatum	Arrow-wood
Wisteria floribunda	Japanese wisteria
sinensis	Chinese wisteria
Zelkova serrata	Zelkova, Gray-bark elm

Coniferous trees

Abies balsamea	Balsam fir, Balsam
lasiocarpa	Alpine fir
Cedrus atlantica	Atlas cedar
libani	Cedar of Lebanon
Chamaecyparis obtusa	Hinoki cypress
pisifera	Sawara cypress
thyoides	White-cedar, False cypress
Cryptomeria	
Cupressus macrocarpa	Monterey cypress
Ginkgo biloba	Maidenhair-tree
Juniperus californica	California juniper, Desert white-cedar
chinensis	Chinese juniper
communis	Common juniper
conferta	Shore juniper
deppeana	Alligator juniper, Checkered-bark juniper
horizontalis	Creeping juniper
monosperma	One-seed juniper, Cherry-stone juniper

Coniferous trees

Juniperus occidentalis	Western juniper, Sierra juniper
osteosperma	Utah juniper, Bigberry juniper
recurva	Squamata juniper
rigida	Needle juniper
scopulorum	Rocky-mountain red-cedar, Western red-cedar, Cedro rojo
virginiana	Eastern red-cedar, Red-cedar
Larix decidua	European larch
laricina	American larch, Tamarack, Hackmatack, Black larch
leptolepsis	Japanese larch
occidentalis	Western larch, Montana larch, Mountain larch, Western tamarack
Picea engelmannii	Engelmann spruce
glauca	Alberta spruce, White spruce
glehnii	Saghalin spruce
jezoensis	Jezo spruce, Edo spruce, Yeddo spruce
mariana	Black spruce, Bog spruce, Swamp spruce
rubens	Red spruce, Yellow spruce
sitchensis	Sitka spruce, Coast spruce, Tideland spruce
Pinus albicaulis	Whitebark pine, Scrub pine
aristata	Bristle-cone pine, Foxtail pine, Hickory pine
banksiana	Jack pine, Gray pine, Scrub pine, Banksian pine
canariensis	Canary Island pine
cembra	Swiss stone pine
cembroides	Mexican pinyon, Nut pine, Pinyon
coulteri	Coulter pine, Pitch pine
densiflora	Japanese red pine
flexilis	Limber pine

Coniferous trees

Pinus jeffreyi	Jeffrey pine, Western yellow pine
mugo	Mugho pine, Swiss mountain pine
nigra	Black pine, Austrian pine
parviflora	Japanese white pine
ponderosa	Ponderosa pine, Blackjack pine, Bull pine, Rock pine, Western yellow pine, Pino real
radiata	Monterey pine
rigida	Pitch pine
sabiniana	Digger pine, Bull pine, Gray pine
strobus	White pine, Salt pine, Northern pine
sylvestris	Scots pine, Scotch pine
virginiana	Virginia pine, Jersey pine, Spruce pine, Scrub pine
Pseudolarix amabilis	Golden-larch
Pseudotsuga menziesii	Douglas fir
Sequoia gigantea	Giant sequoia, Bigtree, Giant redwood
sempervirens	Redwood, California redwood, Coastal redwood
Tamarix juniperina	Tamarisk
parviflora	Small-flower tamarisk
Taxus baccata	English yew
cuspidata	Japanese yew
Thuja occidentalis	American arborvitae, Eastern arborvitae, Swamp cedar
Tsuga canadensis	Eastern hemlock, Canada hemlock
diversifolia	Japanese hemlock
mertensiana	Mountain hemlock, Black hemlock
sieboldii	Siebold hemlock

Broad-leaved evergreens

Buxus	Boxwood
Cotoneaster	
Hedera helix	Ivy

BONSAI

Broad-leaved evergreens	
Ilex crenata	Japanese holly
opaca	American holly
pernyi	Perny holly
vomitoria	Yaupon, Cassena, Christmas berry, Evergreen holly
Kalmia angustifolia	Sheep-laurel, Lamb-kill, Pig-laurel, Dwarf-laurel
Leiophyllum buxifolium	Box sand-myrtle
Myrica cerifera	Wax-myrtle, Southern bayberry, Candleberry
Photinia	
Pieris japonica	Japanese andromeda
Pyracantha	Firethorn
Quercus agrifolia	California live oak, Coast live oak
chrysolepis	Canyon live oak, Canyon oak, Gold-cup oak, Maul oak, White live oak
suber	Cork oak
virginiana	Live oak
Rhododendron indicum	Azalea
mucronatum	Azalea
obtusum	Azalea
williamsianum	Rhododendron
Thea sinensis bohea	Tea

Tropicals and semitropicals	
Acacia	
Bougainvillea	
Calliandra	
Carissa grandiflora	Natal-plum
Casuarina equisitifolia	Horsetail beefwood
Citrus limonia	Lemon
mitis	Calamondin
paradisi	Grapefruit
trifoliata	Trifoliate orange
Cuphea	
Ficus	Fig
Fortunella	Kumquat
Gardenia jasminoides	Cape-jasmine
thunbergia	Gardenia
Grevillea robusta	Silk-oak
Laurus nobilis	Laurel, Sweet bay
Mahonia	
Malpighia coccigera	Holly malpighia

Tropicals and semitropicals	
Myrtus communis	Myrtle
Olea europaea	Common olive
Podocarpus	
Punica granatum	Pomegranate
Serissa foetida	Serissa
Sparmannia africana	African hemp

Bonytip fleabane. See *Erigeron karvinskianus.*

Borage. See *Borago officinalis.*

Borage Family (*Boraginaceae*). A large and varied family. All have hairy stems or leaves, regular flowers, mostly in one-sided spikes or clusters, and nutlike fruit. A partial list of the genera in this family described in this encyclopedia includes: *Anchusa, Borago, Brunnera, Cerinthe, Cynoglossum, Echium, Heliotropium, Lithospermum, Mertensia, Myosotis* (the familiar forget-me-not) and *Pulmonaria.*

Boraginaceae. See Borage Family.

BORAGO (boh-*ray*-go). Borage. Borage Family (*Boraginaceae*). Rough-stemmed and coarse herbs of the Mediterranean region. Grayish-green, bristly foliage and star-shaped, blue flowers. Very attractive to honey bees. Useful in the flower garden and herb garden. Also effective in hilly ground or in sloping rock gardens. Easily grown in ordinary garden soil and full sun. Propagate annuals by seeds sown in spring; perennials by division.

B. laxiflora (lax-if-*floh*-ruh). A low-growing perennial, with pale blue, drooping flowers. This plant is excellent for rock gardens.

B. officinalis (off-iss-in-*nay*-liss). Common borage. A universal favorite since the time of the ancient Greeks, who used the young leaves in cooling drinks for their medicinal and supposedly soothing qualities. It is one of the plants that attract bees to the garden. A hardy annual to 2 ft., with oblong woolly leaves and clusters of ¾-in. blue flowers, sometimes purple or white, blooming all summer. The small, tender leaves have a cucumberlike flavor and are delicious in salads, iced drinks and for pickling. Pick them before the bloom begins. The flowers last well when cut. In late summer, mature plants cut back to a few inches from the ground will send up fresh, new growth for fall bloom. The plants self-sow readily, and are propagated from seed. They do not transplant.

borax. In the garden, borax is used for killing weeds and poison ivy. See Pests and Diseases.

Borax is also used for drying flowers; a mixture of half borax and half cornmeal works well. Place the blossom in a box, and sift the borax mixture in and around the petals until the flower is completely buried. Cover the box and leave it undisturbed for a week or ten days. Then uncover the box, carefully lift out the flower and shake or brush off the borax. You will have a well-preserved flower. Thick-petaled flowers, such as dahlias, take a longer time to dry than those with thin petals—cosmos, for instance. Most flowers dried in this way will retain their original color. Silica gel is used for the same purpose and in the same way. For complete information on drying flowers and foliage, see *dried flowers*.

Bordeaux mixture. An old-time fungicide prepared from copper sulfate and lime, now little used but still effective. See Pests and Diseases.

border. A long, relatively narrow bed of plants such as might parallel a driveway, walk, house, wall or, especially, the lawn. There is no set plan for a border.

Borders may vary in content depending on climate, space and the effect desired. Here, where summer weather is cool and moist, tuberous begonias mix with scarlet sage, lavender-blue ageratum and lobelia, white sweet alyssum, golden French marigolds, plumes of pink astilbe and neat clumps of rosy *Begonia semperflorens*.

Sedum spathulifolium is a candidate for the blue border. Its bluish-green leaves tinged with red are decorative at every season. During May and June it produces clusters of bright yellow flowers that are ½ inch across.

Border Plants with Blue Foliage

By ELSIE LOUISE SCULTHORP

Plants with colored foliage have one great advantage—they stay on the job for a longer part of the year than flowers do, often lasting well into the winter. Foliage of many colors can be used to advantage as accents or to complete a color scheme, but blue foliage is probably the quietest and most restful color for a border. It gives an indistinct and charming effect—a good contrast for the gay colors of the flowers, and if planted in the shade, it makes the shadowy places softer and mistier.

There are numerous variations in blue coloring. Some plants have foliage of a striking steel-blue; some have leaves of varying shades of blue-green; some have whitish, grayish, frosty, or silvery blue; some have opalescent blue. The stronger the shade, the more care should be exercised in its use.

One of the best and most useful of the plants with blue-gray leaves is the plantain lily (*Hosta sieboldiana*). This is a stately border plant; handsome, too, in shady places. A hot, dry situation seems to produce better color in the foliage. The plant makes a large, compact mound of beautiful, large, blue-gray leaves and produces short spires of lavender bells. It is more useful for its leaves than for its flowers, but it has a fine effect wherever planted and is an excellent accent.

We often see the tall, bearded iris with blue-green-gray foliage and recognize the relative of the old-fashioned sweet iris (*Iris pallida*). But when not in flower the clumps of softly colored foliage are striking in the border and the foliage remains good-looking well into autumn.

Lovage (*Levisticum officinale*), a perennial herb planted and loved since the beginning of gardens, is well worth a place in the border. It has many divided leaves of dark, shining blue-green, making clumps about three feet tall, and it bears clusters of green-yellow carrot flowers. All parts of the plant—root, leaves, flowers, and seeds—are edible, with a strong celery taste.

Some of the meadow-rues (*Thalictrum*) have foliage of a lovely soft, bluish tone. Dusty meadow-rue (*T. glaucum*) is perhaps the best of these, with ele-

It may be rectangular; it may be curved, scalloped or free-form. It may conform to the contours of the land or reflect some other element of the total design—or it may be virtually sufficient unto itself. Four feet is about the minimum width that will allow a balance of plant display. And a border wider than 6 ft. is difficult to cultivate. Very wide borders sometimes have a flagstone path through them.

Since most borders are adjacent to grassy areas, they often present an edging problem. Left alone, the grass will spread into the bed. With a sharp spade, an edger and edging shears it can be kept trim. But a much simpler solution—if it fits into your landscaping plans—is to put in a permanent and virtually invisible edging of steel or aluminum strips, or the more assertive brick, flagstones on edge or stone curbing. See *edging*.

Cultivation and maintenance of a border are the same as for any planting bed. Thoroughly spade and fertilize the soil in the fall or early spring. During the summer, cultivate shallowly, or use a mulch to prevent weeds and conserve soil moisture.

The traditional border may be planted with annuals, biennials or perennials. Shrub borders are chiefly comprised of woody plants. These can be intermingled or used separately.

BORDER

UPPER LEFT: *Festuca ovina glauca*, the blue fescue, is a fine, tufted, ornamental grass and one of the most strikingly effective in the blue border.
UPPER RIGHT: *Hosta sieboldiana* has large bluish leaves; pale lilac blooms appear at the beginning of summer.
ABOVE: *Iris pallida variegata*, the sweet iris, is a bearded species with fragrant flowers that are lavender-blue to white. The leaves are blue-green and white.

gant, finely cut foliage of blue-gray and soft, feathery heads of fragrant yellow flowers. It grows three to four feet tall and blooms in July. It's beautiful in the border, with flowers good for cutting.

The old favorite, dianthus, too, with its grassy, bluish foliage, is good for both foliage and delightfully perfumed flowers. It is frequently used as an edging, and the lower kinds could be used as a ground cover in a sunny spot. There are hundreds of species, with much variation in the heights and growth habits from tiny, low mounds to some that grow about a foot high. The foliage of all species, in both texture and color, is indispensable in the garden.

Herb-of-grace (*Ruta graveolens*) is an interesting member of the Rue Family, which includes citrus fruits, gasplant, and many fragrant trees and shrubs. It has been grown since ancient times, and was a necessary flavoring for meats in the days when there was no ice to keep food fresh in summer. It is a beautiful plant, easily grown but seldom seen; a very satisfactory perennial, long-lived, in a permanent cloak of foliage about 2 feet high. The strongly scented opalescent-blue leaves are divided, with rounded leaflets. The plant bears flat clusters of small, bright yellow flowers of not much value. It is one of the best of the fragrant plants for bluish foliage, useful near the front of the border.

Some to Cut

Sea holly (*Eryngium maritimum*), with its hollylike leaves and its spiny, metallic-blue thistlelike flower

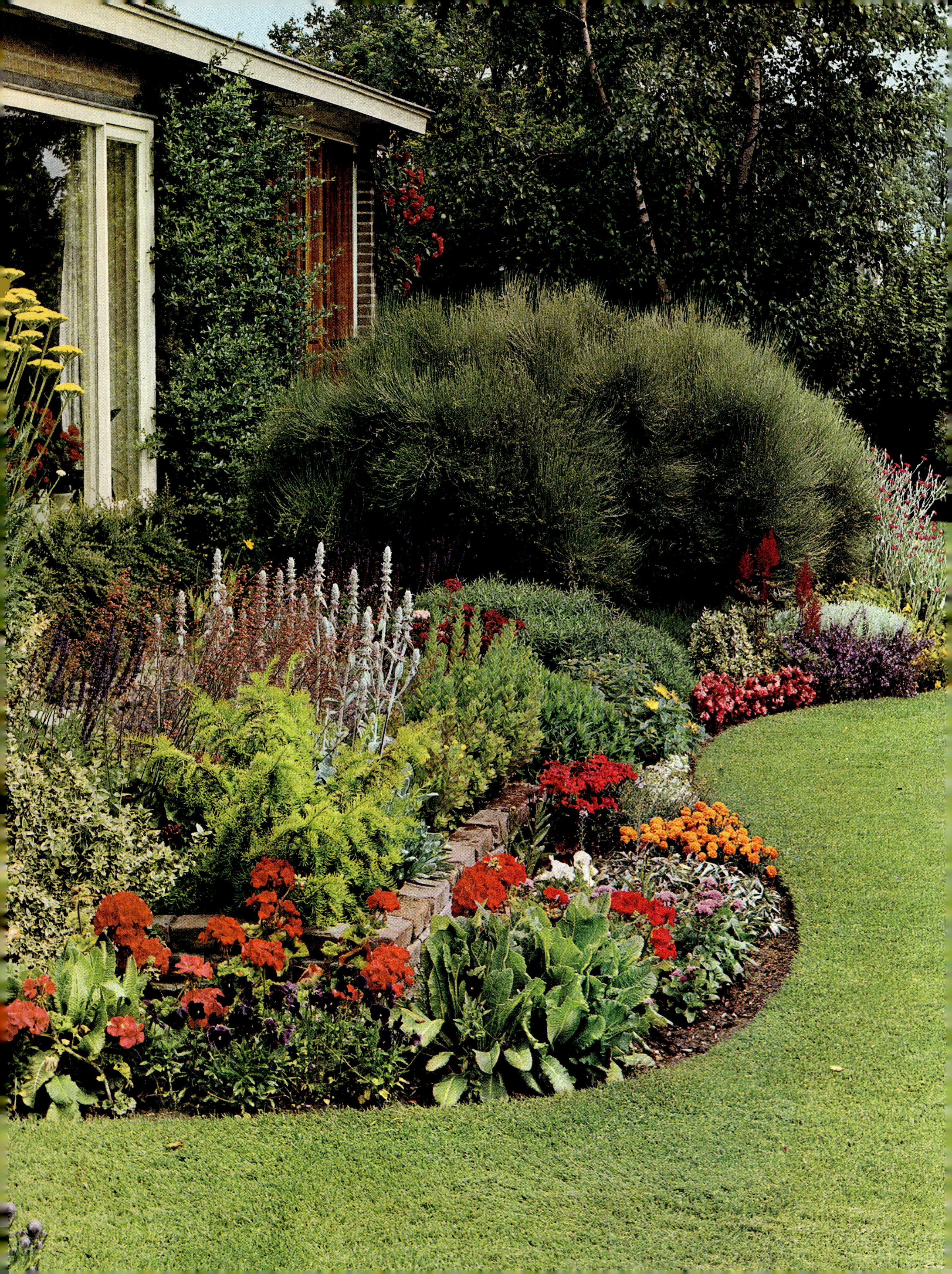

heads, is an attention getter in the border, decidedly attractive, and also useful for cutting. Amethyst eryngium is a beautiful plant that develops into a fine clump of decorative blue-gray foliage, with many amethyst-blue flower heads, creating a stunning effect. It needs sandy loam and a good sunny spot.

For a fragrant plant with silvery-bluish foliage, you can't do better than the charming, aromatic old favorite, lavender. There are different kinds, with flowers varying in color from lavender to a deep purple-blue; the commonest kind has the bluest foliage. They attain a height of one or two feet, and, where hardy, make an admirable appearance.

The horned-poppy or seed-poppy (*Glaucium flavum*) has toothed leaves of bluish white, and bears large poppylike yellow or orange flowers, interesting and showy. It is a biennial, but seeds itself freely and is easily cultivated. It likes plenty of sun.

One of the most delightful of all the blue-tinted foliage plants is the stonecrop (*Sedum*). It's an appealing, small plant with rounded, fleshy, blue leaves, and little clusters of dark pink flowers at the ends of trailing stems. Flourishes in September and into October. This is a popular plant for a hanging basket.

Here are some other suggestions for blue-leaved plants: A small edition of sweet woodruff (*Asperula odorata*), which has narrow, very blue-green foliage and tiny, white, misty flower clusters. Creeping baby's-breath (*Gypsophila repens*), with its small blue-green leaves, is wonderful for small stone walls. Blue fescue (*Festuca ovina glauca*), a lovely grass with blue leaves, grows in small tufts, rather like small dianthus. It has little pale yellow flower plumes about a foot high. Excellent for an edging; it does not spread.

Visit a good nursery and search for plants with blue leaves. You'll find surprising treasures that will be delightful in your garden.

LEFT: Blue foliage, whether it tends to gray or green undertones, intensifies all surrounding colors—greens seem greener, reds redder. And the effect on all kinds of pink and strong purple (like the pansies shown) is quite remarkable. The silvery-blue thread of this garden is spun by velvety spires of *Stachys olympica* FOREGROUND, silver-variegated euonymus LEFT FOREGROUND, gray-blue cerastium and rose-pink flowering corn cockle both BACKGROUND. The intense blue spires are those of salvia; the low-growing lavender-blue is ageratum; the clump of medium blue in front of the cerastium is echium. Other materials in this carefully planned garden of annuals, perennials and shrubs, include: tall, golden *Achillea filipendulina*, *Cotoneaster horizontalis*, pale pink heuchera, ruby-red sedum, orange marigolds, glowing scarlet geraniums, dwarf yellow hypericum, pink *Begonia semperflorens* and a Japanese yew (*Taxus*) in dwarf gold-leaf form. Climbing roses and birch trees grow in the background.

Border privet. See *Ligustrum obtusifolium*.

borealis (bor-ee-*ay*-liss), **-e.** Northern.

borecole. Name used for kale; see *Brassica oleracea acephala*.

borer. One of a wide variety of insects, or their larvae, that drill tunnels into the woody or fleshy parts of plants. Their presence is sometimes betrayed by a small dribble of "frass" (sawdustlike excrement) on the surface of the plant or on the ground nearby. In most cases, borers are the larval forms of moths or beetles. They can be controlled by spraying with malathion. Plug the tunnel openings with mud or asphalt paint after applying the spray.

Rule One

One of the cardinal rules on preparing soil for pot plants is to leave plenty of coarse fibrous material in the mixture. Sifting is generally frowned on as tending to create too fine a consistency—soggy and slow to aerate when wet, powdery and hard to moisten when dry. R.B.

---

boron. Chemical symbol, B. One of the trace elements essential to plant growth. If there is insufficient boron in the soil, terminal buds may die; plant stems and the petioles of young leaves become brittle; root tips die. It should be noted also that boron is very toxic to plants except in minute quantities. It must be fed sparingly—and only when need has been well established—in the form of ordinary borax. For example, an ornamental tree should be given no more than 1 oz. per inch of trunk diameter once in three years; a fruit tree should be given half this amount. For general soil applications it is best to base quantities in accordance with an expert soil test. There is an old rule that if you cannot grow good beets, your ground may be deficient in boron. Indeed it may—but as often it may not.

Boston fern. See *Nephrolepis exaltata bostoniensis*.

Boston-ivy. See *Parthenocissus tricuspidata*.

botany. The science of plants and plant life. Also, the plant life of a region; the scientific literature related to a plant or group of plants. While there is a close relationship between the substance of botany, horticulture and ordinary gardening, in practice the separation is distinct and the differences great.

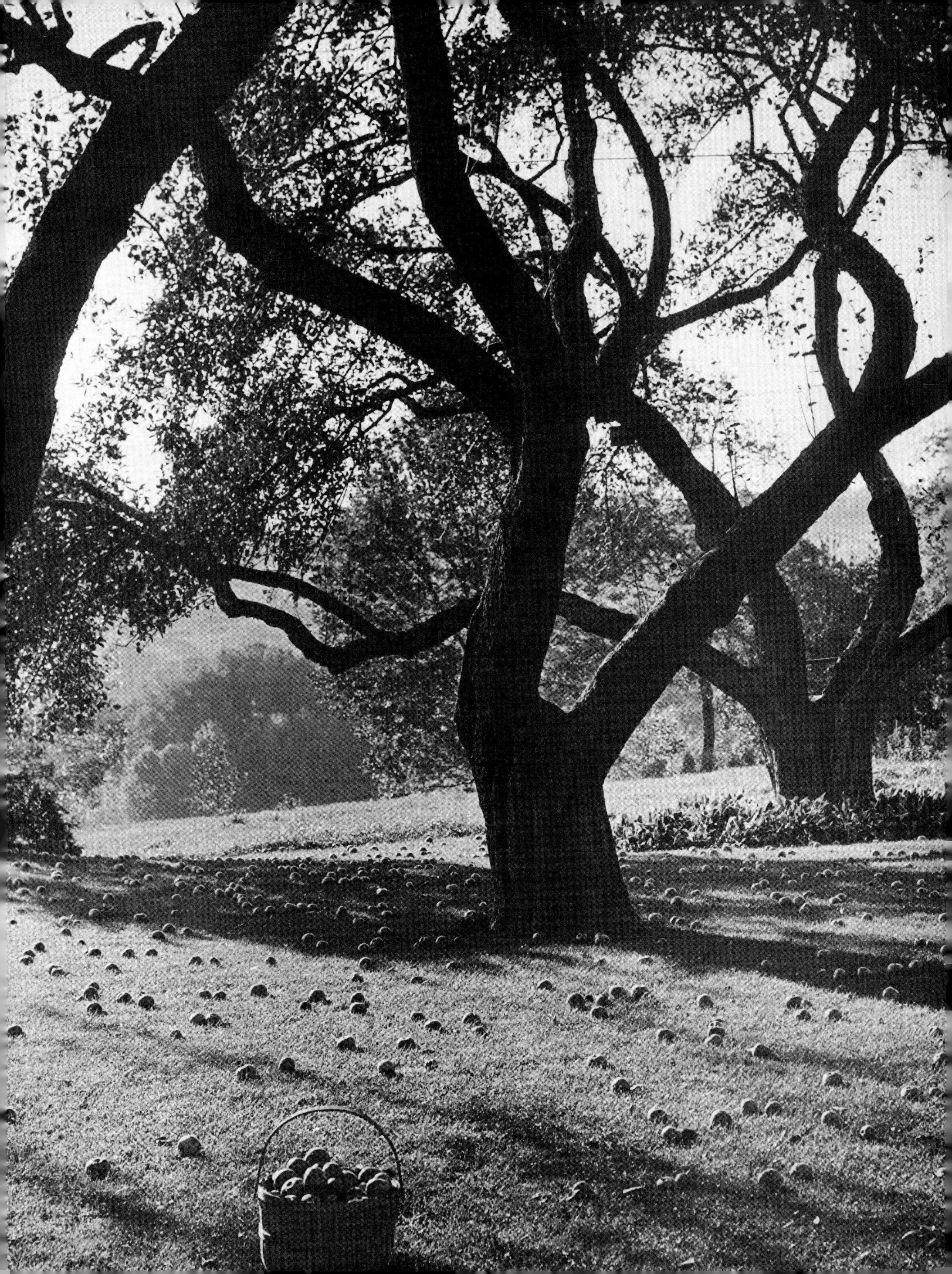

BOTANY

Botany: The Successful Plant

By MAY THEILGAARD WATTS

Success? Must we dally to define it? I am willing to accept the first unedited, unexpurgated concept of success that comes into your mind, if you will reciprocate. But we are about to consider success in a *plant*. That combination is likely to set us to stroking our chins and pursing our lips and judiciously discussing "successful in whose opinion?—from what point of view?—in what relationship?"

Let's look at a plant that seems successful—seems so to me, at any rate—a plant that can endure being kicked by a gardener, chewed by a cow, having its flowers pulled off by children and much, much more. Let's look at a dandelion.

Does it matter, really, whether the individual dandelion plant that we happen to look at is the darling of the conservationist, pegging down its bit of a dust bowl, binding and healing man-made wounds; or whether our individual is a robust, shaggy intruder, marring the crew-cut uniformity of marshalled grass blades in our expensive lawn? Are not both of these dandelion plants successful, though they are not equally popular? Popularity is another thing, in plants, as among men, often incompatible with success.

Let's start by inspecting the dandelion seed. It arrives suspended from a silken parachute, like an invading commando, with full equipment for flying, landing and hanging on. Barbs on the seed can grip the grit of the dust bowl or the humus of the lawn.

This wind-borne, self-braked seed is a well-provisioned package, holding not only the tiny embryo plant, but also sufficient food to give it a good start until the time when it can utilize the local food supply.

This classic study of apples at harvest time was made by photographer Samuel Gottscho. Successful throughout North America, apples require care when planted in the home orchard but wild species thrive
unaided in forests all over the continent.

355

Are not all seeds successful? Let's look at a few other examples.

First, let's look at an orchid seed—no, a hundred orchid seeds. One is too small. Let's look at them in the hands of an orchid grower—these minute specks, without equipment for traveling or for holding fast, and with a meager supply of energy for starting the growth of the embryo, which, indeed, is not finished and must mature before germination is possible. No wonder the orchid grower is painstakingly using test tubes, sterilized instruments, a selected cultural medium, rubber gloves—and must wait for several years for the plant to attain blooming size. When, finally, a flower is produced and extends its purple lip or its mottled pouch toward our admiration, it is the success of the plant man, not of the plant, that we applaud. But (or so), we stamp on dandelions while we coddle orchids.

Some Plants Need Help To Succeed

An orchid seed may need man, but only when outside of its natural range. What about seeds that need the ministrations of humans no matter where they are on the face of the earth? How successful is a kernel of corn, a grain of wheat? Each of these seeds has plentiful provisions for starting off the embryo plant. Our own bodies, largely constructed out of the energy from those two seeds, attests to that provision. But these well-packaged seeds are without any facilities for travel away from their birthplace and out into independence. They are unable even to leave home without help from man. Think of the competition and the struggle for survival of the many plants that could spring up from one fallen ear of corn—if the ear were capable of wrenching itself loose from the plant. Here, then, is a plant that is a successful half of a partnership, but a complete failure without man as its partner. The rigid ear of corn holding fast to its seeds and the stiff ear of wheat gripping its plump grains would have become extinct long ago if they had not chanced to meet up with a hungry partner equipped with hands and tools and plans.

Is the heavenly blue morning-glory another plant that needs man's ministrations? We file its hard seeds, or soak them, to help the embryo plant break its way out through the thick seed coat. And we actually pour boiling water over the seeds of the Kentucky coffee-tree. But this strenuous treatment is not really necessary. Nature, always more concerned for survival of the race than for survival of the individual, seems to have provided for some seeds to wait a year, two years, many years, for germination. If all of one year's seedlings should be wiped out by heat or drought or cold or disease or competition, some seed would still survive to await a better year, a better chance. Because gardeners are not particularly concerned about the survival of the race, but insist on blue morning-glories on the fence this very summer, we file the seeds.

Men, like chickens, like mice, like juncoes, awake in the morning and start eating seeds, or seed wrappings. We start, perhaps, with tomato juice, as seed wrapping. Then coffee, a roasted seed. Then cereal, seeds ironed flat or shot from guns. Then toast, from ground-up seeds, with jam made from seed wrappings. Then eggs—the hen made those from seeds—and bacon, which a useful pig made out of seeds someone put into his trough.

Then, on a spring morning, sustained by seeds, we emerge into the garden with our new handsome seed packages in hand. Perhaps we plant lima beans. How plump with energy they feel. But the seed coat feels like raincoat material. We can't help wondering if the little plant will be able to rupture that coat. But if we investigate with a hand lens, we can detect a minute hole, close to the whitened scar marking the point where the seed was attached to the pod. The point of the new root will be directed at that hole, and will be able to wedge a rupture into the seed coat. Then the arching neck of the little plant stem will give a mighty heave and lift its fat seed leaves up above the soil. When these plump ovals spread open they will reveal, held between them, the first true leaves of the bean plant. To discover whether those two oval seed leaves have any use, we need only to grow several beans in a pot and pinch the seed leaves (cotyledons) off half of them. We will soon be convinced that here is a packaged booster for the new plant.

All this seems to add up to considerable efficiency. It looks as if the lima bean might be called a successful seed. But wait; let's look again.

How did this plump seed get out of its pod? Someone had to pry the pod open—had to pry hard. Who pried these resistant pods open when we were not around?

The wild relatives of beans do not have their seeds nailed to the mast like this. The two halves of their pods spring apart and roll up, ejecting the seed forcefully. The lima bean, then, like corn and wheat, is a seed that can succeed only in partnership with man.

But perhaps, after our seedy breakfast, we have not gone out to install little partners, but have gone to see whether the petunias are up in the pots in the cold frame where we planted the tiny seeds a week, or two weeks ago.

There they come, just pushing up, jostling each other. We sowed them close. They can help each other up through the ground. Then we can thin them

BOTANY

out. Nature uses too many seeds. Why shouldn't we? But we won't stand by, as nature does, watching the weaklings crowded out while the strong survive. We will thin and transplant. In nature it is enough if a minute percentage survives. In gardening that is not enough. We paid for *all* those seeds. Maybe they are special, and sold by count. Maybe we paid a dollar for a hundred seeds that lie in the very tip of a spoon. We don't want any of this struggle for survival. Perhaps the seed we bought represents true doubles that have been hybridized with difficulty and produce seeds sparingly. Perhaps these seeds are the result of deliberate shocking with X rays, or colchicine. Perhaps they have had their chromosome number doubled by this treatment. Probably, if we allow the crowded seedlings to fight it out, the stout survivors would tend to be the plants that most nearly resembled the original wild ancestors of this garden variety. Probably the eliminated plants would, if they had lived, have shown the very characteristics that the hybridizers were seeking. The gardener must stand by to give assistance to *his* chosen strain as against nature's chosen strain.

Plants That Succeed Alone

Here and there among the seeds a gardener has may be one that holds within itself a deep secret—the secret of having been shocked by cosmic rays, or by atomic radiation. The plant growing from this seed may be a mutant, a sport—a genius among conformist relatives. Perhaps it will exhibit a uniqueness that proves desirable, but probably it will be strange but undesirable. Perhaps the unique quality will be undesirable to the plant, but desirable to man—like the ear of corn or the head of wheat with their firmly gripped seeds. Perhaps the unique quality will be desirable to the plant but undesirable to man—like the dandelion seed.

Whether formed by accident or by man's intention, the seeds of hybrids, of mutants, are likely to require man as a partner to success.

But there are plenty of seeds in the garden that need no gardening partner. No one keeps them carefully indoors at the right temperature, the right humidity, during the winter. No one files their seed coats, or soaks them in a sulfuric-acid solution, or pours boiling water over them, to help them rupture their seed coats. No one has inoculated them with nitrogen-fixing bacteria. No one drops them in place. No one covers them two diameters deep with finely

Unlike the successful dandelion, the orchid seed is not built to travel and will require several years to produce blooms. Without the gardener's help it could not prosper here.

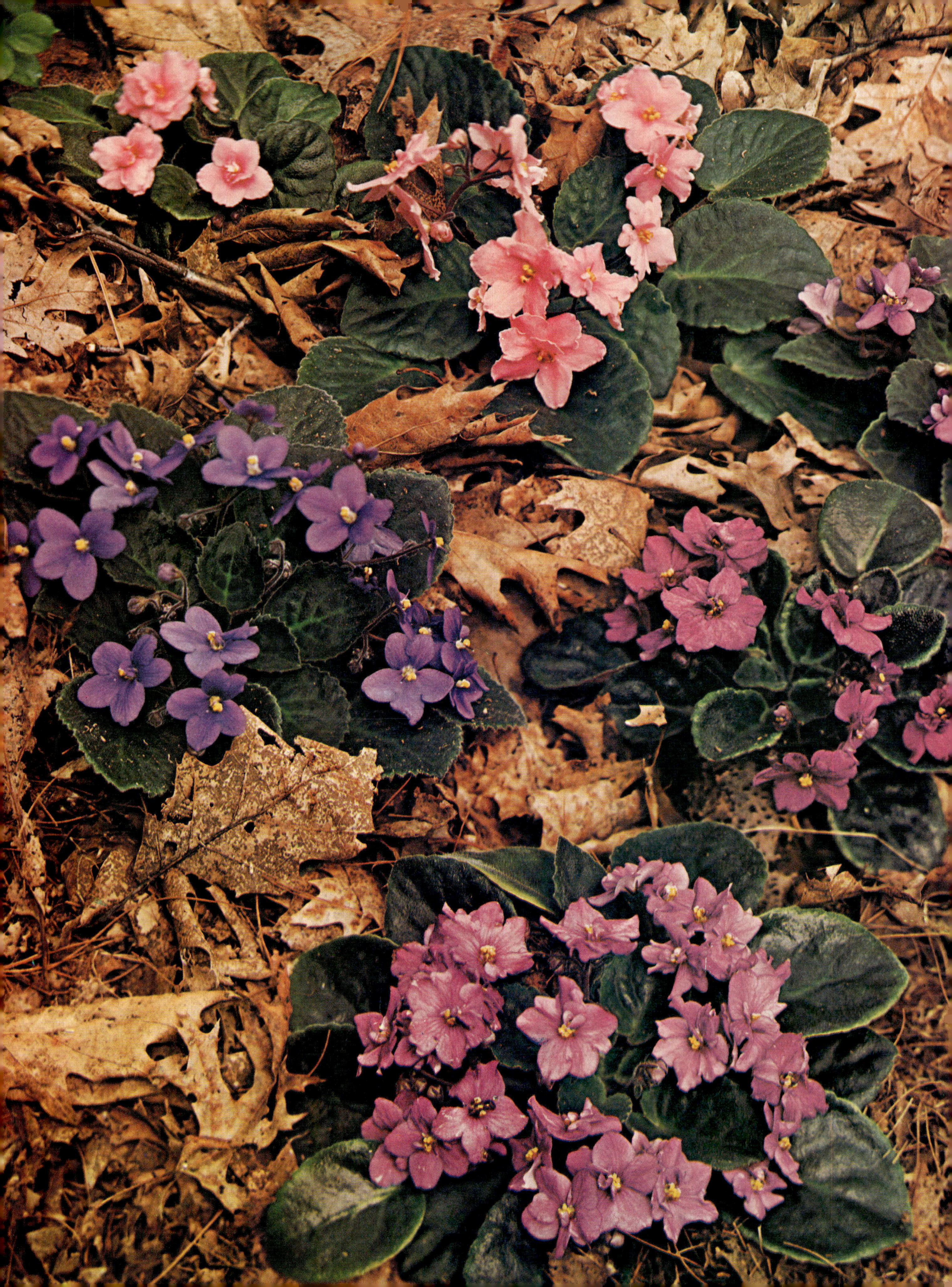

pulverized soil. No one brings them into the garden on a spring morning in colorful seed packets. They fly in on the wind or travel in in a bird's digestive tract or in the mud on a bird's feet. They ride in on a dog's fur. They roll in. They are shot in, by seed pods that work like guns. Or they have been there a while, having a special resource in the capacity to wait and to germinate eventually, when bacteria and fungi in the soil have decomposed their seed coats.

All these, uninvited, grow between the rows, in the rows, among the delphiniums, close to the roses, in the center of a clump of phlox, in the larkspur bed. Unless we help out our partner-seedlings, they will be elbowed out of existence.

Those seedlings in the phlox clumps, and those in the larkspur bed and under the petunia edge and among the bachelor's-buttons, are offspring of plants that we ourselves selected and installed. But we don't want their children. If we should permit the volunteer phlox seedlings to grow, a vigorous magenta-colored clump resembling the wild ancestor will gradually crowd out the large-flowered, delicately colored salmon-rose, or pale pink, or crimson-eyed phlox that we planted. If we let the seedlings of the petunias grow, the flowers will become smaller, more like the original South American ancestor. The bachelor's-button seedlings will show flatter, sparser, simpler heads. The larkspur spikes will become shorter and presently show a rabbit head in the center of each flower, instead of the doubleness of the named variety that we planted.

Wild Flowers That Are Welcome

However not all self-sufficient plants are banned from the garden. Some are invited to come in—some natives that are quite able to hold their own without help from man. What about the native columbines that we sow among the rocks beside the pool, to dangle red for the humming birds? What about the cardinal-flower seed that we scatter so that the crimson spikes may drive deep into the dark pool? What about the violets under the apple tree? We are planting seeds that man has not hybridized, or selected, or shocked or even chosen and treasured from bombarded mutants. But why should we need to scatter seeds of these natives? If they are truly natives of our area, and if this crack between the rocks, this

Saintpaulias that grow in the wilds of East Africa are well equipped to care for themselves in their surroundings, but sophisticated man-made hybrids like these, which we call African violets, need specialized soil, careful watering and the care and interest of the gardener in order to succeed.

The cardinal flower grows in its special water-side habitat without help, but the brilliant red flowers are so appealing that, despite its independence, it receives help from wild-flower enthusiasts and gardeners who scatter seed to increase the crop.

place beside the pool, this dappled shade under the apple tree, are reasonable facsimiles of the native habitats, won't these plants come, unbidden, unbought? Yes, they will come, probably, if the habitat stays the same, and if we are content to wait and wait. But we are not so content, of course, in a small garden, where every square foot counts.

So we assist nature, anticipating her progress. But we are not so prodigal of our seed expenditure as nature would be. We take care that those columbine seeds land *between* the rocks, not *on* them. We drop the cardinal seeds into the dark soil *beside* the water, without dropping any *into* the water. We scatter the violet seeds under the apple tree, not under evergreen shade, and not where the turf is thick. As a matter of fact, we probably decide to avoid a few more of nature's hazards, and start all the seeds in the cold frame, and set them in place in the garden when they are better able to face competition. Even the natives, then, because of this special treatment, when they are invited into our gardens are there in a sort of partnership with the gardener.

Occasionally we gardeners desert our collection of green partners for a while to hobnob with nature's successes on a mountaintop, in a desert, along a trout stream. When we return from our vacations we may find our cherished partners dried up, curled up, brown, collapsed against each other. No one gave

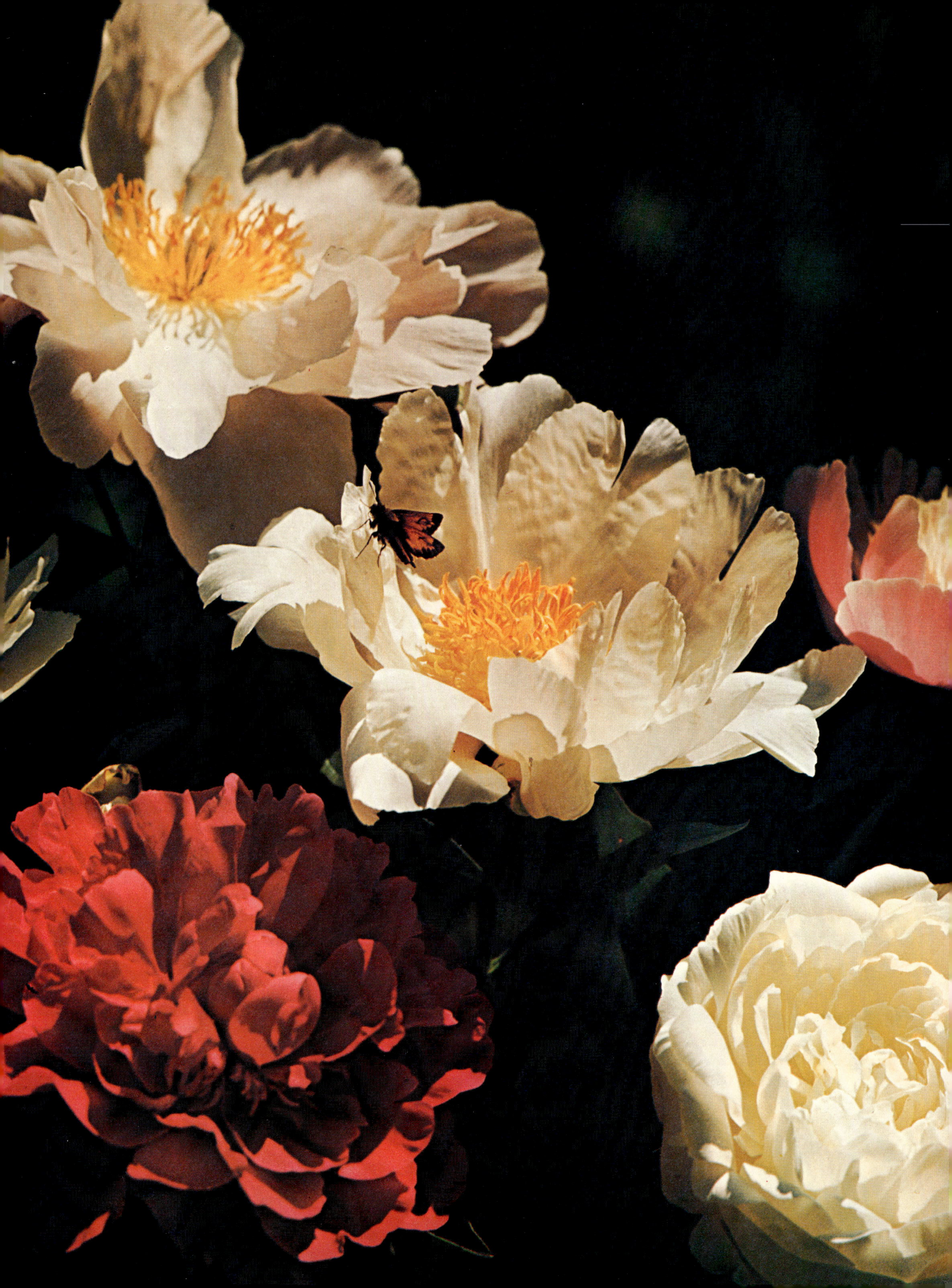

them a drink while we were gone. No one put crutches under them. No one picked off the flowers, thus exercising birth control and keeping them from pouring their strength into unwanted myriads of probably backsliding offspring. But among the ruins stands a plant we failed to notice before we left—green among the tired browns, blooming mightily, with a seed head uplifted and sowing the wind. A dandelion! No one sprinkled it. Why did it survive?

Let's look at the root, where the water intake is. Digging it is not easy. We discard the trowel and get the spade. Even so, the root breaks and we bring it up in two sections. We lay it down, and beside it we lay the short bush of a zinnia's roots and a petunia's roots. Obviously the long root was the one that drank deeper down in the soil. Moist particles of earth still cling to it. Here is a one-way root—a tap root that can drink deep when the top soil, where zinnias and petunias drink, has long since dried out.

But length is not all. This dandelion root is fat, too —fat with food storage that gives a running start to the spring growth. Not only long, and fat, but able to take tucks in itself. If we inspect an old root we can see those tucks—wrinkled, horizontal folds at the ground line. Even these may contribute to success. As the plant grows new leaves constantly from its apex while the old ones die off at the base, the whole green structure would be gradually lifted above the surface of the ground, and be vulnerable to breaking by wind and hoof. But this root has the capacity for contracting, for pulling in its neck. The wrinkled folds are evidence of such contraction.

There are many other roots fat with storage in our gardens. We know them by their swift start in the spring: peonies, asparagus, bleeding-hearts, for examples. There are some garden plants that have tap roots much like the dandelion's. We know them by the difficulty of transplanting them—Oriental poppy, for example. With many minor roots, a few can be spared, but with one main intake line, breakage can be disastrous. The dandelion does not transplant well. Does someone care?

The dandelion's root is not the only feature that might help the plant survive a summer drought. The leaves, too, can take a beating. Let's look at a dandelion's leaves.

We break one off the plant. It drips milky juice. If we examine other plants that, like the dandelion, sometimes stand green among wilted and drooping

OPPOSITE: A quick start in spring is characteristic of plants whose roots are fat with stored foods. Once planted, the peony is one garden favorite noted for its ability to live on without care, year after year. It does need freezing temperatures in winter.

Bleeding-heart, an old-fashioned garden favorite, is another of the plants that store lots of food in the roots. Like the dandelion, it is well equipped by nature for a quick take-off as soon as the weather begins to show signs of warming.

companions, we are sure to find that some of them have a similar milky juice—whether the plant is a stout weed like milkweed, a tough forest-margin tree like sumac, a prairie remnant like flowering-spurge, a garden plant like Oriental poppy or snow-on-the-mountain. There is a noticeable difference between this thick fluid and the water stuff that exudes from the stem of a violet or a trillium.

Leaves Are Shaped with a Purpose

This milky juice is not the only feature that can help a dandelion through a drought. Let's look at the *shape* of the leaf. It looks as if someone had torn, or pinched out, bits of the margin, removing part of the soft green tissue that the thirsty sun might suck dry, but leaving the plumbing system untouched. The veins are intact, but the leaf surface is reduced. Out along the roadsides we can observe plenty of other examples of reduced leaf surfaces—in yarrow, in thistles, in Queen Anne's-lace and many others. To see this leaf reduction carried to its final degree, we must go to the desert and inspect plants like cactus or Mormon tea, where the stems have grown fat and succulent and green, and carry on the food manufacture for which the tiny, spiny leaves are no longer adequate.

Not only the shape of the dandelion leaf and the size of its surface but also its position with relation to the sun may contribute to success. Certainly dandelion leaves do not suggest suppliant hands spread to catch precious filtered light of the forest, as trillium leaves do, on our forest floors, or as hosta leaves do, in the shady corner of our gardens where conditions of their ancestral homeland have been approximated.

The upright leaves of the dandelion plant catch morning and afternoon sun, and let the midday rays slide past, while the more horizontal leaves gain a venetian-blind sort of shading from other leaves of the rosette. The basal leaves may be close to the ground where they efficiently elbow competitors, as they pre-empt a circular plot and make their own mulch against evaporation and where, incidentally, they are usually muddy and distasteful, so that no self-respecting cow will nibble them and no self-respecting lawn mower will cut them, and where they can carry on, should lawn mowers or cows dispatch their more upright partners.

Other plants carry this edge-to-the-sun position to a greater extreme. Prickly lettuce, of roadsides and vacant lots, twist their leaves into such marked north-south orientation that this becomes a "compass plant." Prairie dock assumes something of this position. And in our gardens, the iris leaves form vertical fans.

The dandelion leaf does not have all the features found in leaves that endure beating sun. Hairiness, for example, is lacking—hairiness such as the mullein wears like a felt coat, and the velvet plant wears like a velvet coat, and the Artemisia wears in our sunny gardens or in dunes or in deserts.

A leaf may need to discourage hungry animals as well as the thirsty sun. The dandelion has a bitter taste. It is not relished unless food is scarce. The new young leaves are the most vulnerable. We ourselves eat those. There are no cows in a garden, but I have observed dandelion leaves standing intact where aphids were sucking dry the tender shoots of roses and delphiniums, while caterpillars and grasshoppers were chewing at many other kinds of leaves. (This was somebody else's garden, of course.) To sample the flavor of a sunbeaten leaf equipped with animal discourager, we need only to take a nibble of a marigold leaf, whose ancestors inhabited sunny Mexican fields. But everyone is familiar with success protected by bitterness, in areas other than gardens.

Such a leaf, then, coupled with such a root and started off by such a seed, helps to spell success for a dandelion plant, for one individual dandelion plant. But nature seems ever disdainfully disinterested in the success of one individual. Survival of the race seems to hold the focus of her attention. Reproduction, the future, the "citizens of tomorrow," is the controlling theme in fields, forests, commencement addresses and suburban PTA's.

Let's look at the dandelion's provision for the future of its kind. Let's look at a seed factory—a flower.

It will not be difficult to find a dandelion in bloom. It has a uniquely long blooming period. How different from the period of a week or two when we may find trilliums, or Jack-in-the-pulpits, or hepaticas. Most flowers have a blooming period related to day length. On a lengthening day bloom sweet William, for example, and Canterbury bells and peonies. On a shortening day bloom chrysanthemums, asters, dahlias. If we want blooms at other times we must contrive to tamper artificially with the day length. By means of such tampering, chrysanthemums may be had for Easter. But dandelions may be had for Easter without any maneuvering—and for the Fourth of July and Thanksgiving, and perhaps for Christmas too. There seems to be no sensitivity to day length here.

Yes, it is easy to find dandelions in bloom, but, having found them, it is not so easy to examine one individual flower. Here is no rugged individualist operating alone, like an orchid in the gloom of the rain forest. Here the individual is submerged in the community. What a child picks, and calls a dandelion flower, is, in fact, a city of flowers—a huddle, one for all and all for one.

The Well-Packaged Seed

To inspect an individual flower we have to pull one of the yellow straps, and look closely, probably with the aid of a hand lens, at all that is attached to it. Here is a complete flower, though it is small. And in this little flower we can find the floral features that are the most recent developments in flowers. Here are none of the old-fashioned features that mark such early floral experiments as magnolias, water-lilies, buttercups and other primitives. Among the advanced characters to be seen in this tiny flower of the dandelion are petals united along their sides; stamens reduced in number and united into a tube; the community formation, pooling expenditure of advertising display, using one stem, one green community wall. And here is no mass production of minute seed, as in an orchid flower. Instead, each flower produces a single seed, big, well-packed.

The rugged dandelion is one of nature's most stubborn successes and has more survival equipment than most other plants. Its toughness is a product of civilization developed in primitive villages in Europe where bare feet packed the soil and the sun baked it hard and dry.

All these modern developments are to be expected in the Composite Family to which the dandelion belongs, but the dandelion goes one step—one big step —beyond what is to be expected. Actually it seems to go just a step too far. (You can almost hear two daisies telling each other about this queer business, and wondering what this world is coming to, anyway.)

With all its up-to-date equipment that we associate with cross-pollination; with a dazzling yellow color that is especially visible to bees; with its green involucre closing up the whole floral display at the merest cloud that threatens wet pollen and dilutes nectar; with pollen-bearing visitors, of assorted sizes and tongue-lengths, hurtling in to a landing; with all this flourish of the paraphernalia of sex, this strange seed factory actually operates without benefit of sex.

It actually makes seeds without fertilization. Parthenogenesis, this is called—*partheno* from the Greek word for virgin, and *genesis* for the Greek word for birth, hence "a virgin birth." That dandelion pollen that travels off, so functional-looking, on a bee's importantly hairy hind leg, is sterile stuff. It will probably be deposited on the receptive-looking stigma of some other dandelion. But it will send down no pollen tube to fertilize an ovule. But the ovule will make a seed just the same, without benefit of sex. (Does not the whole structure of our culture, its novels, its advertising, its cosmetics, its stimulants, its foundations, its hair sprays, its tattooed wrists, seem to shudder at this act?)

At any rate the dandelion's future seems assured.

We know that if we have no bees on our apple trees this spring we can expect no apples in the fall. But if no bee should enter our neighborhood all summer (or if we should just happen, as we use the paraphernalia of progress, to poison all those that do enter) we shall have dandelion seeds just the same—enough for all the adjoining neighbors. No need to worry about that supply.

These virgin-birth seeds will be firmly set in a disk. The stem of the disk will elongate and hold this nursery high—this is an efficient stem, hollow, resilient, able to bend without breaking. Finally, when the seeds are ripe and ready and the day is sunny, the disk will bulge upward into a half-dome shape. This bulging will spread each dent that holds the tip of a seed. The released seeds will be off on the first breeze. And they will have a silken parachute for flight, barbs to effect a landing, a good package of food to start off the new plant—but isn't this where we came in?

With so many characteristics of survival value, the dandelion looks practically invincible. A tired gardener may well ask, "Is there no weakness in its armor?" "Is there no way of eliminating it permanently from a garden?"

The answer to both questions is yes.

There is a simple way, which takes advantage of its chief vulnerability, of eliminating it from a garden. If a gardener will turn his back on the garden, stop mowing the grass, stop weeding out the seedling elms, just stop everything, the dandelion will disappear from that place. In other words, if the gardener will go away from the garden, the dandelion will go away too.

No Plant Is Invulnerable

Then shade will come—the shade of tall unmowed grasses, and ragweed, thistles, milkweeds. The dandelion's leaves will lengthen upward, and its circle of soil will be reduced. Perhaps a squirrel will bury an acorn beside it. Perhaps a bird will deposit a hawthorn seed. Surely the wind will bring seeds of cottonwoods or trembling aspen. Under the saplings the shade will deepen. Gradually all the shady niches will be filled wtih plants that tolerate shade. Eventually the permanent native vegetation of the area will take over. There will be no place for a dandelion. They will be completely eliminated from this spot that was once a garden, but so will the delphiniums, the lilacs, the peonies, the apples, the Colorado spruces, the European larches, the ginkgo trees and even the hardy chrysanthemums, Oriental poppies and iris.

The dandelion may come back, but not until a forest giant falls down, perhaps, allowing a chimney of sunlight to enter the forest; or until man comes back, with an ax or a bulldozer—probably a bulldozer.

For this is the weakness in the dandelion's armor, that it cannot tolerate shade and that its tenure is only as permanent as disturbance. But disturbance tends to be the permanent condition wherever men huddle, or trade or beat paths to huddle, or trade or beat more paths.

In those disturbed areas where the dandelion thrives, the landscape is dominated by a band of foreigners. An ailanthus tree, from China, grows out of the areaway there beside the pavement. Bluegrass and clover fill the narrow strip of the parkway in the best places, while dandelion and plantain gather on the beaten places where people wait for the bus. English sparrows are noisy under the eaves. Starlings suck their teeth in the Norway maples. There are German cockroaches in the kitchen, and Norway rats in the basement.

Why this assemblage of foreigners in an American city?

For the answer we need to look at a city in Europe —we need to look at it as it was long ago, long before there were cities in America. The feet of huddled mankind were packing the clay soil. The sun was baking it into a sort of pottery, a compact tile. It was bare of plant life. But not for long. Somehow a tough mutant of a plant developed, and found life possible there on the pavementlike earth—found life possible and competition negligible. This tough plant raised its tough progeny around itself. The line increased and spread to other beaten places. When pioneers came to America the seeds of these specialized toughs came along, uninvited, as stowaways in luggage, in clothing, in bags of seeds, in shoes. When men began to gather in huddles in this country, and to beat the ground into pavement, these seeds were here and ready. They had little competition from native plants, because these natives had been exposed to no more concentrated trampling than that of transient bands of hunters. It is interesting now to find that London

OPPOSITE: The dandelion seed assures its survival. Produced without fertilization, the seed has a silken parachute for flight, barbs to effect a landing and a package of food to guarantee survival in the new environment. Although the dandelion is particularly well equipped to succeed in the temperate regions mankind has inhabited, all plants have equipment developed to make survival possible in the environments that spawned them and will thrive under cultivation almost anywhere if the gardener will take the trouble to provide close copies of the conditions in which the plant first grew.
OVERLEAF: Among the flowers blooming in this field of wild grasses are poppies, bee-balm, baby's-breath. Such a maintenance-free summer vista can be reproduced in almost any sunny field. Plow and harrow the section, and broadcast pounds of hardy annual seeds sold for this purpose by many of the mail order seed houses.

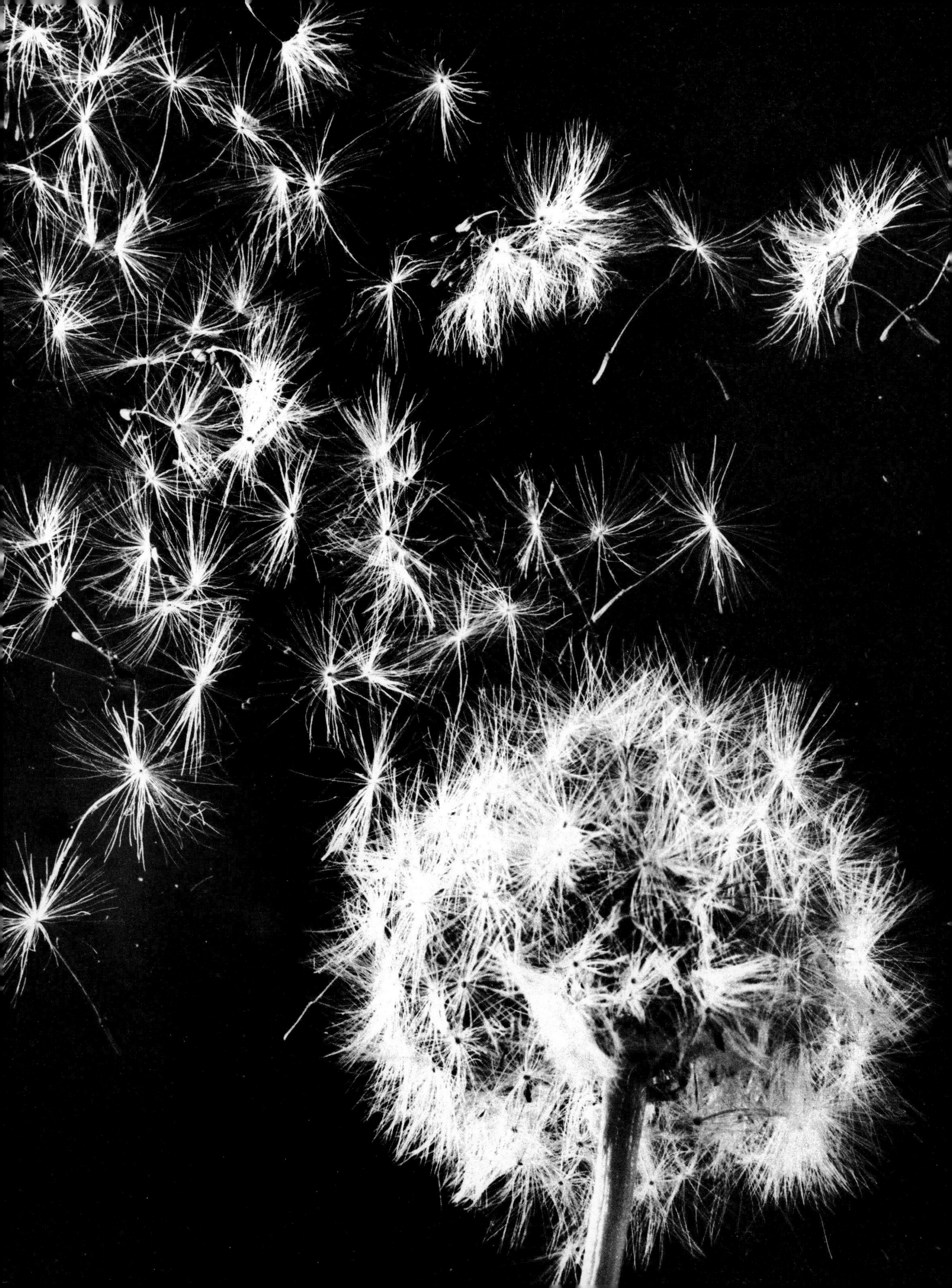

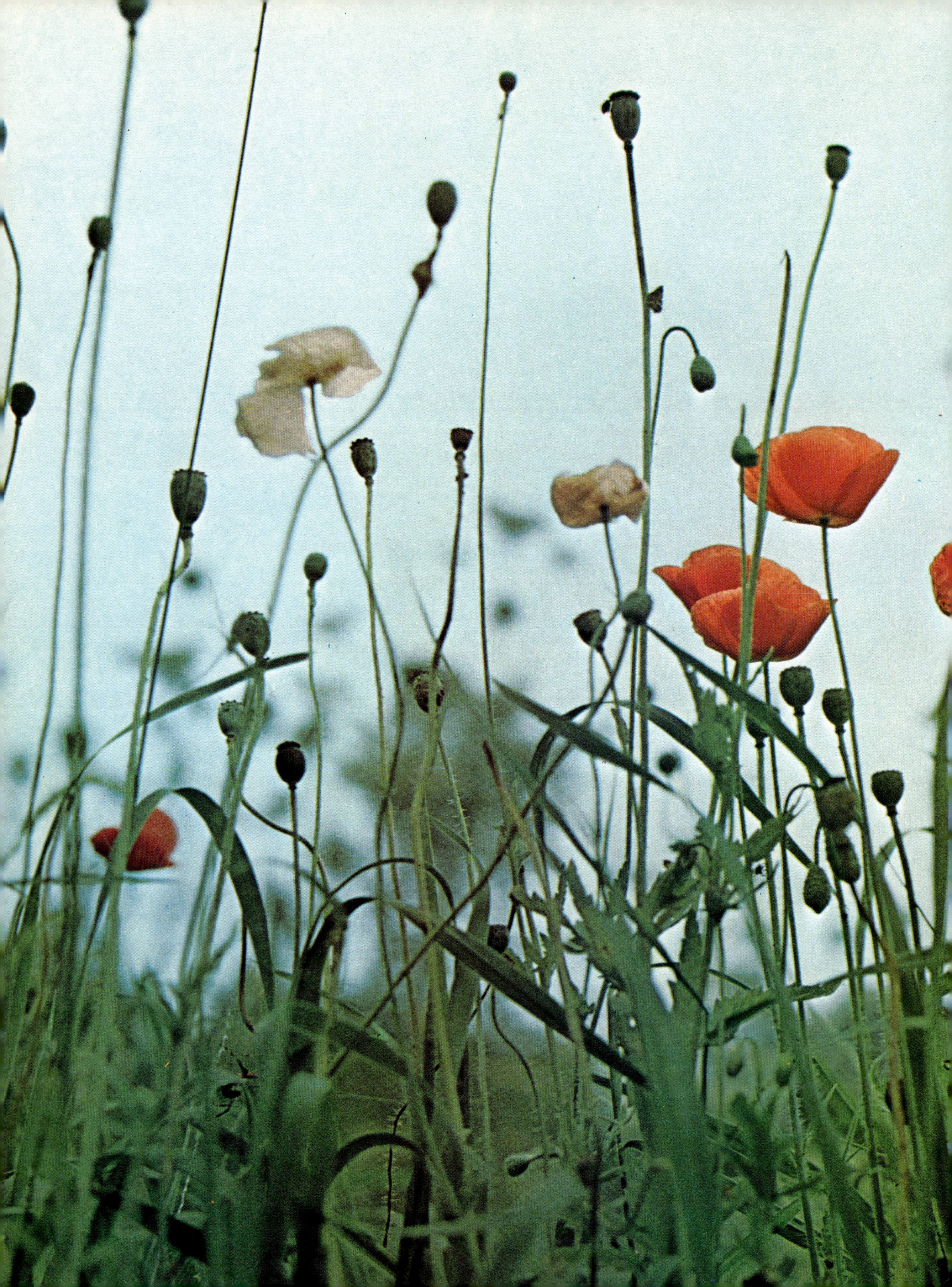

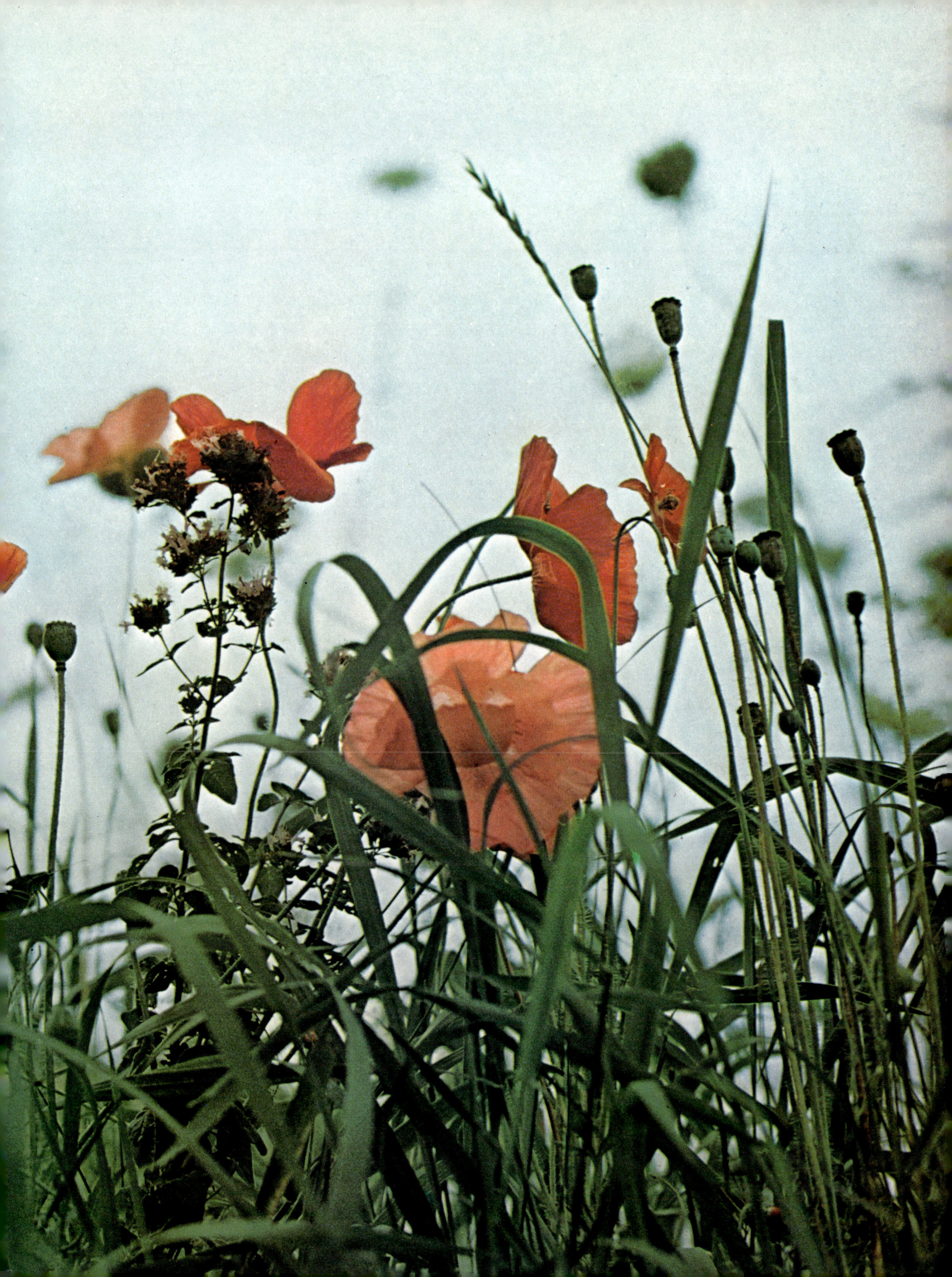

bomb sites are being taken over, in a similar way, by our fireweed, the first plant to come into our northern burned forests. Fires were an important part of the scene in America long ago. We were training plants for London bomb sites while they were training plants for Chicago alleys.

Gradually the band of foreign weeds has followed in the heavy footsteps of progress, further and further west. I saw them invading the heights of the Rocky Mountains, following the paths of the dude-ranch riding horses. But they were not stepping off the trail to invade the closed company of the native forest.

That is the vegetational cover with which the invaders cannot compete—the native plant formation.

What is it then, that makes a plant a native? Not that it can endure the averages of temperature, of rainfall, but that it can endure the *worst* that ever happens in the area. The *worst* times may be far apart, so far apart that only the old-timers remember them. But they come again, inevitably. They come, and they eliminate the weaklings. Suddenly the weather that had been so cooperative for 10 or 20 years narrows its eyes and points a cruel, bony finger of drought or freezing or sudden change at a plant, and counts it out of the game. The ones that stay in the game are the ones that we call natives. Not long ago there were two evil winters that came early and abruptly, and offered extremes of both freezing and thawing. They counted out of the game several shrubs that we, at the Morton Arboretum, on northern Illinois prairie landscape, had been recommending to gardeners for years as being dependably hardy. They *had been* hardy—for 20 years or so. But, when spring came that year, they were dead, to the ground or deeper. But the wild plums in every forest margin bloomed on schedule. The hawthorn, and wild crab apple, and shadbush, and nanny berry, and witch hazel and bur oaks, all acted as if nothing whatsoever had happened since they shed their leaves in the fall. They or their ancestors had seen it all before. Some of their ancestors had died of it—the weak ones.

Cultivation Changes Nature's Balance

The dandelion, then, and all its kind, are successful plants in disturbed areas. In undisturbed areas success belongs to the natives.

Cultivation is a form of disturbance.

A garden is cultivated and planned and shaped by the gardener's hand and eye and mind, or it is hardly a garden. Such shaping by artist and artisan has made gardens the fitting settings for much written and unwritten history.

But wherever man shapes the scene, there he must cope with the plants that he himself has helped make by accident. And while he copes with tough accidents like the dandelion, he must also cooperate with such treasured and fortunate accidents of nature, accepted and embellished by himself, as corn and beans. And while he copes and cooperates with the various accidents, he must also coddle his intentional creations. He must keep the big-headed sunflowers (called Russian) from remembering their many-flowered prairie past. He must keep the dark purple petunias and the maroon nicotianas from remembering how the moths could once find their white moons in the dusk. He must cope with such tendencies toward remembering by thwarting seedlings. And while he copes and cooperates and coddles, he must also imitate.

He must imitate ancestral homelands, for he has introduced into his planting several individuals that were capable of great success when man never entered their lives. But when man *has* entered their lives, to the extent of transporting them to places where weather or soil or exposure or companions are foreign to their needs, then their success depends upon man. Think of a hemlock, for example, brought from a humid, sheltered, shady forest, and set out to face wind and drought and smoky, gas-tinctured air in a city. It needs help. Think of a yew from a permanently shady, snow-filled forest floor, nakedly facing a thirsty winter sun. It needs help. Think of a rhododendron from bitter granite hills finding its roots in limestone soil. It needs help. Think of a sugar maple from well-drained upland, planted in a soggy bottomland. It needs help. These plants, so independently successful in their homelands, will, in the garden, be exactly as good as the success of the gardener in imitating their homeland.

Meanwhile, there thrives the dandelion. It needs no cooperation, no coddling, no imitation of its ancestral homeland. Granted disturbance and sunshine, it is a success.

Always? Well, almost always. There are lapses.

Let's look at the lapses.

A dandelion is not a success in the desert. Its seeds cannot wait several years for rain. Its roots are not spread out close to the surface of the ground in a great lace doily that can capture every drop of rain that falls within that area the instant that it falls, before it has time to evaporate. Its leaves are not fat with the succulence that can store this swiftly gath-

The exquisite hybridized roses we know today were created by gardeners who cross-pollinated by hand to bring about changes in the hardy species. When man shapes the scene, he must help the plants he has made or they will regress to nature's original blueprint.

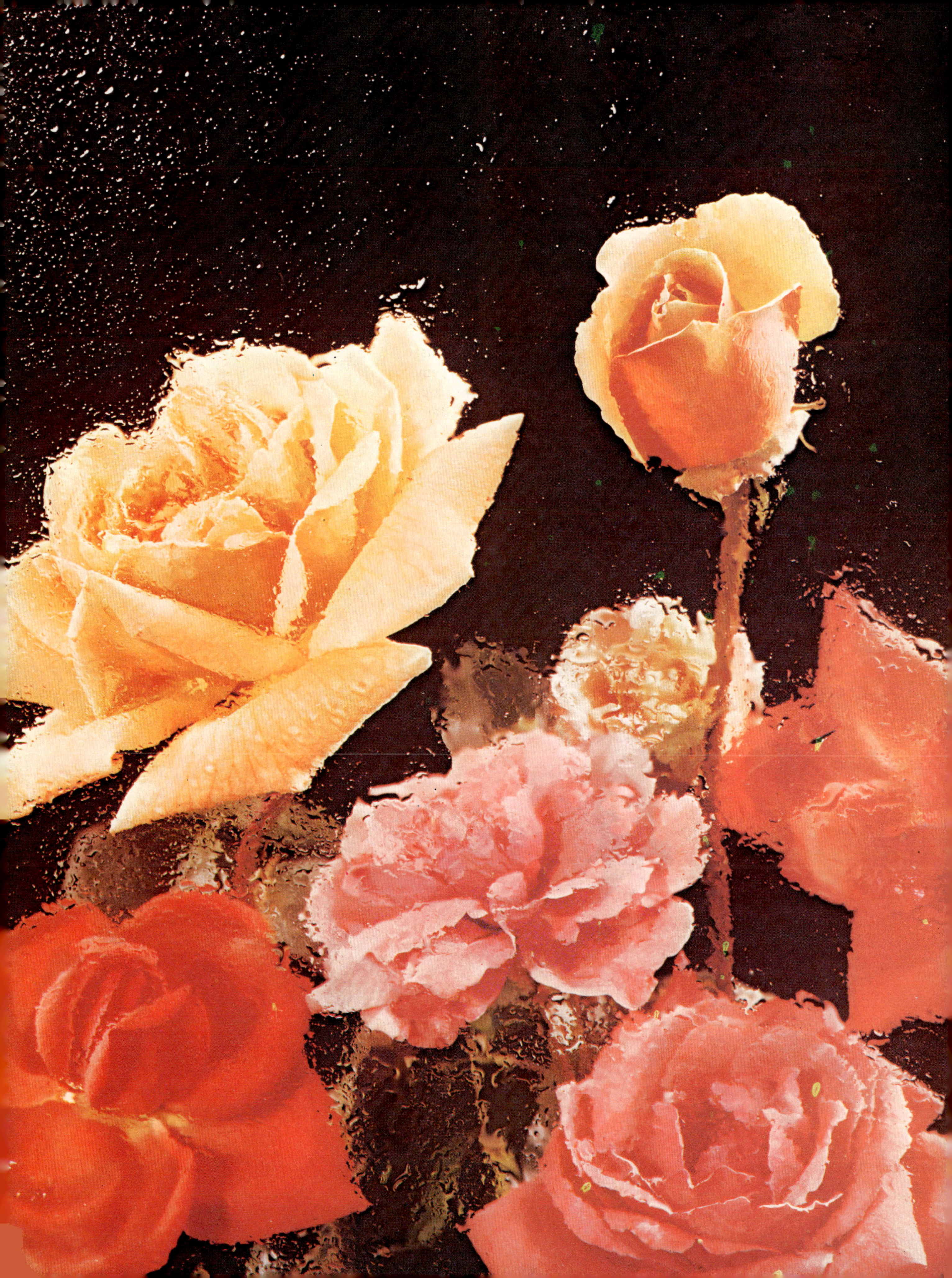

All parts of a plant are designed by nature to help it to survive its particular environment. Many species native to granular soils and arid climates have succulent leaves designed to store every drop of rain that falls within that area the instant it falls and before the moisture has had time to evaporate.

Upper left: The kalanchoe is designed to survive arid conditions and stores its own water supply.

Lower left: Cacti such as *Echinopsis multiplex* would not consider the dandelion a success since it has none of the succulent's aboveground equipment for the retention of water.

Below: Portulaca (rose moss) has plump little leaves and stems showing some of the signs of a succulent, and along with the sedums can be safely planted in the hottest, dryest places. Plants lacking these water storage facilities cannot easily survive arid conditions.

ered rain. (The sedums and the portulaca of our gardens show some of this succulence—enough so that we can safely plant them in the hottest, dryest places.) The cactus would not consider the dandelion a success.

Nor is the dandelion a success in the dripping mists and blue gloom of the rain forests. The strangler fig would not consider it a success. Nor is it a success in the windswept surges of the tallgrass prairie. The big bluestem grass would not consider it a success. Nor is it a success in a bog, in a marsh, on the tundra. The insect-trapping pitcher plant of the bog, the wading cattail in the marsh, the inch-high willow of the tundra, would not consider it a success. Not even those seedling sugar maples growing under the dense shade of the mature sugar maples in that forest not 20 feet from the roadside where the dandelion dominates the scene—not even those would consider the dandelion a success. It cannot pry its way into any closed community, that is to say any community where every ecological niche is filled with the particular plant whose attributes enable it to fill that niche, and keep possession of it, better than others.

There are limits, then, to the success of a dandelion.

In fact, if security (usually pronounced SECU-RITY in our ecological niche) for offspring and permanence of the environment for future generations, are to be considered ingredients of success for a plant, as for man, then the dandelion is not a success at all. Even in a dust bowl it prepares the way for other plants and thus for its own extinction.

And certainly, if, as for man, the good opinion of men is an essential ingredient of success, then, again, the dandelion is far from successful. If, however, the dandelion will substitute publicity for esteem, notoriety for fame (again like man), then the situation is different. Everyone seems to know this plant by name. This cannot be said of most of the pampered beauties of our gardens, nor of the fragile spring flowers of the forest floor. But even in this prestige there is a sort of flaw. Everyone knows it by name—but only one name. It has failed to accrue to itself the rich list of names that gathers through the years around a plant that people, especially close-to-the-soil peasant people, have grown and loved and used, and their children have played with. A collection of names is to a plant something like a string of medals across the chest, denoting long service in home gardens. Three-faces-under-a-hook, the pansy is called, and love-in-idleness, and herb trinity, and little stepmother, and herb constancy, and call-me-to-you, and Jack-jump-up-and-kiss-me, and Kit-run-in-the-fields, and lady's delight, and kiss-her-in-the-buttery, and thoughts, and heartsease and much more. But an orchid is only an orchid. And a dandelion is only a dandelion. It is cold at the top and at the bottom of the ladder. Better stay near the middle.

Not only of pet names does the dandelion have a dearth, but also of stories, legends, superstitions. No one seems to have rubbed it on his rheumatism, or to have slept with it tucked under the pillow on Midsummer Eve, or to have proffered it hopefully in a language-of-flowers nosegay, gathered at sunrise and tendered right-side-up in the right hand. No one? Well almost no one. It is reported that under the Doctrine of Signatures (the school of herbalists that based use of a plant on its appearance), the dandelion was sometimes prescribed for toothache because of the teeth on its leaves. It was also prescribed for diseases of the spleen, because of the shape of its root. And one old book tells that "to dream of dandelions betokens misfortune, enemies, and deceit on the part of loved ones." That sounds a bit like the sort of things that get said in the press about men who are oversuccessful.

But no one can deny the dandelion's popularity with poets and novelists. But neither can anyone deny the popularity of ash-heaps, outhouses, prison walls, alleys, factory districts, hard-beaten city playgrounds, town dumps, corner lampposts, fireplugs, filling stations with modern poets and novelists—and these are the familiar associates of dandelions.

Some Successful Native Plants

How could anyone ignore the dandelion's popularity with children? It can be gathered in tight fistfuls without causing baleful looks. And the hollow stem and some spit make lovely curls. And we have all told time by the seeds, and found out who liked butter by reflecting the buttery glow from under our chins.

Actually, the more I think about it, the better I like the dandelion. I will never forget the two miles of them along the road that I walked (or rode behind a horse that had to be led past the mailboxes) every morning, on the way to the country school where I once taught. One of these days I think I will grow a row of them in my garden. I'll keep the row disturbed —how my bleeding-hearts, and my gasplant, and peonies, and gypsophila and other republicans would hate that. I will let nothing interfere with the beating sun. How my maidenhair ferns, my primroses, my sweet woodruff, and other Emily Dickinsons would shrivel at that.

And for a companion I think I will give this colony of successful Europeans an outstandingly successful American native. That will be a hawthorn tree, standing nearby, but not close enough to shade its naturalized neighbor.

Let's look at this typical native success. It, too, has a seed that arrives on wings—a bird's wings—a seed that can wait a year for the acids of the soil to break down its seed coat. It, too, has a built-in cow discourager, as soon as the thorns have hardened. It, too, bears many seeds, but it provides no parachute for flight. Instead it wraps the seeds in tasty flesh and encloses the flesh in a skin that turns into a stoplight visible to birds when the seeds are mature. It, too, has leaves that are able to endure sun and wind.

So much for the hawthorn's personal success. It has some of the ingredients of the dandelion's success, but it does not come close to equaling it. We can keep hawthorns out of our gardens without half trying. But who wants to try?

We like the layers of white bloom that accentuate the horizontal architecture of the hawthorn in spring. We like the sounds of bees among those flowers. We like the layered light and shade of the summer foliage. Jens Jensen found this pattern symbolic of the way sunlight and cloud-shadow pass alternately across the face of the Illinois prairie. We like the copper and bronze of the fall, and the abundance of red fruits. And, when fruits and leaves have fallen, we like, almost best of all, the gray mist of the bare twigs. And we like the way the flat thorny branches hold their inevitable bird nest each spring and receive snow with such distinction that we can hardly savor a fresh snowfall until we have gone out to see how it lies on the hawthorns. And it is reassuring to know that, no matter how bitter the winter, the hawthorn will not mention it in the spring, when the exotics are showing their scars.

The Hawthorn Has Many Legends

Nor does this little tree lack for legends. For a fact, one should be wary of abusing it, such dire fates have been reported as overtaking any who have taken liberties with this chosen tree of the fairies, though birds may have their way with it. That is because of the act of a bird in pulling free the thorn that was pricking Christ's brow on Calvary. One of the English hawthorns, the Glastonbury thorn, is said to flower at Christmas. The hawthorn flowers have good standing in the language of flowers. They symbolize hope. And parts of the tree have been used as a heart tonic and to relieve vertigo, depression and palpitations. Certainly it has not been forgotten by poets, having supplied the flowers that the older poets lauded, especially by moonlight, and supplying plenty of thorns and fallen rotting fruit to stimulate the younger poets, especially in a miasma. And for children the earth-sweeping branches form a retreat, a playhouse, a wigwam. Of names it has only a few in America. Farmers call it haw, or thornapple. But the English hawthorn has achieved a long list of names: bread and cheeses, cuckoo's beads, hagthorn, pixie pears, quickset, May and many others.

Are there no exotics in our plantings that can compete with the hawthorn for popularity coupled with hardiness? Let's use the hawthorn as a sort of measuring stick for evaluating others.

We can find several plants that approach the measuring stick in the matter of more-than-one-season display. The cotoneasters pay for their place with both flowers and fruit, as does Cornelian-cherry dogwood, as do many honeysuckles, cherries, apples, plums, apricots, viburnums, roses, quinces (the quinces offer an extra dividend by producing their display of flower and fruit even if the plant is pruned for a hedge), and mountain ash or "rowan" (the little rowan tree has held extra value for many people through many centuries in its well-known propensity for protecting people from witches—so that, when we plant a rowan tree we plant white flowers, orange fruit, flocks of robins and cedar waxwings, witch-protection and, alas, probably a few borers, too). The little Callery pear offers abundant bloom, winter interest and the glossiest and richest of fall coloring. The winged euonymus offers explosive fall color and winter interest in its corky angled twigs. Korean barberry offers flowers, dazzling fruit and varied fall colors. All of these measure up well against the hawthorn, but they do not have the dependable hardiness of a native. Outstanding among the natives, the dogwood, in its range, offers flowers, fruit, fall color and winter interest in its tam-o'-shanter buds. The elderberry offers bloom (especially fragrant by moonlight), abundant edible fruit, pithy twigs for making popguns and the raw material for wine and tea and pancakes. The wild plum offers flowers, fall color and fruit that makes a superior jelly. The buckeye offers flowers, fall color and glossy nuts (that can be carried, as they have been so long carried, in the pocket as protection against rheumatism). Birches, in their range, offer a big package of charms: clear fall color, food for winter birds, material for poets, Indians, folktales galore and all-season beauty. Jens Jensen planted them where they would reflect moonlight into a room. They, like the rowan tree, have long been used as a protection against witches. (It seems that witches can pass a birch, but only after they have

Caught in an unusually clear silhouette, this dandelion reveals the raised stems on which the plant's seeds are cradled while ripening. One warm, airy day, conditions will be exactly right and the seeds with their parachutes will be dispersed to the winds to find new sites on which to grow and reproduce.

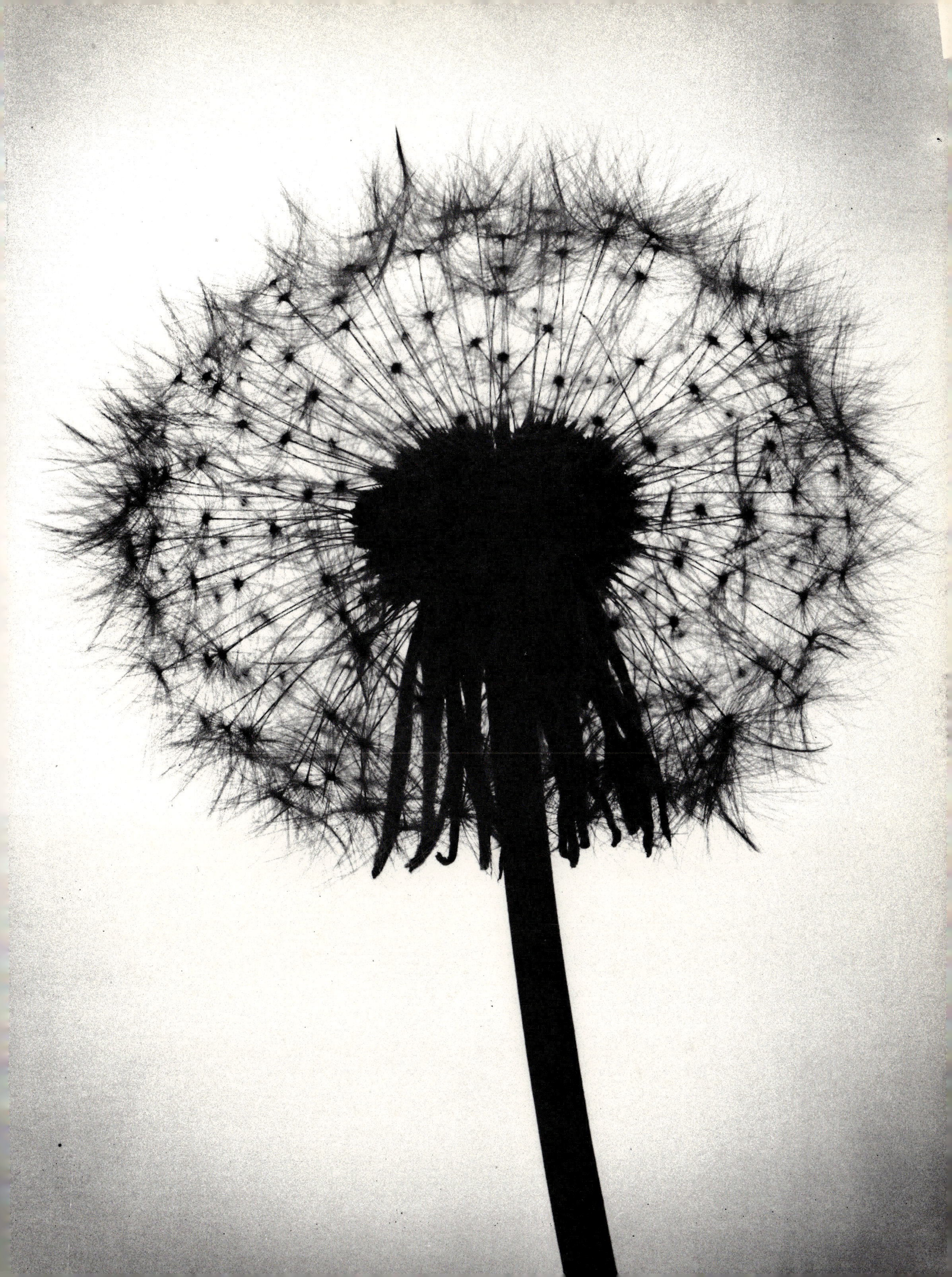

BOTANY

counted all its leaves, and that gives the pursued one a head start.) (Perhaps I should have warned all serious, practical-minded gardeners to skip all the parts of this section that lie between parentheses, but it is too late now—and part of the success of plants in my garden is made up of the plant's long-established place in men's lives.)

If we had a plant for our gardens that incorporated all the best characteristics of that outstanding native success, the hawthorn, together with all the characteristics of that overwhelming naturalized success, the dandelion, would we gardeners all be satisfied?

One weekend in April years ago, in the buoyancy of spring and under the lure of new catalogs, there were many new homeowners who came to us at the Morton Arboretum for advice about plant material. If a plant were really to fill *all* of their requests and wistful wishes that I listed as I listened, it would have to be something like this:

It should be rare, not common—but inexpensive.

It should have showy flowers from spring to fall that don't shed petals and mess up the lawn.

It should have showy fruits that hang on all winter —but make good jelly.

It should be evergreen—but have good fall color.

It should attract birds—but not too early in the morning.

It would be nice if it could keep people from looking in through the picture window—but it should not obstruct the view looking out.

It would be helpful if it could produce interesting material for arrangements, including a little driftwood, or reasonable facsimile.

It should be fragrant—but repellent to dogs.

It should have sweet flavor in the fruit—but unpleasant flavor in the leaves to discourage chewing and sucking insects, and in bark and twigs to discourage nibbling rabbits.

It should grow fast at first, until it attains the desired height, and then stop.

It should be different from anything the neighbors have—but be available at a neighboring nursery.

Perhaps it should be plastic, wired for birdsong and the sound of rustling leaves, with Christmas lights built in, and a soft-drink spigot in the trunk. Then there would be no problems of sun and wind and drought and flood; no need for crutches, or cultivating or spraying (actually we should probably still need to weed if we wanted our technological achievement to remain visible—unless we installed it in the middle of green-colored cement lawn). There would be no need to sprinkle (except for coal dust, and the dung of subnormal birds, and dog visitations). No fertilizers. And no need to go out first thing in the morning and last thing at night to see how it was getting along, how it had changed, how buds were unfurling or new leaves unfolding. No need to wander out in the afternoon to see whether hummingbirds were hovering or moths unrolling their tongues or bees shouldering through the floral entrances. No need for watching clouds or winds, or for crumbling a handful of soil and sniffing at it. No need for stooping to smell flowers in the moonlight—any fragrance would be efficiently synthesized elsewhere and dispensed here by the touch of a foot on a pedal. There would be no longing for spring, no uncertainty about the vigor of the fall coloring. Spring would be on call at the touch of a switch, with dynamic evocative leaf designs produced by famous designers. There would be an end to over-the-fence bragging about green thumbs and raising things from seeds or cuttings or making a triumphant graft. There would be an end to dirtying-up the station wagon with trophies from faraway fields and forests and friendly gardens. There would be an end to silly old legends and the lore of herb gatherers and the sentimental messages of the language of flowers. There would be no leaves to rake, no faded flowers, no winter covering. No seed catalogs in the winter mail. No mulch, no compost, no concern about the earthworm population, no staking, no pruning, no girdling by rabbits or mice—just a general overall numbness.

Gardeners Like To Garden

Would that be a successful plant? Any honest gardener I know, however harried and horny-handed, would prefer to have a welter of dandelions, thistles, ragweed and box-elders complete with beetles.

In a garden it is not a successful plant, ready-made, insured against failure, that we seek. Rather is our pleasure founded on the establishment of a successful, and challenging, partnership. We minister to the needs of the garden; it ministers to ours.

If the medium resists the hands of the artisan or the artist, so much more interesting is the result. Sculpture, etchings, woodcuts, arrowheads, clipper ships, represent work in mediums that fought back. A plastic plant would represent manipulation of spineless stuff.

We do not speak of successful paints in a masterpiece. We look for the craftsman who chooses raw materials that fit the accomplishment of his dream, but makes his raw materials successful by the way he uses them.

May Theilgaard Watts was the recent recipient of a citation by the American Horticultural Society for her lifelong work as an interpretive naturalist with children and adults in the Greater Chicago area.

BOTTLE GARDEN

BOTRYCHIUM (boh-*trik*-ee-um). GRAPE FERN. MOONWORT. Adder's-tongue Family (*Ophioglossaceae*). A large genus of ferns, widely distributed in temperate regions of the world. Two kinds are quite common in N. America. Ornamental plants with underground stems and triangular, compound, evergreen fronds. A separate stalk rises above the fronds, bearing branched clusters of spore cases. These ferns need shade and moist, rich soil. They are good in the wildflower garden or fern garden and are propagated by spores. All native species of grape fern are on the preservation lists of Conn., Me. and Md. and are protected, that is, are not to be picked or dug up.

B. dissectum (dis-*sek*-tum). A hardy species, growing about 1½ ft. high, with finely dissected foliage giving a delicate, lacy appearance. Zone 3.

B. virginianum (vir-jin-ee-*ay*-num). RATTLESNAKE FERN. A handsomer and larger species than *B. dissectum*, growing to 2½ ft. The broadly triangular fronds branch horizontally outwards in a graceful way. The bright yellow spore cases are clustered on a short stem that rises above the lacelike fronds. Zone 3.

botryoides (bot-rye-*oy*-deez). Grapelike or, more often, with grapelike clusters.

botrytis (bot-*rye*-tis), **-e.** With grapelike clusters. Used as a specific plant designation, it is not to be confused with the disease botrytis blight.

botrytis blight. A disfiguring, often serious, fungous disease, particularly of gladioli, lilies, peonies and tulips. It develops and spreads most rapidly in cool, damp weather. Brown rot areas—sometimes preceded by spotting—appear on petals, leaves and soft stems. Flower stems may topple over, buds turn black and dry up. Remove and burn infected plant parts as they become affected; cut off and burn all tops in fall. Spray or dust weekly with botran, ferbam, maneb or zineb. Space susceptible plants as far apart as possible and plant in open locations where air circulation is good. See Pests and Diseases.

Bottle-brush. See CALLISTEMON; MELALEUCA.

Bottle-brushgrass. See *Hystrix patula*.

bottle garden. Growing a garden inside a bottle requires the same kind of patience and skill used in building a model ship under similarly cramped quarters. Beyond this the rewards are infinitely greater, because living plants provide a constantly changing, always fascinating study of nature in miniature. By careful design and selection of the plants, the effect can be a garden with dreamlike quality that could

A bottle garden of compatible plants can exist for months with little or no care. Cut yellowing leaves with a razor blade attached to end of long stick; remove with tongs. Colorful foliage used here includes purple- and silver-leaved strobilanthes, pink-veined fittonia, variegated peperomia, 'Glacier' English ivy and baby's-tears.

exist under no other circumstances. And when a balance of the various elements is achieved, the garden will thrive literally for years with a minimum of care, and often in a room where humidity- and moisture-loving tropicals would never survive in the open air.

There are really only two requisites for bottles to be planted. They need to be transparent and colorless in order to admit light to plants, and waterproof so as to keep moisture from seeping onto the display area. You may use anything from an antique demijohn to a gallon apple-cider jug. The five-gallon bottles in which spring water is delivered are ideal for this kind of gardening.

Planting in a Bottle

For planting the bottle, you will need enough charcoal chips (available wherever house plants are sold) to make a half-inch layer in the bottom of the container; some humusy potting soil; and enough sheet moss (from the woods or your florist) to carpet around the plants. Before you begin planting, clean the inside of the bottle and allow it to dry completely.

Use a large sheet of stiff paper and coil it into a

funnel that will fit all the way inside the bottle to within an inch of the bottom. This directs the growing media exactly where they belong and helps prevent soiling the glass inside. First add the half-inch layer of charcoal chips; gently shake the bottle to even them out. Then add about an inch of potting soil which is just moist enough to crumble nicely after you squeeze a handful of it lightly in your hand. (Soil that is too wet won't slide down the funnel and spread out well; if too dry it puts a layer of dust on the glass.)

Positioning Plants in Cramped Space

To position the plants, you will need sheets of tissue or wax paper, a long piece of wire (a piece of coat-

UPPER LEFT: Drainage material and growing medium may be placed in bottle garden by using a funnel and coil of paper or cardboard mailing tube.
CENTER LEFT: Piece of wire firmly attached to stick and lightly coiled around plant positions it in the bottle.
LOWER LEFT: Spoon taped to stick assists in positioning root system. Spool attached to another stick firms soil.
ABOVE: The finished bottle garden with moisture-preserving cover. The plants used here are shade- and moisture-loving ferns, mosses and selaginellas, with pebbles and small stones artfully arranged to resemble a woodland dell. Kept in moderate house temperatures, in bright light but no direct sun, this bottle garden could exist for a year or more without care.

hanger works well), slender tongs or chopsticks. Remove plants from pots, wash the earth from the roots and pat dry with a piece of soft cloth. Clip off any damaged or yellowing leaves, or flowers, and prune away any unusually long roots. Gently coil each plant in a piece of wax or tissue paper, furling it until it is small enough to fit through the bottle neck. Slip the coiled paper inside and shake lightly to release the plant. Remove the paper and begin work with the wire, or sticks. Place the plant in an upright position, in approximately the place where you want it, then, using the paper funnel, add just enough soil about the roots to hold it in place. Repeat until all plants are inside, and then begin the final maneuvering with wire, sticks and tongs, adding more soil as necessary to hold everything in place and cover all roots.

Add Moss for Ground Cover

Crouch low and look through the walls of the bottle to achieve the most pleasing arrangement of the plants. If the bottle is to be viewed from all sides, design in the round. If it will occupy a position on a bookshelf, design as a shadow box. When all plants are finally placed, begin to add swatches of the moss, first working them down along the sides between the soil and the glass, moss side out. Then cover all spaces around the plants, carefully working the moss around the stem bases. When complete, pour small amounts of water inside to settle the moss and soil about the roots, and to remove any particles of earth that may adhere to the glass and leaves. Be sure to not add so much water that the plantings float.

From this point on, the only key to successfully maintaining a bottle garden is to provide the right amount of light. Hot, direct sun shining on the glass will spoil the leaves. A place where the light is bright, but with little or no direct sun, is ideal. After a week or so if the plants appear to be losing color and leaning in an ungainly position, move the bottle closer to strong light. Once the lighting requirements are established, you can move a garden under glass to any similarly lighted spot in your home.

Water, But Not Much

The amount of water required by bottle gardens varies according to the size, the kind of plants, the room temperatures and the amount of light. The moss makes a fairly accurate gauge for telling when to add water. If it appears a dark, healthy green, no water is likely required. If the moss looks dry and faded, add water, but not much. Bottle garden plants will benefit from an occasional misting with a fogger or atomizer filled with clean water. The only other maintenance needed besides watering and occasional feeding is to immediately remove any yellowing leaves or spent flowers. Feeding with a very small amount of liquid house-plant food can be done three or four times a year. If you feed too much, the plants will be forced into excessive growth that requires an unnecessary amount of tedious pruning to keep them in proper scale for the bottle.

Plant Choices for Bottles

Plants that look well together include a miniature spathiphyllum, two fernlike selaginellas (*S. kraussiana* used to form a delicate design tracery up the glass walls, and the tuft-forming *S. k. brownii*), cathedral windows plant (*Calathea makoyana*) and silvery-leaved miniature *Philodendron sodiroi*.

Other small-growing plants that will do well in a bottle garden include miniature African violets, *Allophyton mexicanum*, baby's-tears (helxine), *Caladium humboldtii*, begonias Baby Rainbow, It and Winter Jewel, bertolonia, chamaeranthemum, *Cissus striata*, *Erythroides nobilis argyroneurus* (jewel orchid), *Ficus repens pumila*, fittonia and maranta. Also useful for bottle gardens are small ferns such as *Polystichum tsus-simense*, *Pteris ensiformis victoriae* and adiantum (maidenhair), *Sinningia pusilla* (and other miniature gloxinias), small-leaved English ivies, *Neanthe bella* (dwarf palm), pellionia, pilea, *Saxifraga sarmentosa* and variety *tricolor* and *Siderasis*.

Terrariums offer another form of gardening under glass in miniature. See *terrarium*.

BOTTLE-GARDEN PLANTS

GROUND CARPETERS

   English ivy, miniature
   Ficus repens pumila
   Helxine (baby's-tears)
   Selaginella

UPRIGHT FOLIAGE

   Begonia rex miniatures
   Bertolonia
   Caladium humboldtii
   Calathea
   Chamaeranthemum
   Cissus striata
   Small ferns: *Adiantum,*
      Polystichum tsus-simense,
      Pteris ensiformis victoriae
   Philodendron sodiroi
   Saxifraga sarmentosa tricolor

FOR FLOWERS

   African violet, miniature
   Allophyton
   Gloxinia, miniature (*Sinningia*)

BOTTLE GENTIAN

Bottle gentian. See *Gentiana clausa*. This species is also known as closed gentian.

Bottle-gourd. See LAGENARIA.

Bottletree. See *Brachychiton populneum*.

bottom heat. Heat applied under a plant bed, usually in the greenhouse, hotbed or propagation case, to hasten germination or rooting and to stimulate growth. The heat source may be an electric soil-heating cable, hot-water or steam pipes. Fresh manure was the old-time heat source, now generally superseded by other methods. See *hotbed*.

Bott's godetia. See *Godetia bottiae*.

BOUGAINVILLEA (boog-in-*vill*-ee-uh). Four-o'clock Family (*Nyctaginaceae*). Tropical, evergreen, woody vines of S. America, grown outdoors in the warmer parts of Fla. and Calif. These plants can be trained as shrubs; they are strong-growing, with alternate leaves and small flowers enclosed by large, showy bracts, usually three together, blooming over a long season, but generally concentrated in summer. They are not particular as to soil, but need full sun. Excellent climber for arbors and trellises. As a greenhouse plant, bougainvillea should be pruned back severely every spring and, if possible, placed outdoors in full sun for the summer. With this care, it will bloom from early fall until late spring. It requires a night-time temperature of 55° to 65° and a soil of equal parts garden loam, peat moss and sand, with an application of fertilizer every two weeks. To propagate, take 3-in. tip cuttings any time from April to June and root in moist soil. Zone 10.

● **B. glabra** (*glay*-bruh). Train this species as a vine to cover large spaces, or keep it dwarfed as a pot plant in greenhouse or on a sunny window sill. The woody stems usually have straight spines, smooth leaves, to 4 in. long, tapering at the base. Flowers are scattered on slender stems, with bracts from yellow through orange and peach to a brilliant magenta or purple. These plants begin to flower when small and blossom best in temperatures of not less than 60°. *B. g. sanderiana* (san-der-ee-*ay*-nuh) is a particularly floriferous white variety.

B. spectabilis (spek-*tab*-il-iss). A stronger grower than *B. glabra*, with larger and less pointed, hairy leaves on stems with stout spines and large flower panicles and bracts, in shades of red.

Boulder-fern. *Dennstaedtia punctilobula*.

Bouncing Bet. *Saponaria officinalis*.

Bourbon rose. See ROSA. (The Bourbon strain of roses came about from a cross between *Rosa chinensis* and 'Rose de Quatre Saisons,' the latter being a Damask rose cultivar.)

LEFT: Bougainvillea, a vine that flourishes outdoors in warm climates, is grown in the greenhouse in cooler regions. The species *glabra*, dwarfed, is grown as a pot plant in the greenhouse. Carmine-rose flowers bloom in summer.
OPPOSITE TOP: Close-up shows tiny flowers of the bougainvillea set off by colorful bracts which are the decorative feature of this handsome vine.
OPPOSITE BOTTOM: A bougainvillea pergola is only for the Far South and warm climates where bougainvillea can succeed all year outdoors.
This vigorously climbing vine is undemanding about soil but does require full sunlight. As a greenhouse plant, bougainvillea should be pruned back severely every spring and placed outdoors. With care, greenhouse specimens will bloom from early fall until late in the spring.

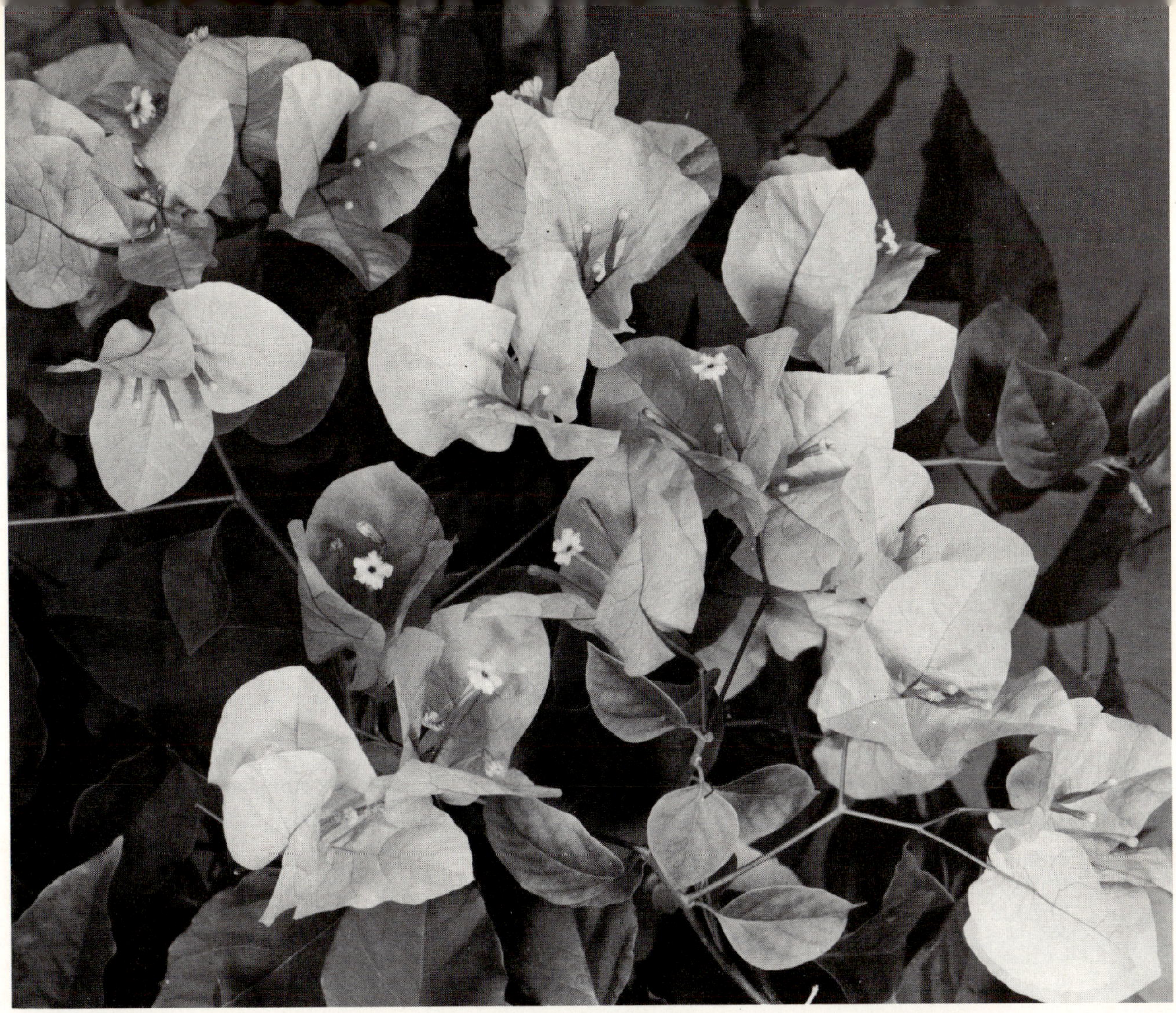

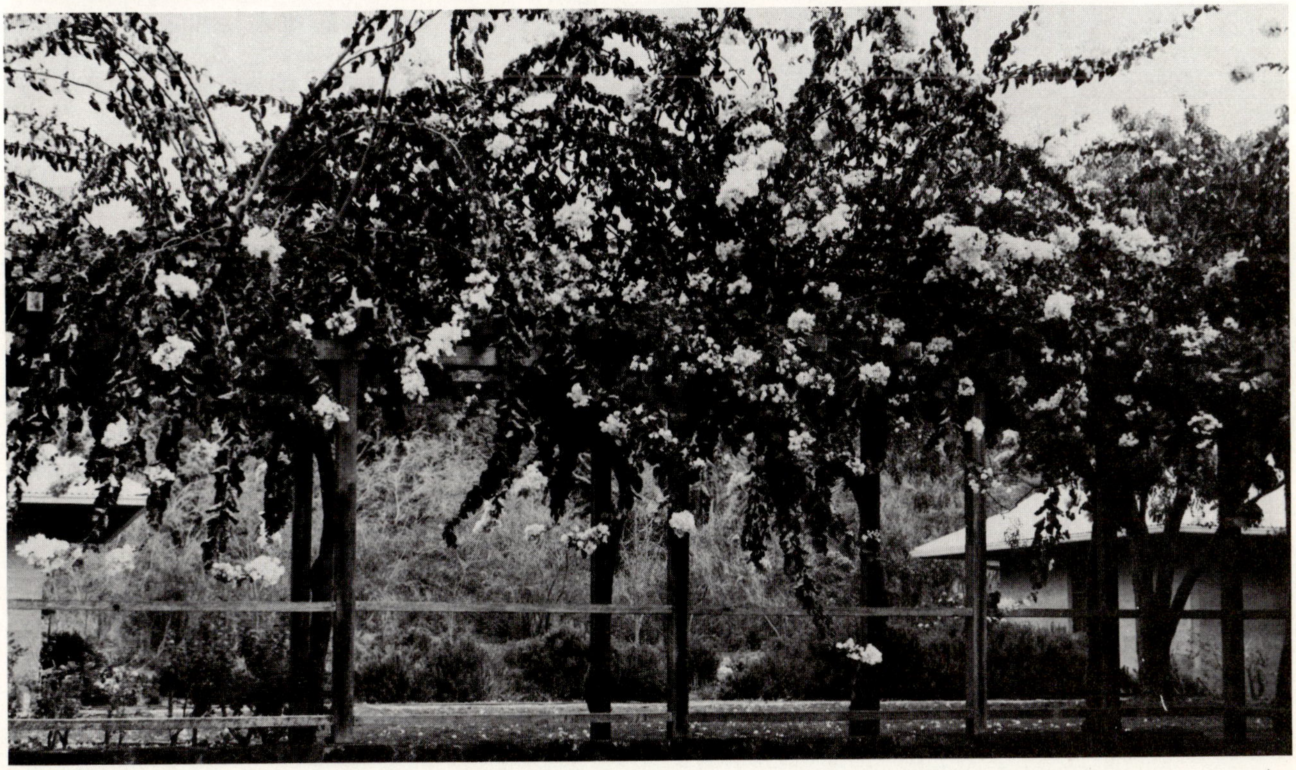

Fragrant clusters of white or red flowers make the bouvardias favorite evergreen shrubs for use in the warm greenhouse. Excellent for use as cut flowers.

BOUSSINGAULTIA (boo-sin-*gol*-tee-uh). Basella Family (*Basellaceae*). Perennial vines of tropical America. The bright green leaves (alternate) cover the branches densely, giving a lush, tropical effect. The sweetly fragrant flowers are small, but appear in long, showy, spikelike clusters and bloom profusely in late summer and fall. Useful as a screen or to cover trellises. Prune back in early spring to keep the proper shape. Grown outdoors in warm regions in rich, well-drained, sandy loam in sun or partial shade. Vines tend to become rampant if the ground is too moist. Propagate by seeds, root division or by small tubercles that appear in the leaf axils. Zone 9 and southward. It can also be grown farther north if roots are lifted and stored over winter.
B. baselloides: *B. gracilis*.
B. gracilis (*grass*-il-iss). MADEIRA VINE. MIGNONETTE VINE. This plant, often listed as *B. baselloides*, is correctly the variety *pseudo-baselloides* (soo-doh-bas-el-*loh*-id-eez). It is a tall, vigorous, tendril-climbing vine with a much-branched woody stem growing from a tuberous root. It may extend as much as 20 ft. or more. Lustrous, evergreen, heart-shaped leaves 3 in. long and a profusion of white flowers combine to make this a desirable vine, especially good near the house where its delightful fragrance may be appreciated. It is evergreen and can be grown in the greenhouse if kept under control.

BOUVARDIA (boo-*vard*-ee-uh). Madder Family (*Rubiaceae*). Small evergreen shrubs of tropical America, with opposite or whorled leaves. Grown especially for the showy, fragrant clusters of white or red flowers, tubular in shape. Popular as warm-greenhouse plants and for cut flowers. They require a rich potting mixture, plenty of water and frequent pinchings to retain proper form. Propagate by root cuttings. Zone 10.
B. humboldtii (hum-*bolt*-ee-eye). SWEET BOUVARDIA. From 2 to 4 ft. tall, with tapered, opposite leaves and fragrant white flowers 2½ in. long, 1 in. wide. This is a popular plant for greenhouses in the North; it can be placed outdoors in summer.
● **B. leiantha** (lyc-*anth*-uh). Shrub to 3 ft. or more, with hairy stems and leaves about 3 in. long. The tubular flowers are red, ½ in. long, and grow in close, full clusters.
B. longiflora (lon-jif-*floh*-ruh). This shrub grows to as much as 5 ft. tall and has fragrant white flowers 3½ in. across. An excellent plant for cut flowers.
B. ternifolia (ter-nif-*foh*-lee-uh). The leaves of this 3-ft. shrub grow in whorls of three or four, each one 2½ in. long. The red, tubular flowers are 1 in. long and grow in clusters.

Bower actinidia. See *Actinidia arguta*.

Bower plant. See *Pandorea jasminoides*.

Bowiea. See SCHIZOBASOPSIS.

bowling green. A greensward for the game of bowls, which is played with so-called biased balls, made of wood. The object is to hit a stationery target ball. This ancient game, well-known in Great Britain and played extensively by the American colonists, is becoming popular once more. Many city parks in America are installing bowling greens for use by teams of players of all ages. The bowling green in New York City's Central Park is in constant use during the summer and they have always been common in Pacific Northwest towns and cities.

The most important requirement of a bowling green, aside from its length of 100 ft. or more, is that the turf be perfectly level and even. 'Washington' creeping bentgrass is often used to produce fine turf. Bocce, a highly informal variant of bowls that is played with round rather than flattened balls, can be played on any surface from turf to cobbles.

Bowstring-hemp. See SANSEVIERIA.

Box, Boxwood. See BUXUS.

Box blueberry. See *Vaccinium ovatum*.

Box-elder. See *Acer negundo*.

boxes. For sidewalk and store-front use, see the article Children's Projects.

Box Family (*Buxaceae*). A small but important family of mostly evergreen shrubs and trees. *Buxus* (box), *Pachysandra*, *Sarcococca* and *Simmondsia* are the most important genera and are discussed separately in this encyclopedia.

Box huckleberry. See *Gaylussacia brachycera*.

Box sand myrtle. See *Leiophyllum buxifolium*.

Box thorn. See LYCIUM.

Boysenberry. See *Rubus loganobaccus*.

brachiatus (brak-ee-*ay*-tus), **-a, -um.** Having spreading branches arranged in alternate pairs at right angles to the stem, as in maple trees, which are said to have a briate form.

brachy- (brak-ee). Prefix meaning short.

BRACHYCHITON (brak-ik-*kye*-ton). Sterculia Family (*Sterculiaceae*). A group of showy Australian trees, sometimes having swollen trunks. They are grown for their ornamental value and for their ability to withstand hot, dry weather. Almost any soil is suitable. Propagate by seeds and cuttings of ripened wood.

B. acerifolium (ay-ser-if-*foh*-lee-um). FLAME BOTTLETREE. This species grows to 60 ft. or more and has shiny, alternate leaves 10 in. long, which fall off just before the scarlet blossoms appear in July and Aug. The brilliant flowers grow in clusters 1 ft. long, without petals. Although these trees are grown for their ornamental value, they have the disadvantage of dropping their leaves, flowers and black fruit. Zone 10.

B. discolor (dis-*kol*-or). PINK FLAME BOTTLETREE. Hav-

ABOVE, TOP: *Brachychiton acerifolium*, the flame bottletree, is one of a group of showy Australian trees of special value for their resistance to hot, dry weather. This species has brilliant scarlet flowers in summer, and is grown outdoors in California and in Florida.
ABOVE: *Brachychiton discolor* has pink blossoms.

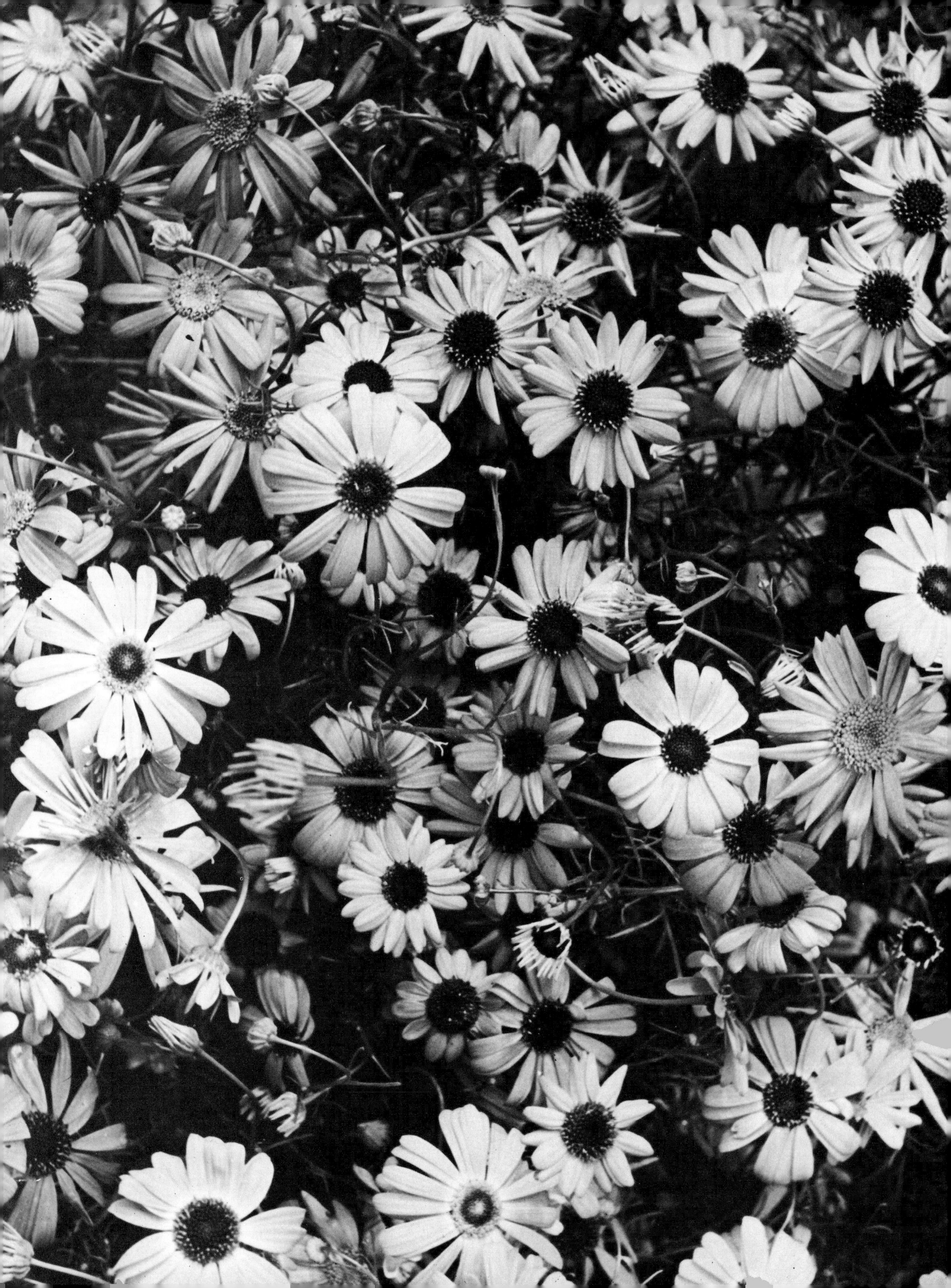

ing the largest flowers of this group of trees, it blooms in June and July, with terminal spikes of pink, bell-shaped flowers. Its leaves are 4 to 6 in. across and its fruit 6 in. long. It is a faster grower than *B. acerifolium*. Especially popular in Fla. Zone 9.

B. populneum (pop-*ull*-nee-um). BOTTLETREE. Formerly known as Sterculia diversifolia, this tree gets its common name from the shape of its trunk. It grows to a height of 60 ft., and is sometimes used as a windbreak, particularly in Calif. Like the others in this group, it is inclined to be untidy. Zone 9.

BRACHYCOME (brak-*kik*-om-ee). Composite Family (*Compositae*). A genus of Australian herbs, containing one popular, tender annual with feathery, alternate leaves. This easily grown plant, flowering six weeks after planting, has small, daisylike blossoms. Since the period of bloom is short, successive sowings are desirable.

B. iberidifolia (eye-ber-id-if-*foh*-lee-uh). SWAN RIVER DAISY. An easily grown annual, 8 to 18 in. high. Seeds can be sown indoors or out. The plant is very free-flowering, with individual flowers 1 in. across. The blue, white or rose blossoms, with yellow centers, are abundant enough to fill in bare spaces in the garden. Sow seeds ¼ in. deep in garden loam, in full sun. It is an excellent plant for massing in borders and for edging.

BRACHYSEMA (brak-iss-*seem*-uh). Pea Family (*Leguminosae*). Evergreen, spreading or semiclimbing shrubs of Australia. Sometimes grown in greenhouses, and outdoors in southern Calif. Propagate by seeds or cuttings.

B. lanceolatum (lan-see-oh-*lay*-tum). A shrub to 3 ft. with mostly opposite leaves (some are alternate) to 4 in. long, silvery beneath. It has bright scarlet flowers, about 1 in long. Zone 10.

Bracken. See *Pteridium aquilinum*.

bract. One of the small, scalelike leaves that emerge from a flower stalk and enclose a flower bud before it opens. Although usually green, bracts may be beautifully colored. The "flowers" of dogwood and poinsettia, for example, are really made up of bracts. The actual flowers of these plants are relatively small and inconspicuous.

OPPOSITE: *Brachycome iberidifolia*, the Swan River daisy, a charming annual from Australia that bears small blue, white, rose or mauve-rose flowers in summer. Seeds may be started in the greenhouse and set out 6 inches apart when danger of frost is past. An attractive pot plant for the greenhouse, brachycome blooms in spring.

bracteatus (brak-tee-*ay*-tus), **-a, -um.** With bracts; bracteate.

Bracted iris. See *Iris bracteata*.

Brake. Also known as bracken, it is a name commonly applied to any coarse fern. But strictly, the brake is *Pteridium aquilinum*, which see; also PTERIS.

bramble. In general, any shrub with thorns or prickles. But strictly, it is a plant of the genus *Rubus*. The best-known brambles (or bramble fruits) are the raspberry and blackberry.

bramble fruits. Small, soft fruits as raspberry and blackberry. See article on growing fruit listed under *fruits* and also Plant Finder section in Volume 16.

branch. A limb; any stem growing from the trunk of a tree, or, often, from another branch. Also, as a verb, it denotes a spreading aspect of a plant's growth.

brasiliensis (braz-il-ee-*en*-siss), **-e.** From Brazil.

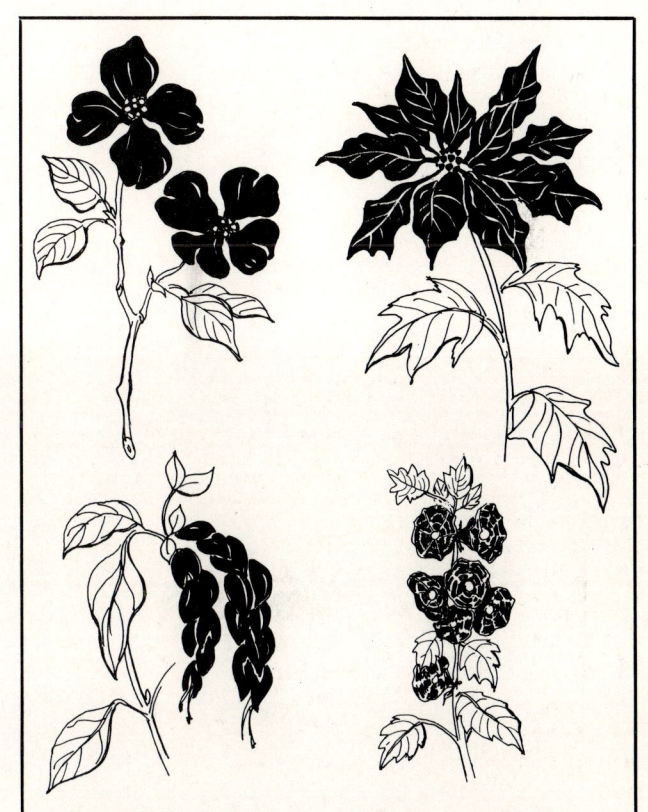

The most showy parts of many plants are the bracts surrounding small, insignificant true flowers. Examples: UPPER LEFT, dogwood; UPPER RIGHT, poinsettia; LOWER LEFT, shrimp plant; LOWER RIGHT, bells-of-Ireland.

BRASSAIA (brass-*say*-ee-uh). Octopus-tree. Aralia or Ginseng Family (*Araliaceae*). A tree native to Australia, grown as an ornamental in southern Fla. The strange, long flower stems give the plant its common name. Propagate by cuttings or seeds. Zone 10.

B. actinophylla (ak-tin-oh-*fill*-uh). Queensland umbrella-tree. Schefflera of florists. Evergreen tree to 40 ft. with large glossy leaves of six to eight elongated leaflets. Red flowers on branches that stretch out like arms of an octopus. Best known as one of the "cast-iron" house plants (don't expect bloom indoors). However, it does not thrive on neglect. It needs the strongest light you can provide, short of direct sun through glass, even though it grows in full sun outdoors where it is hardy (freezes at 25°). If plant is not receiving enough light, leaf stems grow too long and sag under weight of leaflets. No harm to plant if you have no objection to the slightly droopy appearance. Water well, preferably by immersion, every two weeks. If large pot size precludes immersion, water well, let soil dry out, then water thoroughly again. Soil should be porous; brassaias do not like a soggy growing medium. They have no humidity problem, but do better away from drafts of dry winter air. Zone 10.

BRASSAVOLA (brass-*av*-vol-luh). Orchid Family (*Orchidaceae*). Epiphytic (tree-perching) orchids from tropical America. One cylindrical leaf grows from the stemlike pseudobulbs of these plants, some of which resemble the familiar cattleyas. The large and showy flowers usually bloom singly. These are characterized by narrow sepals and petals with an enlarged lip. Easily grown in orchid baskets or cribs in an intermediate greenhouse with high humidity (above 50 per cent). For abundant bloom provide bright, diffused light in summer, direct sun in winter. For potting use fir bark or osmunda fiber. Propagate by division.

B. cucullata (kuk-yew-*lay*-tuh). This species has orange, yellow or white flowers and is an excellent and spectacular plant.

B. digbyana (dig-bee-*ay*-nuh). May be listed in catalogs as Laelia digbyana or Rhyncholaelia, this orchid has a single, fleshy leaf up to 8 in. long and barely 1 in. wide. The fragrant, greenish-white flower has a large, heart-shaped, white lip that is deeply fringed. The flowers are about 5 in. across and bloom during the summer in greenhouses. Much used for hybridizing. Zone 10.

B. glauca (*glaw*-kuh). May be listed in catalogs as Laelia glauca or Rhyncholaelia. The 6-in. fleshy leaf grows from the slender, grayish pseudobulb. Olive-green flowers about 4 in. across bloom in winter.

B. nodosa (nod-*doh*-suh). Small greenish-white flowers appear in fall. The plant has one pencil-shaped leaf to 9 in. long. The flowers have a delightful fragrance at night.

BRASSIA (*brass*-ee-uh). Orchid Family (*Orchidaceae*). Sturdy and interesting epiphytic (tree-perching) orchids of tropical America, grown for the spiderlike flowers. From the large pseudobulbs grow one or two tonguelike leaves and lateral racemes of flowers on arching stems. The yellowish flowers are made up of narrow, long-pointed sepals and petals, resembling

OPPOSITE: Brassia is a sturdy tree-perching orchid grown for its elegant, spidery yellow-cream flowers. This species is the named hybrid 'Edvah Loo.'
ABOVE: Brassavola 'David Sander' was developed from *B. digbyana* and *B. cucullata*. It is an excellent hybrid.
RIGHT: Sturdy *Brassavola digbyana* is a fragrant orchid.

the legs of a spider. Easily grown in fir bark or osmunda fiber in an intermediate greenhouse, or as house plants if high humidity can be maintained. They show to best advantage in orchid baskets or cribs. Propagate by division.

B. caudata (kaw-*day*-tuh). The pseudobulbs of this species are up to 6 in. long. From them grow the oblong, pointed leaves, which may be 1 ft. long. Arching spikes of greenish-yellow flowers, spotted with brown, bloom in spring and summer. The 6-in., taillike sepals grow in a lateral direction.

B. maculata (mak-yew-*lay*-tuh). Plant resembles large *B. caudata* with 5- to 8-in. flowers, waxy, scented, long-lived, mainly cream-yellow to gold with purple.

B. verrucosa (vehr-roo-*koh*-suh). Arching, wiry

flower stems bear long, threadlike sepals and petals to 5 in. long. The white lip is spotted with fine brown warts.

BRASSICA (*brass*-ik-uh). Mustard Family (*Cruciferae*). A large genus of annuals, biennials and perennials containing the cabbagey spices and the mustards and many vegetables, as well as several weeds. They are erect, branching plants with toothed leaves and yellow or yellowish-white flowers in spring. Most of the perennials are hardy as far north as Zone 4. Brassicas are subject to an assortment of wormy pests, and it is good garden practice to avoid planting a *Brassica* species where another *Brassica* was the previous crop.

B. alba: B. hirta.

B. caulorapa (kaw-lor-*ray*-puh). KOHLRABI. A low biennial to 18 in., with bluish-green leaves and cream-colored flowers. The edible turniplike tuber is actually the swollen stem 1 to 3 in. above the ground. It is known also as stem-turnip. Kohlrabi is a hardy, cool-weather plant. Sow seeds in early spring in rows 2 ft. apart and thin the plants to leave about 5 in. of space between. The secret of good flavor is fast, unchecked growth; for this they need good, enriched, loose soil with plenty of moisture—but never let them become waterlogged. A planting every three or four weeks will provide a continuous crop well into the autumn. Used like turnips, the tuberous stems are at their best when not more than 2 in. across, about two months after planting. Spraying may be necessary to control the aphids. Good varieties include 'Early Purple Vienna' and 'Early White Vienna.'

B. hirta (*hert*-uh). WHITE MUSTARD. Sometimes listed in catalogs as B. alba. This is a sturdy annual, 2 to 4 ft. tall, with oval-shaped divided leaves and small yellow flowers, ½ in. long, that bloom from June to Aug. It is considered a weed in much of the U.S., but is often grown as a crop in Calif. and also in Europe.

B. juncea (*joon*-see-uh). LEAF MUSTARD. An easily grown annual that reaches 4 ft. Widespread as a weed in N. America, it has yellow flowers and blooms from June to Aug. The variety *crispifolia* (kris-pif-*foh*-lee-uh), known as 'Southern Curled,' is grown for greens. It has thin, ovalish leaves with scalloped edges.

B. napobrassica (nap-oh-*brass*-ik-uh). RUTABAGA. This hardy biennial has edible roots similar to the turnip. Seeds are sown in early summer in drills 18 in. apart and thinned to stand 6 in. apart. Harvest in

ABOVE: Leaf mustard, *Brassica juncea*, is a cooking green grown in the South and related to cabbage and cauliflower. Cultural requirements are similar.
RIGHT: Kale, *Brassica oleracea acephala*, is a curly-leaved cooking green. It is considered to be a particularly good source of vitamin A, of ascorbic acid and thiamine.

Oct. or after the first frost and after roots have fully matured. They need a longer season and can withstand more frost than the closely related turnip. For winter storage, place them in a cellar in moist sand. These plants need a rich, moist soil, but if they are planted too early they are likely to bolt, especially if the temperature goes down to 50°. Very popular and widely available varieties include 'American Purple Top,' 'Long Island Improved,' 'Laurentian' and 'Macombre.'

B. napus (*nay*-pus). RAPE. Popular salad in Europe, rape is an annual, used here as a forage or cover crop for late autumn and early spring. Sow seeds broadcast or in drills in early summer.

B. nigra (*ny*-gruh). BLACK MUSTARD. A tall annual, to 6 ft. or more, with lobed leaves and clusters of small yellow flowers. It is a widespread weed in N. America and is grown commercially for table mustard.

B. oleracea (oh-ler-*ray*-see-uh). A thick-leaved perennial that is known in cultivated form only for its varieties:

B. o. acephala (ass-*sef*-al-uh). KALE. Sometimes known as borecole, kale is related to cabbage but does not form heads or dense rosettes of leaves. It has, instead, many long leaves, sometimes curled or finely cut. It is an excellent source of vitamin A, ascorbic acid and thiamine. It is a cool-season plant and is grown as a fall, winter and spring crop in the South and is best in the North when planted in spring for fall harvest. Sow the seeds in rows 2 ft. apart in good garden soil with plenty of moisture and added fertilizer. Thin the seedlings to about 12 in. apart when they are 3 in. high. Collards, unlike true kale, of which they are a variety, have short trunklike stems and need warm weather. Collards are widely grown in the South for their loose crown of cabbagelike leaves. Start seeds indoors in spring and set the seedlings out in rows 3 ft. apart. Collards withstand hot weather better than kale or cabbage. An excellent variety of kale for the home garden is 'Vates,' a dwarf kind with tender leaves that are beautiful enough to use in flower arrangements if they are not used in cooking.

TOP RIGHT: A culture sequence that produces excellent rutabagas requires that the seedlings be thinned drastically when they are a few inches high.
SECOND FROM TOP: To grow rutabagas in a small area, thin seedlings to a double row alternating plants and spaces. Cultivate and hill plants slightly when seedlings begin to form bulbs.
THIRD FROM TOP: Organic growing of rutabagas calls for the application of an organic mulch which will decay. As the mulch decays, nutrients are washed into the soil where they become immediately available to the plants. Photo shows how little remains of 6-inch coat of mulch applied only four to six weeks before.
BOTTOM: Rutabagas grown by the organic method described.

B. o. botrytis (bot-*rye*-tis). CAULIFLOWER. A biennial of the cabbage tribe. The edible part of cauliflower is the thickened flower cluster rather than the leaves. Seeds can be started indoors and set out in early spring, after the last frost, in a rich soil with a pH range of 5.5 to 6.5. The plants need plenty of moisture and cool weather. They cannot withstand heat or freezing cold. Space the plants about 15 in. apart in rows 3 ft. apart. Sowings about three weeks apart through spring will give a continuous crop into the fall. For a pure-white head, the cauliflower must be blanched. When the head is about an inch in diameter, pull the leaves up from the bottom of the plant and tie them over the head, to keep out direct sunlight. About ten days later, just as soon as the head reaches maturity, it will be ready to harvest. In warm weather, do not blanch until two or three days before harvesting, as the plant may rot in the heat. The Snowball varieties are some of the best for home gardens.

B. o. capitata (cap-ih-*tay*-tuh). CABBAGE. This is the most important and most widely used vegetable of the *Brassica* genus, and, like the others, it is a cool-weather plant. It can be grown throughout the summer, but not if the heat is extreme. Sow seeds indoors in early March and transplant outdoors in late April or early May. Place seedlings 1 ft. apart in rows that are 3 ft. apart. These plants need a fertile soil and plenty of moisture, with extra feedings of fertilizer high in nitrogen and potash. The soil should have a pH of 6.5. For early crops, a sandy loam is best; for later crops use a heavier soil, one that will retain more moisture. For home gardeners the Savoy varieties are superior. Also fine for the home garden is 'Morden Dwarf,' a Canadian variety. The heads are ready for

TOP LEFT: To harvest huge white heads of cauliflower, incorporate organic matter high in nitrogen into planting holes or throughout bed. Here a handful of compost mixed with well-aged cow manure is being spread along the trench in which cauliflowers will be planted. When short of nitrogen, cauliflower leaves droop and die and heads are stunted and yellowish.
SECOND FROM TOP: As cauliflower matures, small heads begin to form in the center of the upper leaves. One method for blanching heads is to tie leaves together over the newly forming cauliflower with raffia, twine or tape. Blanched heads are better formed, whiter and sweeter.
THIRD FROM TOP: Heads form quickly after they have been covered. Untie one every few days to keep track of progress, and harvest when they are on the young side.
BOTTOM: Cauliflower heads are ready when the curds are well formed but still pure white and very crisp. Soak cauliflower florets in salt water before cooking to eliminate insects. Cauliflower keeps well for several weeks if the whole plant is pulled and then hung up in a cool dark place.

The many forms of cabbage grown in gardens today are derived from the wild cabbage, *Brassica oleracea*, and belong to the Mustard Family. It is one of the oldest recorded vegetables. Several species, including red cabbage, have been in general use for more than 2,000 years. They require from 60 (early varieties) to 100 days (late varieties) to mature. A few are mid-season varieties and mature through the summer.
ABOVE: The Savoy cabbages have curly leaves, and are ornamental as well as delicious. Two good varieties of Savoy are 'Perfection Drumhead' and 'Chieftain Savoy,' both requiring about 90 days to produce a crop.
LEFT: Both green and red cabbages are subject as are all the brassicas to attack from a number of wormy pests, and it is good practice to avoid planting one *Brassica* where another *Brassica* was the most recent crop. Brassicas are cool-weather vegetables and are easy to grow. They may be started early from seed indoors.

use as soon as they are fully formed. If left too long, heads may split.

Several kinds of leaf-eating caterpillars find cabbage and its relatives delectable. These can be controlled with sprayings of malathion or diazinon. Avoid planting where a *Brassica* was the previous crop.

B. o. gemmifera (jem-*mif*-er-uh). BRUSSELS SPROUTS. This is primarily a fall and winter vegetable. It will withstand light frosts and is best when harvested in the fall after cold weather has set in. Plant seeds in late May, and transplant to their permanent place in the garden in late July or early Aug. Space the plants 2 ft. apart, with 3 ft. between the rows. They require well-prepared garden soil enriched with fertilizer. Harvest in Sept. and Oct.

Brussels sprouts have a single stalk on which numerous little heads or "sprouts" appear, growing in the leaf axils, two or three months after planting. The heads are best when they are 1 to 1½ in. across. Pick those at the bottom of the stalk first, breaking off the leaf below the head. New leaves and sprouts will continue to grow at the top of the stalk for a period of six to eight weeks. One well-grown plant will produce about a qt. of sprouts. This vegetable is rich in calcium, iron and vitamins. The variety 'Jade Cross,' an F_1 hybrid, is disease-resistant and superior in flavor. As with cabbage, spray with malathion or diazinon to control leaf-eating caterpillars, and avoid planting where a *Brassica* was the former crop.

B. o. italica (it-*tal*-ik-uh). BROCCOLI. A mineral-rich green vegetable, related to the cauliflower, with several flower heads on fleshy stalks. It is one of the easiest of green vegetables to grow. Since it requires

TOP LEFT: Mixture of compost and well-rotted cow manure is a first class fertilizer for cabbage which requires a soil humusy enough to hold moisture and rich in nitrogen. One method recommended is to apply the fertilizer over the entire bed where the cabbage is to grow at least two weeks before cabbage is set out and then to plow or dig the fertilizer into the soil.
SECOND FROM TOP: Cabbage seedlings started indoors in early March are ready to set out in early May. These six-week-old seedlings will be about 7 inches tall.
THIRD FROM TOP: Cultivate soil around young cabbages; the more light and air they receive the more quickly they will grow. The quality of the cabbage crop is related to the speed at which it matures. Cultivation allows lots of air and water to penetrate to root levels and helps the seedlings grow rapidly.
BOTTOM: Cabbage must be kept well watered, especially during hot dry spells, and needs constant moisture to form large firm heads. When checking to see if a head is ready for harvest, press down firmly on the top. If the leaves feel spongy to the touch the head is not yet full and ready to be harvested and stored.

a long, cool season, seeds can be started indoors in Feb. or March and the seedlings set outdoors as soon as danger of frost is past. A second planting in late summer will provide a fall crop. Place the plants 2 ft. apart in rows with 2 ft. between them, in well-prepared garden soil with added fertilizer. Both the flower heads and the stalks are edible and should be cut for cooking before the flowers open. A second growth of stalks and heads will appear after the first cutting. The variety 'Cleopatra' is resistant to weather, minding neither heat nor drought, and is especially vigorous. 'Zenith' and 'Spartan Early' are also good varieties for the home garden. 'Spartan Early' is especially good for freezing.

B. pekinensis (pee-kin-*nen*-siss). CHINESE CABBAGE. This plant has crisp leaves and is used like lettuce. The outer leaves can be cooked as greens. Chinese cabbage does not have the pronounced cabbage flavor

UPPER LEFT: Harvest broccoli while flower buds are still tight and tender. When cutting off the main head, leave behind a fairly long stub of stem so that the plant can produce the smaller secondary heads which are the second crop. Culture is similar to that of cauliflower.
UPPER RIGHT: Brussels sprouts are a popular *Brassica* crop and simple to grow. Keep soil around sprouts cultivated to speed growth. Young plants benefit from a high hilling in hot weather.
CENTER RIGHT: Mulch Brussels sprouts in midsummer with grass clippings to keep soil porous, cool and damp through droughts. Like other brassicas they require constant moisture in the soil. Mulching is a good way to assure the supply, and helps to keep weeds down as well.
LOWER RIGHT: Lower heads on this well-formed stalk of Brussels sprouts are ready to harvest. To produce tight, firm heads, remove all lower leaves in late September so the plant can concentrate its energy on the food crop.

of the other plants in this genus. Sow seeds in the early spring as soon as the ground can be worked. This planting will mature in early summer. A second sowing, about July 1, will provide heads for the fall and early winter. When the seedlings are 2 or 3 in. high they should be thinned to about 8 in. apart. These thinnings make excellent salad or cooked greens. Popular varieties are 'Chihli,' 'Michihli' and 'Wong Bok.' The Nagao hybrid is shorter than other varieties but has excellent flavor.

B. rapa (*ray*-puh). TURNIP. A green-leaved biennial with a white or yellow, fleshy, edible tuber. Turnips are hardy, cool-season plants, but will not tolerate as much frost as rutabagas. They will produce two crops. Early varieties, such as 'Purple Top White Globe,' should be planted as soon in spring as the ground can be worked, and harvested in early summer. Turnips do not develop well in summer heat or drought. Another sowing made in late July or early Aug., about two months before freezing weather is expected, will produce a fall and winter crop. The Japanese variety 'Just Right' is an excellent fall type. A loose, friable soil gives the best results, allowing the tubers freedom to develop. Sow seeds where they are to remain, ½ in. deep in drills 15 in. apart. For turnip greens, plant the variety 'Seven Top.' Turnip greens of varieties such as 'Foliage' or 'Shogoin' can be eaten as greens in 30 days after planting; the root is ready in 70 days. Early varieties can be pulled in 25 to 30 days and later varieties in 60.

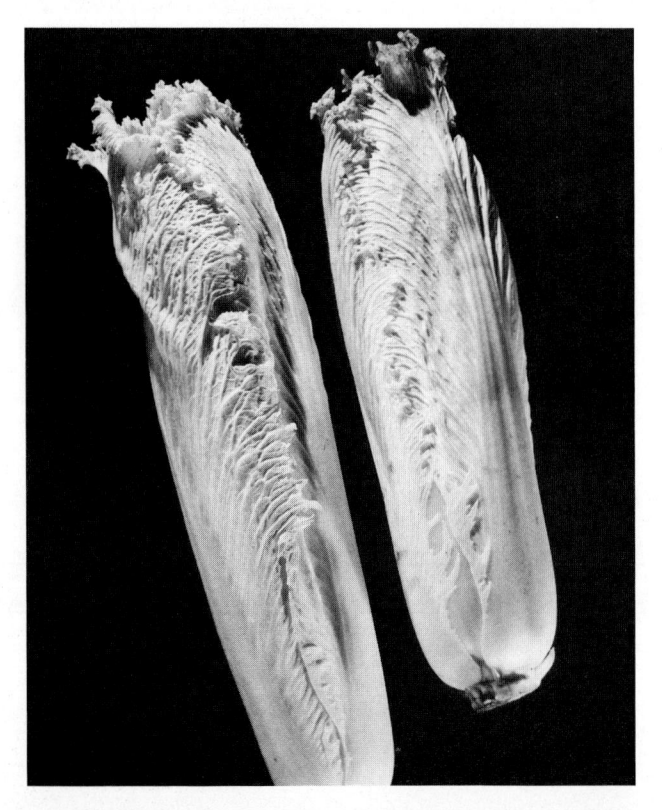

Kohlrabi, the Crisp Cabbage

By WILLIAM A. BUCK

The name of this vegetable is German for cabbage turnip. It may not be botanically sound, but the plant combines some of the best aspects of those two old dependables. Kohlrabi has a number of claims to our attention. As scholars have pointed out, nearly all of our field and garden crops were developed from the wild by Stone Age men.

Ages before they learned to smelt metals and carve their story in stone, men built towns, created the great myths, tamed the cow (9000 B.C.), and worshipped heavenly deities who made the cabbage grow and the ewe bear her lamb in spring.

But they did not create kohlrabi. For it, along with two other close relatives in the genus *Brassica*—the rutabaga (or Swedish turnip) and Brussels sprouts—are brash newcomers.

All three apparently first turned up in the gardens of northern Europe in the late Middle Ages—the only crops the people of the North ever tamed from the wild, as far as we know. Luther Burbank believed that kohlrabi was the most recent of all our cultivated crops.

A botanist described the vegetable in A.D. 1554, and this was the first sure mention of it that we have found. By the end of that century, men were planting it in Germany, England, Italy, Spain and all around the sea that the Romans once called their own. As far as the record shows, it did not reach our shores until 1806.

Kohlrabi is a biennial, which produces flowers and seed in its second year, and a descendant of the wild cabbage of the shores and islands of Europe, *Brassica oleracea*, which has such strange talents. The parent plant bestowed the gift of enthusiasm on its offspring. If a plant has a cabbage habit of growth, almost the entire plant becomes one monstrous bud.

LEFT: Chinese cabbage, *Brassica pekinensis*, is sweet and crisp and is used as lettuce in salads. The outer leaves can be cooked as a green. This is one more member of the large family of edible vegetables that belong to the genus *Brassica*.
OPPOSITE: Another edible brassica, kohlrabi, has a flavor somewhere between that of the cabbage and the turnip. It looks a little like an extravagant flying saucer.

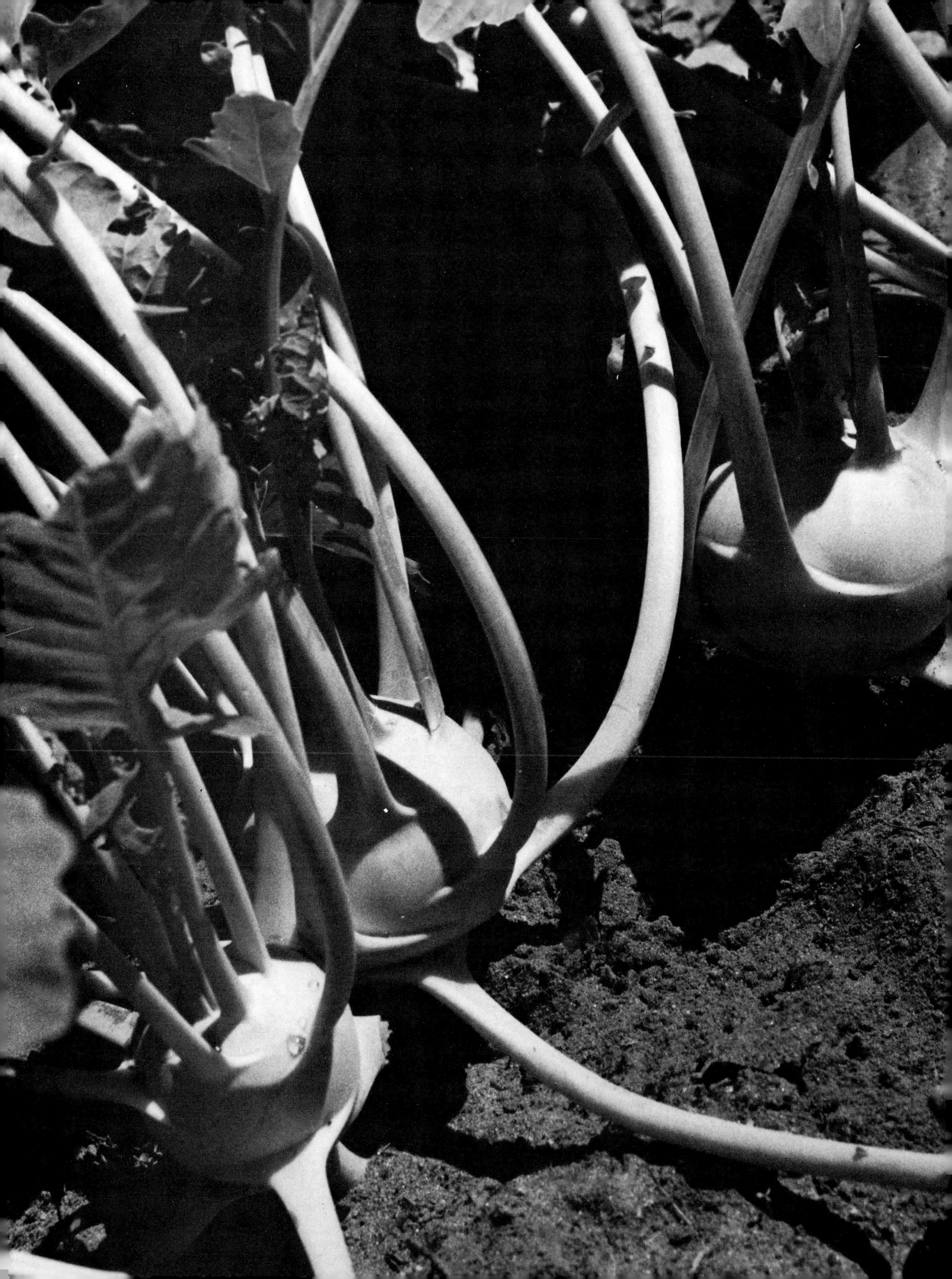

BRASSICA

The edible portion of kohlrabi is the fattened root stalk which in the garden sits just above the ground. This vegetable has an unusual crispness that makes it a good companion to many cheese dips and sauces, an excellent addition, shredded, to any salad.

If it has the cauliflower habit, the flowers and flower stems grow together, making the "curd." There is a kale of the Channel Islands that makes so tough a stem that it is used as a cane, and a Mediterranean type that grows as tall as a tree. The turnip, a close relative, *Brassica rapa*, has put its evolutionary faith in its root and it is there that the plant stores its supplies for the year.

A Clown

Kohlrabi looks like the clown of the gang, with its strange, enlarged stem. All of these members of the cabbage side of the crucifers will cross like alley cats. Did someone crossbreed the two, bringing the turnip upstairs, you might say, both in quality and place?

Perhaps taxonomy can give us a thought. The *Encyclopedia Britannica*, Burbank, and Victor Boswell, Head of Vegetable Crop Research of the U.S. Department of Agriculture, give it the botanical name, *Brassica oleracea caulorapa*, which identifies it as a variety, race or cultivar of the parent, virtually the same plant. *Taylor's Encyclopedia of Gardening*, *The Wise Garden Encyclopedia* and *Hortus Second* all agree on *Brassica caulorapa*, which would make it a different species, though closely allied.

If you hold the notion that European taste in food is better than American you may be impressed by the fact that kohlrabi has always been much more popular in Europe than here. Those disciples of the good life, the Viennese, have cherished it so long and to such hearty purpose that the only varieties you will find in most American catalogs today are the White and the Purple Vienna.

The white, which some say is better in quality, actually has a light green bulb; the purple has a slight tint on the bulb and leaves. Some say the taste is like a very superior turnip, some say it is like a cabbage, though the best-tasting of all the tribe. In fact, the flavor is best described as a combination of both.

An Easy Crop

Kohlrabi is easy to grow, and produces generously. It will do well in almost any soil, can withstand some frost on transplanting, and will even survive some mild neglect. It will mature for the kitchen at high altitudes and high latitudes, almost anywhere that has a growing season 80 days in length or more.

While it is a cool-weather crop, like all the family, it can endure heat much better than the others, and should do well as a succession crop, following early peas, for example. It matures in 60 to 70 days, in my experience, and so one can make a sowing after the June peas, then another a couple of weeks later, until the hard frost looms 80 days away.

In spring it is best to start the plants indoors to get a lead on the season, or, at any rate, to sow the seed with the earliest crops, before April 15 in my locality, near New York City.

Like all the clan, kohlrabi thrives best on a rich soil, mellow with organic decay, well-drained but amply watered; quick growth is important for the best flavor. In sandy soils, the ideal plant food is an 8-16-16 formula and a light side dressing of nitrogen some six weeks after planting. Otherwise, 5-10-5 or thereabouts is good enough.

If you plant a fall crop to succeed a spring one, treat the earth to a second fertilizing. Cover the seeds a half-inch deep. After thinning, plants should stand 8 inches apart and rows 18 inches. A mulch is better than cultivation for all of the cabbages with their cool-weather persuasion, for it keeps the soil cool.

Diseases and bugs have never troubled my kohlrabi; this seems to be the common experience, though

Kohlrabi is picked as soon as it is 2 inches in diameter; an overly large crop can be stored buried deep in the soil and covered with a thick mulch. It keeps well in the root cellar through the winter and will stay crisp.

we do know that there are several plagues of the crucifers which it can catch and several pests that can feed on it. My guess at the reason for this immunity is that the bugs prefer to chew on other members of the family.

If you want to be careful with your kohlrabi, you can use baits to kill off the slugs and snails, and a general garden dust or spray should do for any other visitors, except the harlequin bug which infests the country south of 40° north latitude. For controls, see the article Pests and Diseases.

Harvesting

Kohlrabi is not really a slow grower, but it seems to be. You hardly believe that curious bulb will actually appear, but it does. Do not allow it to grow much more than 2 inches in diameter before you pull up the plant and trim out the bulb, for if it gets too big it will become woody and lose its flavor. Some say that you must not peel the globe before cooking, because the skin holds in the pristine goodness.

If some bulbs are getting too big and there is no room on the menu for kohlrabi, harvest it anyway;
kohlrabi stored in a cool place for a couple of days is better than the woody thing it becomes if you leave it in the garden to toughen its storage house against the future. Many like it best chopped raw into cubes for a salad, or eaten by hand in the field as we used to like turnips when I was a boy. Some like it cooked *au gratin* or with sour cream.

In our neglect of this vegetable we are missing something. After all, to the Romans cabbage was the best of table vegetables and, moreover, good for what ails you, from colic to insomnia, and kohlrabi is a superior kind of cabbage.

Some Like It Cold

Usually it is better to mulch a heaved plant than simply to wait for a muddy thaw and push the roots back into the ground. At least a mulch will not damage vulnerable tissues, and it will stabilize temperatures to a remarkable degree, at the same time preventing the plant from drying out.   R.B.

x BRASSOCATTLAELIA

x *Brassolaelia* is a cross between the orchid genera *Brassavola* and *Laelia*. The hybrids are available to orchid enthusiasts in a wide range of colors. This one is B. x 'Helen,' bronze, green and rose. The fringed flowers are also fragrant.

x BRASSOCATTLAELIA: Outmoded name once used for trigeneric crosses of the orchids *Brassavola, Cattleya* and *Laelia;* see x *Brassolaeliocattleya.*

x BRASSOCATTLEYA (brass-oh-*kat*-lee-uh). Orchid Family (*Orchidaceae*). A group of bigeneric hybrids, crosses between two genera—*Brassavola* and *Cattleya*. These plants are available to orchid fanciers and are grown like cattleyas, in fir bark or osmunda fiber.

x BRASSOLAELIA (brass-oh-*lee*-lee-uh). Orchid Family (*Orchidaceae*). A group of bigeneric hybrids, crosses between *Brassavola* and *Laelia*. They are available to orchid enthusiasts in a wide range of colors and are grown in fir bark or osmunda fiber.

x BRASSOLAELIOCATTLEYA (brass-oh-lee-lee-uh-*kat*-lee-uh). Orchid Family (*Orchidaceae*). This is the name given to a group of trigeneric hybrids, combining three genera—*Brassavola, Laelia* and *Cattleya*—crossed to produce plants that are more vigorous, more colorful and generally more desirable in some way than the original genera. Interesting plants for the orchid specialist, they are grown like cattleyas, in fir bark or osmunda fiber. There is a large number of named varieties, and new ones are being developed by professional hybridizers every year.

Brazilian bower plant. See *Adhatoda cydoniaefolia.*

Brazilian edelweiss. See *Rechsteineria leucotricha.*

Brazilian morning-glory. See *Ipomoea setosa.*

Brazilian peppertree. See *Schinus terebinthifolius.*

Brazil nut. See BERTHOLLETIA.

Breadfruit. See *Artocarpus communis.*

Breadfruit tree. See ARTOCARPUS.

break. A change or alteration of genes not produced by crossing; a mutation or sport. Also, loosely, a term denoting the emergence of a growth bud from a stem, as on a rosebush in spring.

breeder tulip. An important class of tulips with long stems, round or oval flowers, and a slightly bronzed or muddy cast to its flower colors.

brevi-. Prefix meaning short.

BREVOORTIA (brev-*voor*-tee-uh). FLORAL FIRECRACKER. Lily Family (*Liliaceae*). Only one species is known, *Ida-Maia* (i-duh-*my*-ee-uh). which is called the floral firecracker, and in some areas, firecracker flower. It was formerly *Brodiaea coccinea*, and is a cormous herb that grows in California in shady, well-drained places. It is on the preservation list of Ore. and is protected, that is, not to be picked or dug up.

brick. For information on the uses of bricks in various home landscape structures, see article, Paths, Walks, Walls listed under *construction*. The extensive treatment under that heading gives complete instructions.

Bridal wreath. See *Spiraea prunifolia.*

x *Brassolaeliocattleya* is the name given to a group of hybrid orchids bred from three genera, *Brassavola*, *Cattleya* and *Laelia*, crossed to produce plants more vigorous and colorful than the parents.

bridge graft. See *grafting*.

BRIGGSIA (*brigg*-see-uh). Gesneriad Family (*Gesneriaceae*). A group of about 20, mostly stemless, rosette-forming herbs from the province of Yunnan in particular, but found in mountains from northeastern India to the southwestern provinces of China, generally. Most also have thick rhizomes, but a few have slender rhizomes and develop stems.
B. muscicola (mews-*sik*-oh-luh), with rosettes to 8 in. across of lightly haired leaves, has greenish-yellow tubular flowers an inch long and half as wide. Grow it in a cool, shaded greenhouse.

Brisbane box. See *Tristania conferta*.

Bristle-cone pine. See *Pinus aristata*.

Bristly aralia. See *Aralia hispida*.

Bristly sarsaparilla. See *Aralia hispida*.

Brittle-fern. See *Cystopteris fragilis*.

Brittle maidenhair fern. See *Adiantum tenerum*.

BRITTONASTRUM (brit-tohn-*as*-trum). Mint Family (*Labiatae*). Tender, perennial herbs native to Ariz. and Mexico. Grows to 2 or 3 ft., with opposite leaves and two-lipped flowers in purple, red or white. Propagate by seed or division in spring. Zone 8.
B. canum (*kay*-num). Formerly listed as Agastache. Grows to 3 ft. with 1½-in.-ovate leaves and pink flowers to 1 in. long.
B. mexicanum (mex-ik-*kay*-num). This species has creeping rootstocks and grows to 3 ft. Aromatic dark pink to crimson flowers.

BRIZA (*brye*-zuh). QUAKING GRASS. Grass Family (*Gramineae*). Low, annual and perennial grasses with flattened, nodding spikelets on threadlike stalks. Useful for winter decoration when dried. These plants can be grown outdoors for ornament. Propagate annuals by seeds sown where plants are to stand; perennials by division of the clumps.
B. maxima (*max*-im-uh). Annual from the Mediterranean region, between 1 and 2 ft. high. The leaves are 6 in. long and ¼ in. wide. The plants are popular because of their delicate 3-in.-long clusters of golden-brown fruits. Seed is planted in mid-May in any soil.
B. media (*mee*-dee-uh). Naturalized in N. America,

BRIZA

LEFT: Briza is quaking grass, an ornamental especially suited for use in vases, in table decorations and in bouquets both dried and fresh. The best species is *Briza maxima*, an annual which flowers during June and July.
OPPOSITE: *Brodiaea uniflora* is the spring star-flower which bears white and pale lilac blossoms early in spring. Brodiaea corms are best set out in October.

this is a perennial species from Europe and Asia. Narrow, slender leaves to 3 in. long and ⅙ in. wide. The ovalish spikelets, 5 to 10 in. long, are often purplish in color. Zone 6.
B. minor (*mye*-nor). Similar to *B. maxima*, it reaches to about 1½ ft. and is easily grown from seed.

Broad bean. See *Vicia faba*.

Broad beech-fern. See *Dryopteris hexagonoptera*.

broadcast. A method of sowing seed or applying dry material evenly over all the ground rather than in rows or drills. This may be done by hand or by machine, some as simple as a canvas shoulder pouch with a hand-cranked, disk-like spreader plate at the bottom. The value of a broadcast technique over strip applications is the feather-edged swaths that may be readily overlapped to avoid both "skips" and double applications. Especially useful in irregular areas.

broadleaf evergreen. A plant other than a conifer or a tropical species having fairly wide (actually, wider than a "needle") evergreen leaves. Well-known examples include species of *Berberis*, *Buxus*, *Cotoneaster*, *Daphne*, *Euonymus*, *Ilex*, *Leucothoe*, *Kalmia* (mountain-laurel), *Pachysandra*, *Pieris* and *Rhododendron*. Such plants do best in relatively mild, moist climates. They require an annual rainfall of 30 in. or better and grow best with a permanent leaf mulch above their roots.

Broccoli. See *Brassica oleracea italica*.

BRODIAEA (broh-dih-*ee*-uh). Lily Family (*Liliaceae*). A large group of cormous plants, mostly from the western U.S. They have sparse, grasslike leaves, which disappear in the summer. The long-lasting white, purple, red or yellow flowers in clusters on slender stalks appear in spring. Brodiaeas are fine plants for naturalizing in frost-free climates, and particularly in the drier sections of the rock garden, since they like a gritty, well-drained soil. Note that *Brodiaea volubilis* is on the preservation list of Calif. and is protected, that is, is not to be picked or dug up, and *hyacinthina* is protected in Tex. They become dormant during the summer, after the leaves have ripened off. Keep them completely dry during this period. Especially good among low ground covers, as the flowers will grow up through them and the dying

Ways to broadcast seeds (usually lawn grass) or fertilizer: By hand is the classic, but not most efficient way. With drop-through spreader, LEFT, or cyclone spreader, RIGHT, is better. Pattern on RIGHT for spreading is preferable.

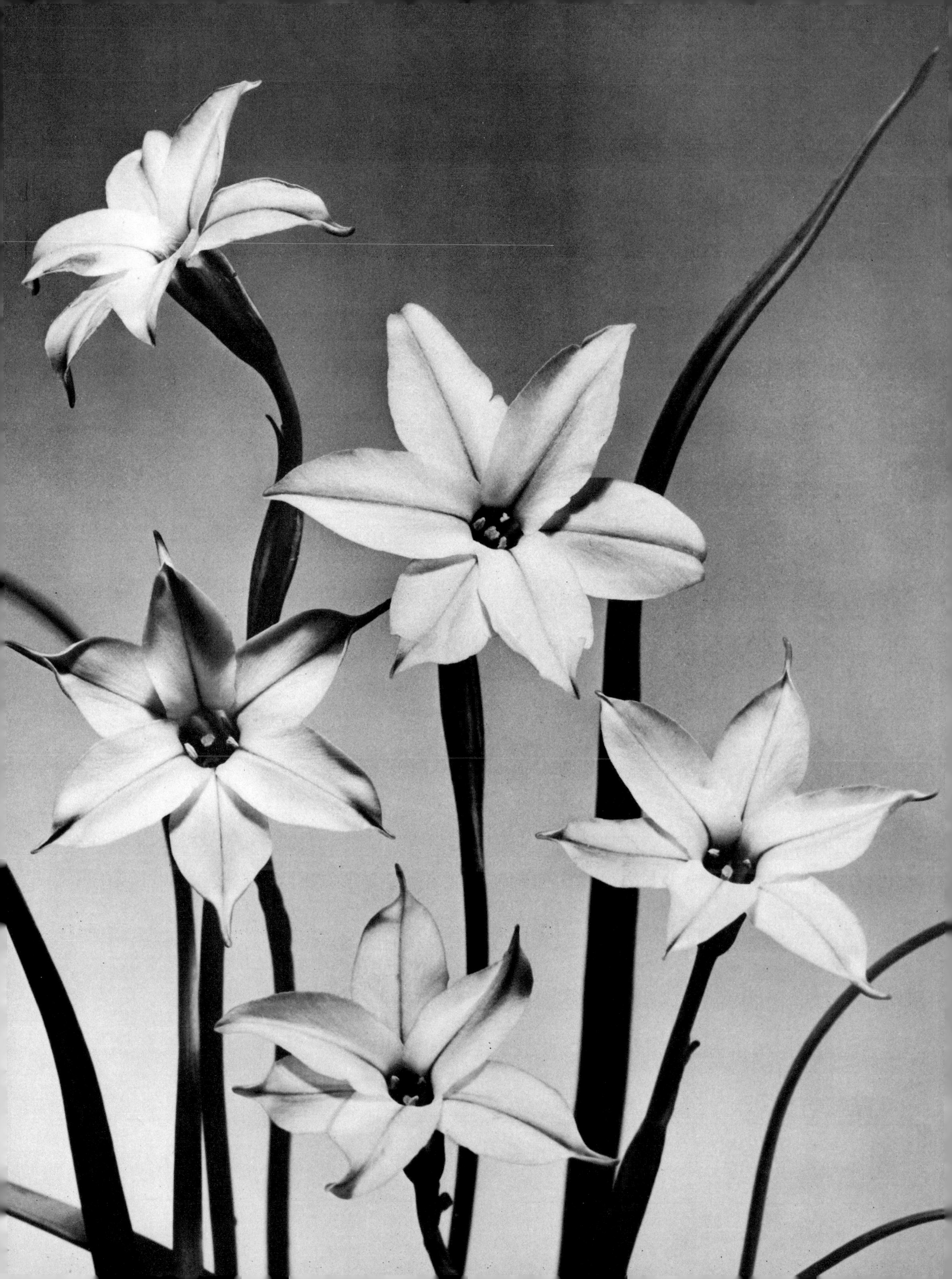

Brodiaea volubilis, the snake-lily, is native to California. It grows to about 4 feet if free-standing, but will climb to 8 feet or more if it finds a support.

foliage will be hidden. Although often listed in catalogs as hardy bulbs, these plants are reliably hardy only on the West Coast and in the Southeast. Propagate by offsets and seeds. Zone 9.

B. bridgesii (*bridges*-ee-eye). Grows about 1 ft. high with slender leaves 12 to 15 in. long and clusters of lilac flowers about 1½ in. across, in early May.

B. capitata (cap-ih-*tay*-tuh). BLUE-DICKS. The blue flowers, ⅔ in. wide, are borne in clusters on this plant, which grows to 2 ft. Native to Ore. and Calif., it is hardy along the West Coast and in the South.

B. crocea (*kroh*-see-uh). This species grows about 1 ft. high, has bright yellow flowers.

B. grandiflora: B. coronaria.

B. ixioides (iks-ee-*oh*-id-eez). PRETTY FACE. Grows about 18 in. high with salmon-colored flowers. Several varieties are available, some with yellow flowers streaked with purple.

B. lactea (*lak*-tee-uh). WILD HYACINTH. With white, sweet-scented flowers, a green stripe down the center of each petal, this species grows about 12 to 18 in. high. A lilac-colored form is often found. It can stand more moisture than other species.

B. laxa (*lax*-uh). A strong showy species which grows to 2 ft. and has 1¾-in.-long purple flowers. Occasionally a white bloom appears.

B. uniflora (yew-nif-*floh*-ruh). SPRING STAR-FLOWER. Sometimes listed in catalogs as Milla uniflora, Triteleia uniflora or Leucocoryne uniflora. From S. America, it is smaller than the native species—only 8 in. high. The leaves are onion-scented if crushed. Solitary white flowers with a purple midrib in each petal; they bloom in April. It is also grown as a greenhouse plant.

B. volubilis (vol-*yew*-bil-iss). SNAKE-LILY. Sometimes listed in catalogs as Stropholirion californicum. This is an odd plant, since it will grow about 4 ft. high when freestanding, but if it has something to twine on, the flower stalk will climb from 6 to 8 ft. Very long-lasting, rose-pink flowers. Native to Calif.

broken tulip. A broad classification of tulips that have petals of two or more colors and leaves that may be blotched or striped. Among the more important groups of broken tulips are the Bizarres, Biblooms, Parrots and Rembrandts. The cause of the broken effects originated with a virus infection, which may or may not recur after the planting of new bulbs.

Brome grass. See BROMUS.

Bromelia Family (*Bromeliaceae*). Also called the Pineapple Family. Bromeliads are herbaceous, often epiphytic (tree-perching), plants of tropical America. They are characterized by rosettes of stiff, fleshy, fibrous leaves often in the shape of a funnel that holds water. Regular flowers, showy in themselves or with vividly colored bracts. The following genera are grown in greenhouses, or outdoors in mild climates: *Aechmea*, *Ananas* (pineapple), *Billbergia*, *Cryptanthus*, *Dyckia*, *Guzmania*, *Hechtia*, *Neoregelia*, *Nidularium*, *Pitcairnia*, *Tillandsia* and *Vriesia*.

The Bromeliad Society is a nonprofit educational organization formed to promote interest and knowledge in this family of plants. Membership is worldwide and includes every phase of grower from apartment dweller to botanic garden personnel. Regular membership in the Society also includes *The Bromeliad Society Bulletin* issued six times a year. Other memberships are available, including a commercial one. In addition the Society fosters affiliates, awards medals, sponsors plantings in botanical gardens and parks, encourages exhibits, answers members' questions and distributes seeds through the Seed Fund. It also publishes the only handbook in English on these epiphytes, *Bromeliads in Color and Their Culture*. For more information write to The Bromeliad Society, Inc., 1811 Edgecliffe Drive, Los Angeles, Calif. 90026.

Bromeliaceae. See Bromelia Family.

bromeliad. Colloquially, any plant of the Bromelia Family.

BROMUS (*broh*-mus). BROME GRASS. Grass Family (*Gramineae*). Annual and perennial grasses with flat leaves and drooping spikelets in open clusters. Some species are grown in gardens for use in dried bouquets. Propagate by seeds sown in June.

B. brizaeformis (briz-ee-*form*-iss). QUAKE GRASS. From Europe and Asia, this annual grass has been naturalized in N. America. Up to 2 ft. high, with leaves to 8 in. long and ¼ in. wide, it has oblong to oval-shaped spikelets 1 in. long in clusters 8 in. long. A graceful plant, popular in gardens and in dried arrangements.

B. japonicus (jap-*pon*-ik-us). An annual grass, to 2 ft. high, with leaves 8 in. long and ¼ in. wide, grown in gardens as an ornamental. Native to Europe and Asia, sparsely naturalized in N. America.

Broom. See CYTISUS.

Broom-corn. See *Sorghum vulgare technicum*.

BROUGHTONIA (braw-*toh*-nee-ah). Orchid Family (*Orchidaceae*). A genus of epiphytic dwarf species from Jamaica, thought to contain several species by some taxonomists but combined by most into a single species, *B. sanguinea* (san-*gwin*-ee-uh). Recently the similar *B. negrilensis* (neg-ril-*en*-siss) has been described. Pseudobulbs of broughtonias are tightly clustered, about the size of a 50-cent-piece, each with a pair of rigid leathery leaves 6 to 8 in. long. The thin inflorescences grow from the apex of each bulb, fall to spring, reaching 18 to 24 in. before the six to 15 1-in. bright crimson sparkling flowers open over a period of weeks at the tip of each spike. Clones with yellow and light pink flowers have been found and recently broughtonia has been crossed with allied genera (*Cattleya*, *Epidendrum*) to produce floriferous hybrids of bright color and low growth. Mount plants tightly on slabs of tree fern. Provide bright light to full sun, excellent drainage, intermediate to warm temperatures and good air circulation. Broughtonias do best when permitted to become established and resent frequent disturbance. Several commonly used insecticides (Cygon, for example) injure broughtonias so check with an orchid grower for names of currently acceptable preparations which are safe.

BROUSSONETIA (broo-soh-*nee*-she-uh). PAPER-MULBERRY. Mulberry Family (*Moraceae*). The only species usually cultivated is a deciduous tree native to eastern Asia, where its gray bark is used in making paper. It has a wide-spreading round head, irregularly and boldly lobed leaves (alternate) and flowers in catkins, male and female on separate trees. Round fruit, usually orange to red, appears in Sept. While not the

Broughtonia sanguinea belongs to a small group of West Indian tree-perching orchids grown in greenhouses in cooler regions. Flowers of this species are crimson.

best ornamental shade tree, it is valuable for poor soils where other trees won't survive. It is often used as a street tree since it tolerates abuse, dust and heat. Unless controlled, it tends to spread rapidly by root suckers. Propagate by seeds, suckers or cuttings. Zone 6.

B. papyrifera (pap-ihr-*rif*-er-uh). Grows about 25 to 40 ft. high, with oval-shaped leaves 6 to 8 in. long and deeply lobed. Forms are available with finely dissected leaves, with white fruit or with variegated foliage. The characteristically gnarled and knobby trunk makes for easy identification.

BROWALLIA (broh-*wall*-lee-uh). Nightshade Family (*Solanaceae*). Bushy, branched annuals, 1 to 2 ft. high, from tropical America. The small lavender-blue tubular flowers bloom abundantly all summer. It is an effective plant in borders, the cutting garden, window boxes, hanging baskets, indoors as a pot plant and in the cool greenhouse. For early bloom outdoors, start seeds indoors in Feb. and plant outside when ground has warmed up. The plants will be bushy if you pinch them back when they are about 5 in. tall. They like full sun indoors, dappled sun outside and garden soil enriched with humus and well dug to a spade's depth. For winter bloom in the greenhouse, sow seeds in midsummer and pot seedlings in Basic Potting Mixture.

B. americana (am-eh-rik-*kay*-nuh). Sometimes listed

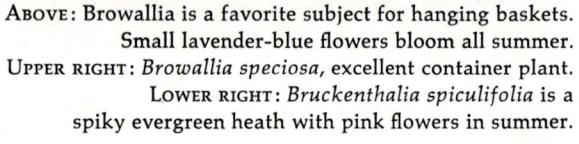

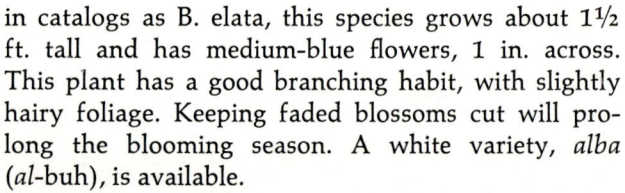

BROWALLIA

ABOVE: Browallia is a favorite subject for hanging baskets. Small lavender-blue flowers bloom all summer.
UPPER RIGHT: *Browallia speciosa*, excellent container plant.
LOWER RIGHT: *Bruckenthalia spiculifolia* is a spiky evergreen heath with pink flowers in summer.

in catalogs as B. elata, this species grows about 1½ ft. tall and has medium-blue flowers, 1 in. across. This plant has a good branching habit, with slightly hairy foliage. Keeping faded blossoms cut will prolong the blooming season. A white variety, *alba* (*al*-buh), is available.
B. elata: *B. americana*.
B. speciosa (spee-see-*oh*-suh). Grows to 2 ft. tall, and is fine for summer flowering in the garden or for the greenhouse. A clear violet color, the flowers are 1 to 2 in. across. It thrives on the West Coast and will do well as far as Zone 3 if started indoors in Feb. and given a sheltered spot. The variety *major* (*may*-jor) is an especially good house plant in the winter. Dig sturdy specimens in autumn, well ahead of frost, and cut them back. An excellent plant also for use in hanging baskets, either in the house or on porch or terrace in summer.

Brown bentgrass. See *Agrostis canina*.

brown canker. A fungus disease that attacks roses, particularly teas and hybrid teas. It causes circular, tan, dead spots with black centers and reddish-purple margins on the canes. Control by cutting out and destroying infected canes and spraying with lime-sulfur solution (one part solution to nine parts water), while dormant or with maneb, ferbam or captan during the growing season.

Brown-eyed Susan. See *Rudbeckia triloba*.

brown patch. A fungus disease that causes more or less circular brown spots, often bordered by a dark green ring, in lawns. The spots may be as much as several feet in diameter and may appear suddenly during warm, wet weather. For treatment, see *lawns*.

Brown's lily. See *Lilium brownii*.

brown-tail moth. A white-winged, brown-bodied, brown-tailed moth common in New England. The caterpillar is 1½ in. long and has broken white stripes on each side of a dark brown body. It feeds on the leaves of deciduous trees, notably the oak, in late summer, fall and spring, and lives in a small web-like nest on the tips of branches. Control by picking off and burning the nests in winter; by spraying in early spring with methoxychlor or lead arsenate.

BRUCKENTHALIA (brook-en-*thay*-lee-uh). SPIKE-HEATH. Heath Family (*Ericaceae*). From southeastern Europe and Asia Minor, a small, pretty shrub, useful chiefly in the sunny rock garden. Propagate by seeds or cuttings. Zone 6.
B. spiculifolia (spic-yew-lif-*foh*-lee-uh). Evergreen, heathlike plant, the only species in this genus. It grows to 10 in. high, with erect stems, crowded with very short, narrow leaves. Attractive pink, bell-shaped flowers bloom in summer.

Brunella. See PRUNELLA.

BRUNFELSIA (brunn-*fel*-zee-uh). Nightshade Family (*Solanaceae*). Evergreen shrubs of the tropical Americas, grown for ornament in intermediate to warm greenhouses and outdoors in southern Fla. and Calif. Glossy, alternate leaves and large, showy, often fragrant flowers, usually blooming in winter and spring. These plants are free-flowering indoors when pot-bound and fed liberally. Use Basic Potting Mixture. Propagate by cuttings of new wood in the spring. Zone 10-9.
B. americana (am-eh-rik-*kay*-nuh). LADY-OF-THE-

UPPER RIGHT: *Brunfelsia calycina* is a shrubby evergreen of tropical America that produces dark purple flowers, fading to near-white and fragrant.
CENTER RIGHT: *Brunfelsia calycina* flowers close up.
LOWER RIGHT: *B. undulata* is the most attractive of the flowering species and produces long white blooms.

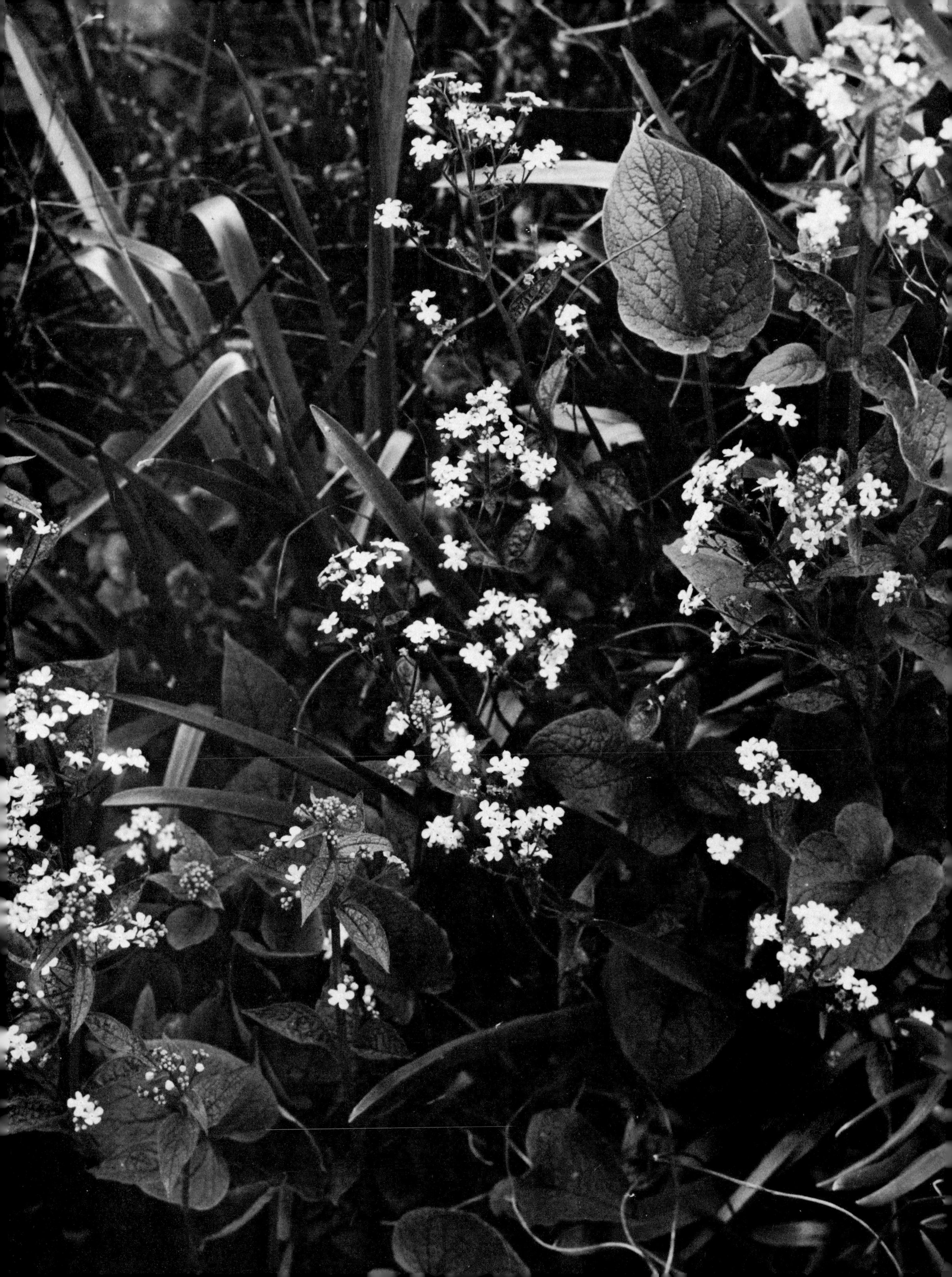

NIGHT. An attractive shrub, growing to 8 ft., with oval leaves to 4 in. long. The handsome, single flowers, 2 in. across with a tube 4 in. long, are white and fade to yellow. The blossoms are very fragrant at night. Yellow berrylike fruit ¾ in. across.

● **B. calycina** (kal-*liss*-in-uh). YESTERDAY-TODAY-AND-TOMORROW. A well-branched shrub to 4 ft. or more, with elliptic leaves to 4 in. long. It has clusters of rich, dark purple, fragrant flowers, 2 in. across with a tube 1 in. long. These fade, day by day, to pale lavender, hence the common name. The variety *floribunda* (floh-rib-*bund*-uh) is dwarf, very free-flowering, and has rich violet flowers with small white eyes.

B. latifolia (lat-if-*foh*-lee-uh). Smaller than *B. americana*, this shrub grows to a maximum of 6 ft., and has an abundance of blue flowers that fade to lavender and white. They are about 1½ in. across and appear intermittently during spring and fall.

● **B. undulata** (un-dew-*lay*-tuh). One of the handsomest and most dramatic of the flowered species, it reaches as much as 15 ft. Long, drooping, fragrant salver-formed flowers are produced even when the plant is small. Opening white, the flowers turn creamy with age.

BRUNNERA (*brunn*-er-uh). Borage Family (*Boraginaceae*). There is only one species in cultivation, an attractive perennial of Asia, with small blue flowers. In masses, the effect is a shimmering blue. It is effective in the early perennial border, with spring bulbs. Give it sun or partial shade and ordinary garden soil. Propagate by seeds or division. Zone 3.

B. macrophylla (mak-roh-*fill*-uh). Often listed in catalogs as Anchusa myosotidiflora, this plant grows to 2 ft. high, with tiny, sky-blue, forget-me-not-like flowers in great abundance in April or May. The flower stems rise above large, rough-textured, heart-shaped leaves at the base of the plant.

brush. The twiggy branches lopped off shrubs and trees, or a thicket of shrubs and trees. Also, the material (traditionally birch saplings) used to support tall varieties of garden peas—and the act of applying such material, "brushing the peas."

Brush-cherry eugenia. See *Eugenia paniculata*.

Brussels sprouts. See *Brassica oleracea gemmifera*.

Bryophyllum. See KALANCHOË.

Brunnera macrophylla is sometimes called forget-me-not anchusa. It is a perennial that bears a quantity of small blue flowers in early spring. The flower stems rise above large heart-shaped leaves at the base of the plants.

BUCHLOE (*buck*-low). Grass Family (*Gramineae*). A grass used for lawns in very dry areas. It roots along stems and has rather stringy leaves.

B. dactyloides (dak-til-*oy*-deez). BUFFALOGRASS. This grass is used for lawns where rainfall is not enough to maintain more desirable lawn grass. It is grown in the high plains of western Tex. and northern Mont. Leaves are pointed, a grayish green, and are somewhat hairy. This grass turns to straw color in exceptionally dry seasons or if the weather becomes exceedingly cold.

BUCIDA (bew-*cye*-duh). Combretum Family (*Combretaceae*). Trees and shrubs native to tropical America. The leathery leaves are clustered at the ends of twigs. Small flowers are borne in spikes, the fruits are small drupes.

B. buceras (bew-*ser*-us). BLACK OLIVE. A tree to 75 ft. tall. The leaves are 3½ in. long, the flowers greenish yellow in spikes about 5 in. long. The fruit is about ⅓ in. long. Native to the West Indies and Fla.

Buckeye. See AESCULUS.

Buckthorn. See RHAMNUS.

Buckthorn Family (*Rhamnaceae*). Except for a few showy plants (notably, *Ceanothus* and *Paliurus*), this family is of secondary garden importance. Trees, shrubs or woody vines, with simple alternate leaves and small, regular flowers. As the common name implies, most species tend to be spiny. *Ceanothus*, *Paliurus*, *Rhamnus* and *Zizyphus* are included in this encyclopedia.

Buckwheat. See *Fagopyrum esculentum*.

Buckwheat Family (*Polygonaceae*). Also called the Knotweed or Rhubarb Family. A varied group of herbaceous plants (many of which are undesirable weeds), woody vines, shrubs and trees, some grown for ornament and a few for their value as food crops. They have jointed stems, simple leaves (usually arranged in sheaths encircling the stem) and small inconspicuous flowers, often in handsome clusters. *Antigonon*, *Eriogonum*, *Fagopyrum* (buckwheat), *Polygonum* (ornamental vines), *Rheum* (rhubarb) and *Rumex* (sorrel) are included in this encyclopedia.

bud. The small plant part, protruding from a stem, branch or root, that develops into a new stem, foliage or flower growth. A leaf bud consists of an outer covering of scales and embryonic flower parts and stalk.

On most trees, shrubs and plants that do not die

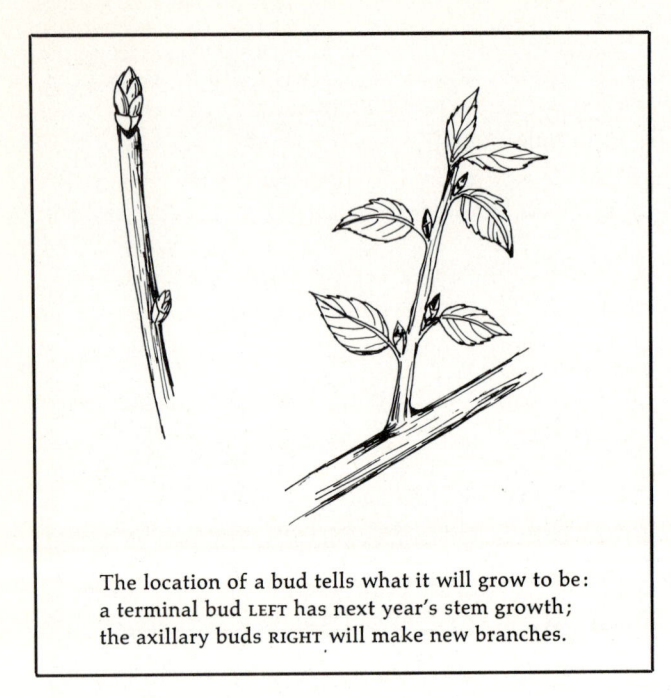

The location of a bud tells what it will grow to be: a terminal bud LEFT has next year's stem growth; the axillary buds RIGHT will make new branches.

back over winter, buds begin to develop in the summer, and by about the middle of fall they are completely formed. Over winter they remain relatively dormant, beginning to swell in Jan. or Feb. Then in spring, following a period of higher temperatures, they begin to open. On some plants, however, only the leaf buds are formed so far in advance of opening. The flower buds on hybrid tea roses, for example, develop on the current season's growth just a short time before they burst into flower. The same is true of many plants that flower in summer and autumn. Buds of spring-flowering plants require a definite period of dormancy, or rest, at low temperatures in order to grow into their final form. You cannot normally bring a branch indoors in the fall and force it to flower. Even forsythia and pussy willows, which seem to flower so easily indoors, must be allowed a dormant period at low temperatures before they will flower indoors.

Leaf buds are differentiated by their location on a plant. A terminal bud is the topmost bud on the stem (axis) of a plant. From it develops the stem growth of the plant next year. In many plants, if it is snipped off, bushy side growth develops. In other plants, such as pine, a single branch starts growing straight up, and the bud at its tip becomes the terminal bud. Axillary buds (or lateral buds) are those that develop in the axils or along the stem (axis) of a plant. From them come new branches (or lateral growth).

Bud is also a term designating a point at which a graft union is made. See *budding*.

bud blast. A disease that causes buds to turn brown and stop growing before they open. They usually do not drop (as in *bud drop*). The problem is mainly attributable to poor growing conditions.

Buddha's belly bamboo. See *Bambusa ventricosa*.

budding. A widely used method of grafting in which a single bud, rather than a branch, is inserted in the stock. All rose grafting is called budding. It is generally done outdoors in July and Aug. The most popular budding technique is called shield-budding or T-budding. In this process, the bud is slipped into a T-shaped cut in the stock bark. See *propagation*.

BUDDLEIA (bud-*lee*-uh). BUTTERFLY-BUSH. Logania Family (*Loganiaceae*). Attractive, deciduous or semi-evergreen shrubs of tropical regions. They can be grown in cool greenhouses for graceful sprays of winter bloom, but they are most often seen outdoors in warm-temperate parts of the U.S. They do best in rich, well-drained soil and full sun. Propagate by cuttings taken in late summer or by seeds.

● **B. alternifolia** (al-ter-nif-*foh*-lee-uh). A beautiful shrub from China, growing to 12 ft., with graceful, arching branches. Alternate, lance-shaped leaves to 4 in. long, held late in the fall. Decorative lavender-purple flowers, in dense clusters along stems of the previous year, bloom in June and July. Although this species is less well-known and generally less winter-hardy than the following more publicized species, it has greater grace and refinement of form. Zone 7.

B. davidii (day-*vid*-ee-eye). SUMMER-LILAC. One of the hardiest species, growing to 10 ft., or less where stems are winter-killed. Soft gray-green, opposite leaves to 10 in. long, toothed, whitish beneath, on tall slender branches. Beautiful fragrant lilac flowers with orange eyes, in dense spikes to 1 ft. long. Popular for its midsummer bloom where it is not reliably top-hardy, but new growth starts quickly from the base if the stems are cut low in spring. This species is a favorite of butterflies. Several varieties with different colorings are available. Zone 6.

B. globosa (gloh-*boh*-suh). A tender species partially evergreen, which is originally native to Peru and

OPPOSITE: An unusual *Buddleia* species, *globosa*, the orange ball tree of Chile and Peru, is evergreen and bears sprays of fragrant round orange-yellow flowers in spring.
RIGHT: Called summer-lilac and butterfly-bush for its appeal to butterflies, the buddleia is an attractive deciduous or semi-deciduous shrub. It produces striking panicles of red, pink, lavender or white flowers in summer. Hardy only in warmer regions, it dies down farther north, rarely reaches a height of more than 10 feet.
BELOW: Butterfly-bush in bloom is a handsome lawn feature.

Chile; but may be grown in this country in southern Calif. This shrub may reach a height of 15 ft. with 10-in. wavy-toothed, lance-shaped leaves which are yellow and hairy beneath but dark green and wrinkled above. The orange-yellow flowers are fragrant and the dense ball-shaped heads are formed of groups of individual ¾-in., long-stalked blooms. The 3-in. globes bloom at the ends of the branches. Zone 7.

> *Seasonal Justice*
>
> There is nothing that so epitomizes the real nature of gardening as the creation and enjoyment of the herbaceous border. In failure or triumph they tempt, challenge, exasperate and reward the gardener, always generously but always, with even-handed justice, according to his desserts. —R.B.

bud drop. A physiological disease that causes buds to shrivel, turn brown and drop before opening. It is especially common in gardenias that are grown indoors in too-high temperature and with too little light and humidity. The problem can be prevented if growing conditions are improved in all ways. Avoid applying too much nitrogen.

bud grafting. See *budding*.

bud mutation. A character change that appears in one of the buds of a plant. It results in a leafy branch or flower that is different from those on other parts of the same plant. The alteration may result from an inexplicable change in one of the plant genes and may be duplicated by asexual propagation of the changed part. Many fruits and roses are bud mutations.

bud sport. A bud variation; one that is different from the other buds on the same plant. The navel orange is a bud sport. Except technically, a bud sport is the same as a bud mutation.

bud stick. A plant shoot containing buds that may be removed for propagation by budding. See *budding*.

Buffalo-berry. See *Shepherdia argentea*.

Buffalograss. See *Buchloe dactyloides*.

bug. The true bug is an insect that belongs to the Hemiptera (half-winged) order—so-called because the outer pair of wings is thick and stiff at the base, membranous at the tip. When these wings are crossed over the back, they form an X. The inner pair of wings is entirely membranous. Bugs are sucking insects. They often give off an unpleasant odor. While some may live in water, most live on land. They usually produce eggs only once a year. Their number includes such common garden pests as chinch bug, lace bug, squash bug and stink bug. (June bugs and potato bugs are not true bugs; they are beetles.) In general, bugs may be controlled in the garden with pyrethrum or a synthetic insecticide such as dylox, diazinon or malathion. For instructions for specific measures, see entries for individual bugs.

Bugbane. See CIMICIFUGA.

Bugle-lily. See WATSONIA.

Bugle plant. See AESCHYNANTHUS.

Bugleweed. See AJUGA.

Bugloss. See ANCHUSA.

building. For information on building garden structures for the landscape, see article, Paths, Walks, Walls, listed under *construction*.

bulb. Loosely, any globular or markedly swollen underground stem that produces top growth and basal roots. Strictly speaking, a true bulb is a modified plant bud enclosed in thick, fleshy scales held together by a fibrous base that sends forth roots. Examples of the true bulb are the daffodil, hyacinth, lily, onion and tulip. On the other hand, crocus, dahlia, gladiolus and iris are produced from related rootstocks classed as corms, rhizomes or tubers.

Bulbs vary widely in their growing habits. Some, like the cardiocrinum bulb, shrivel up after they have produced growth and flowers; their place is taken by a new, larger bulb and a number of small, flat bulbs that develop as the original bulb shrivels. Other bulbs, such as the daffodil, continue to grow larger each year, producing one or more new side bulbs annually. Still others, like the lily, are rough and scaly; each scale, if separated from the parent, can be propagated as a bulb.

All bulbs require a moderately rich soil and good drainage. After flowering, they should be left undisturbed in order to encourage top growth, which restores the strength that is required to form the foliage and flowers for the following season. The bulbs can be left in the same spot year after year until they begin to develop additional stems.

The planting depth for bulbs varies. For specifications, see separate entries for plants growing from bulbs and the chart on pages 412 and 413.

FLOWERS FROM BULBS

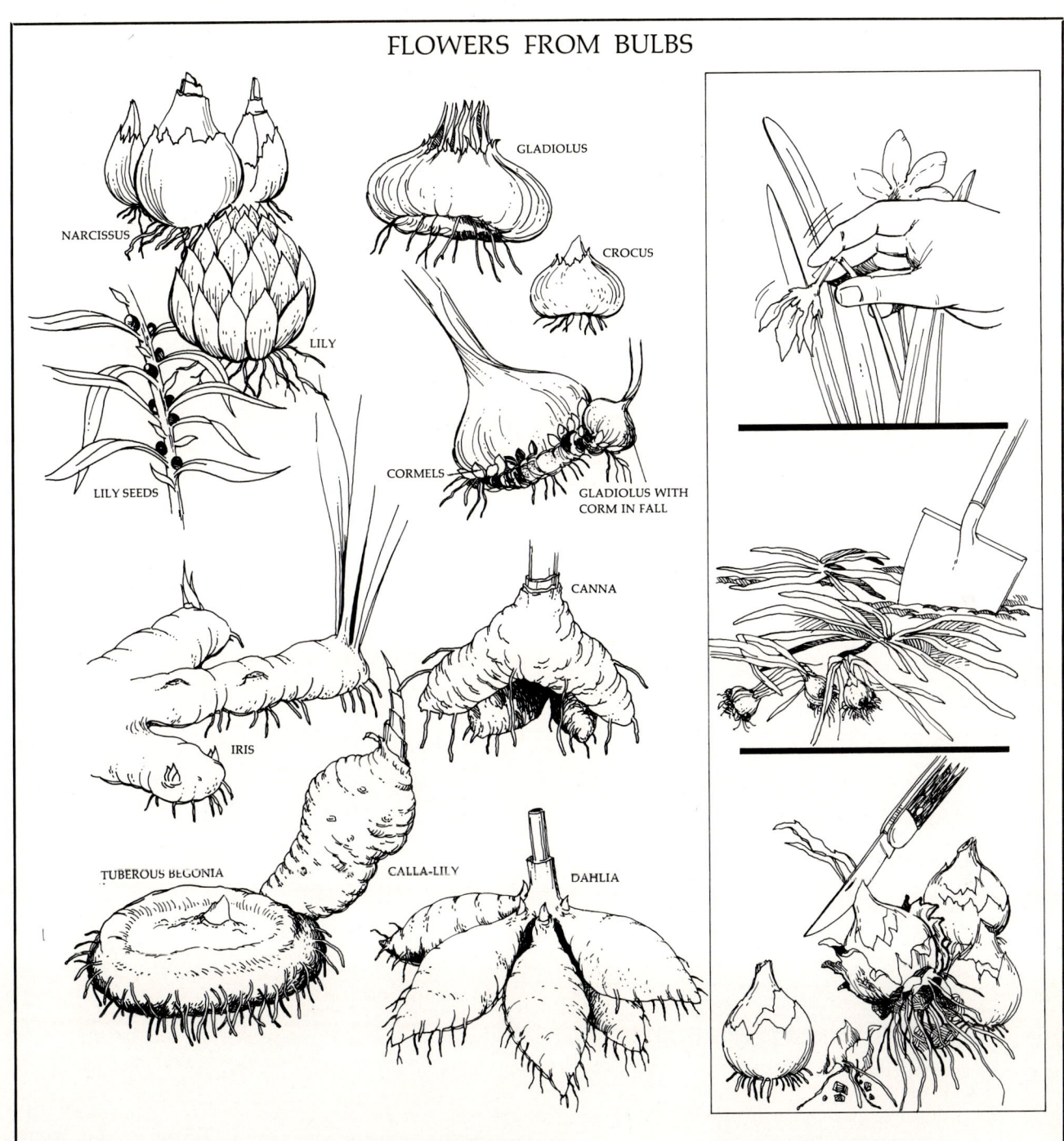

A true bulb is a plant bud enclosed in thick scales held together by a fibrous base that sends out roots. Lilies, narcissus and tulips are true bulbs. Dahlias, gladiolus and iris are produced from rootstocks classed as corms, rhizomes or tubers. Bulbous plants vary in methods of propagation, but many increase by the development of bulb offsets and simultaneously by the production of seed. Offsets exactly duplicate the parent bulb, including hybridized species, but seeds of hybrid species may not exactly reproduce the parent plant. The reproduction system of the lily differs: The lily may be grown from seed or propagated by planting individual scales which will grow into the bulbs which will be true to the parent plant. Other bulbs and corms propagate by seed, and also by root division, for instance dahlias. With few exceptions, the true bulbs are planted in the fall.

Top: To encourage production of large flowers in narcissus and many other bulbs, it is important to break off flower heads once they have faded to prevent the ripening of seeds.
Center: Allow foliage to yellow and die down before digging bulbs for storage or for transplanting.
Bottom: Cut foliage back to the bulb before storing or transplanting so that the bulbs can thoroughly dry out.

Bulbs for All Seasons

By ELIZABETH LAWRENCE

Bulbs are the gardener's best friends. Spring would not be spring without them. But gardeners who think of bulbs as blooming only in spring miss a great deal, for some of the most beautiful ones belong to summer and fall. There is a wide choice of bulbs for all seasons, and every year long-sought treasures turn up in the catalogs.

The majority of bulbs are easy to grow, have few troubles and require little care. Order your bulbs early. Apply bone meal or superphosphate at planting time. Place the top of the bulb twice its height beneath the surface of the ground, though depth is not too important as bulbs seek their own level. Always allow the foliage to die away completely after flowering. This enriches the bulb for the following season.

Hardy Spring Bulbs

Earliest. The first flowers of spring come to my North Carolina garden with the new year. A few years ago, for example, *Crocus sieberi* was in bloom on New Year's Day, narcissus 'Nylon' on January 7, crocus 'Snow Bunting' on the 12th, *C. etruscus* on the 21st. On the 28th the summer snowflake bloomed, and on the 30th, crocus 'Vanguard,' the spring starflower, narcissus 'Bambi,' *Anemone blanda*, *Scilla turbergeniana*, *Eranthis hyemalis*, *Crocus moesicus* and *C.* 'Whitewell's Purple' all came to flower. This does not happen every year, but it is indeed a cold January when we have no bulbs in bloom.

Perhaps so much bloom is not surprising in North Carolina, but even in colder climates the little bulbs are early risers. Winter aconites (*Eranthis*) bloom at the end of January in Ohio and West Virginia, the first flowers of *Crocus tomasinianus* appear in the Brooklyn Botanic Garden some time in February, and *Narcissus bulbocodium romieux* has been reported to open in January against a south wall in a garden on Long Island, New York.

Most crocuses will establish themselves anywhere and flourish and multiply. They will bloom in the open, or under deciduous trees, or even under pines if the branches are high. *C. etruscus*, *C. sieberi* and *C. tomasinianus* flower in tones of translucent violet; *C. moesicus* is a dark golden-yellow, 'Whitewell's Purple' a dark but glowing violet; and 'Vanguard' is violet within, pearl-gray without. 'Snow Bunting,' white with a yellow throat, and 'E. A. Bowles,' a clear soft yellow, are two of the best forms of *C. chrysanthus*. All of these crocuses are easily grown.

Anemone blanda is just as easy and just as enduring as the crocuses. Like winter aconite, glory-of-the-snow (*Chionodoxa*), snow drops (*Galanthus*), snowflakes (*Leucojum*), some of the squills (*Scilla*) and *Hyacinthus azureus*, it becomes naturalized if it is in the right spot and will bloom under trees if there is enough spring sunlight to open the wide flowers that look like hepaticas, to which they are related. The flowers of the various forms are in tints of lavender and lilac, but most beautiful of all is the intense gentian-blue of the variety *atrocaerulea*. If you are in doubt as to the top and bottom of the anemone tubers, put them in the ground horizontally.

You may have some difficulty in getting the winter aconite started, but once established it blooms indefinitely. Success depends upon getting fresh tubers and planting them at once. Unlike crocuses, they are insignificant when they are planted in small groups. Plant them in quantity to make a carpet of gold.

The pale flowers of *Scilla tubergeniana* are very good performers. The best of the early squills are *S. sibirica* 'Spring Beauty' and *S. bifolia*. 'Spring Beauty' is such a brilliant blue that the little flowers are striking even as they emerge from the ground—already open, it seems—sometimes at the end of January in North Carolina, early February in colder places, and early May in Massachusetts. They bloom profusely, often for two months, and the stems lengthen as they bloom until they are four inches long. *S. bifolia* blooms a little later. Its flowers are a softer blue, but equally beautiful.

Even in New York snowdrops bloom in sheltered places early in February, sometimes before that. *Galanthus elwesii*, which is larger, handsomer and earlier than *G. nivalis*, the common snowdrop, is almost always in bloom before the end of January. Both grow in shade and in soil that has enough humus to keep it from drying out in summer, but *G. elwesii* blooms better in full sun.

The true spring snowflake (*Leucojum vernum*) flowers in February or March. It is very rare in Amer-

---

Among the earliest and most rewarding of the spring-flowering bulbs are the bright low-growing crocuses. They bloom in shades ranging through the purples, yellows and white, sometimes with streaked effects. Crocuses establish themselves easily almost anywhere, and will flourish and multiply. They bloom in the open or under trees, even shady evergreens.

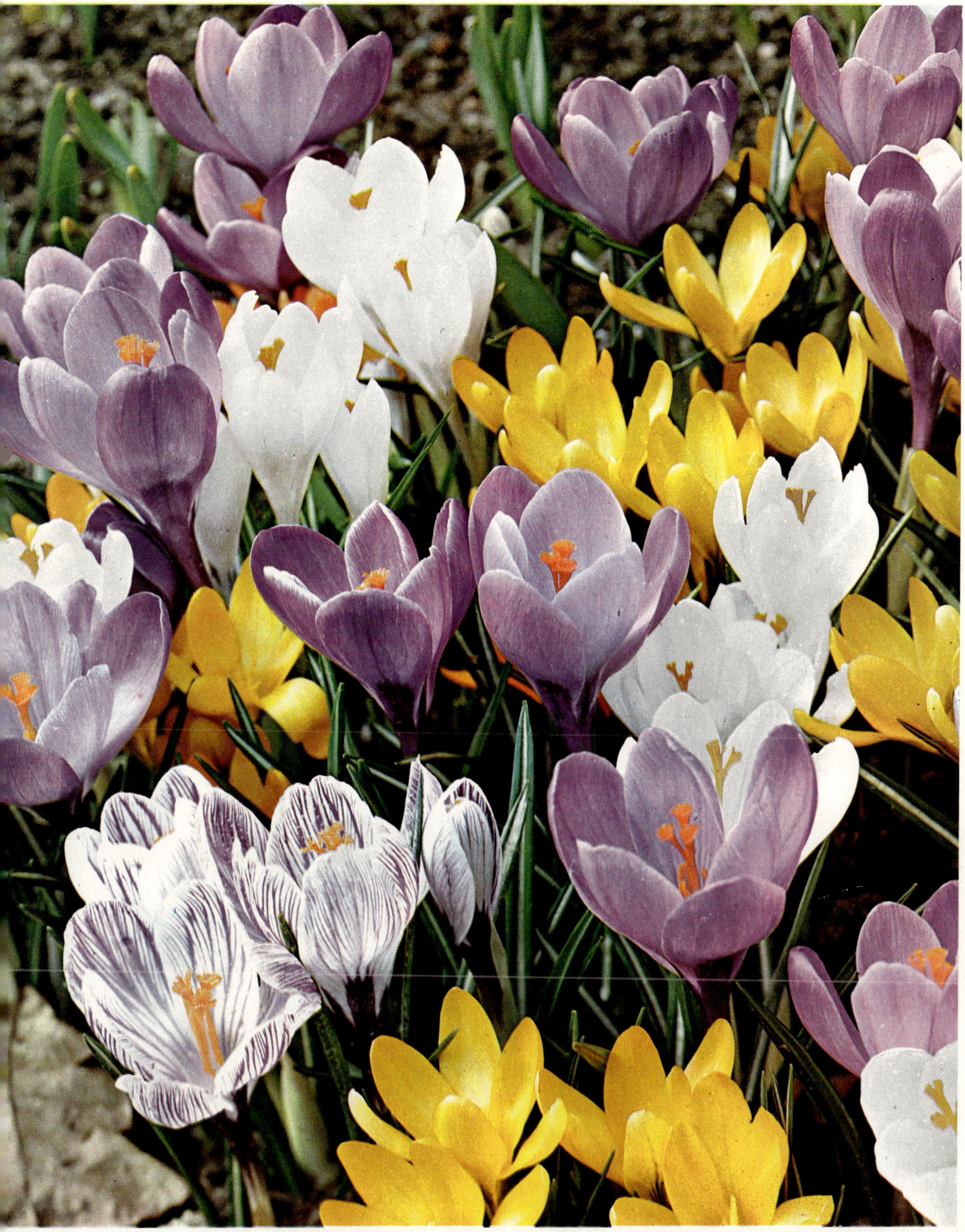

BULB PLANTER:
DEPTH OF PLANTING, HEIGHT OF BLOOM

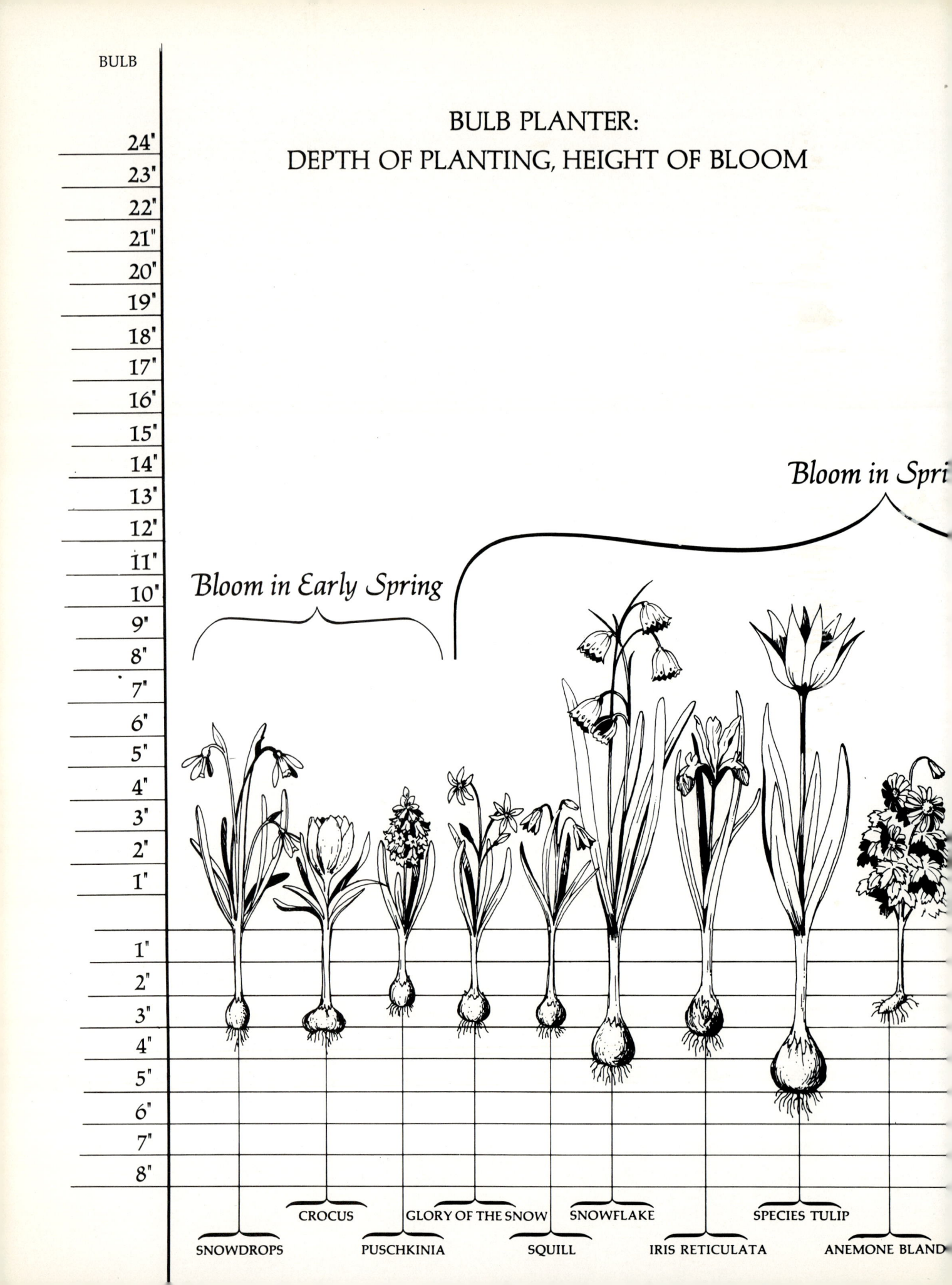

Bloom in Early Spring

Bloom in Spring

BULB

24"
23"
22"
21"
20"
19"
18"
17"
16"
15"
14"
13"
12"
11"
10"
9"
8"
7"
6"
5"
4"
3"
2"
1"

1"
2"
3"
4"
5"
6"
7"
8"

SNOWDROPS · CROCUS · PUSCHKINIA · GLORY OF THE SNOW · SQUILL · SNOWFLAKE · IRIS RETICULATA · SPECIES TULIP · ANEMONE BLAND

Bloom in Summer

BULB
24"
23"
22"
21"
20"
19"
18"
17"
16"
15"
14"
13"
12"
11"
10"
9"
8"
7"
6"
5"
4"
3"
2"
1"

1"
2"
3"
4"
5"
6"
7"
8"

PE HYACINTH   DAFFODIL   SCILLA NUTANS   MADONNA LILY
HYACINTH   TULIP   ALLIUMS   LILIES

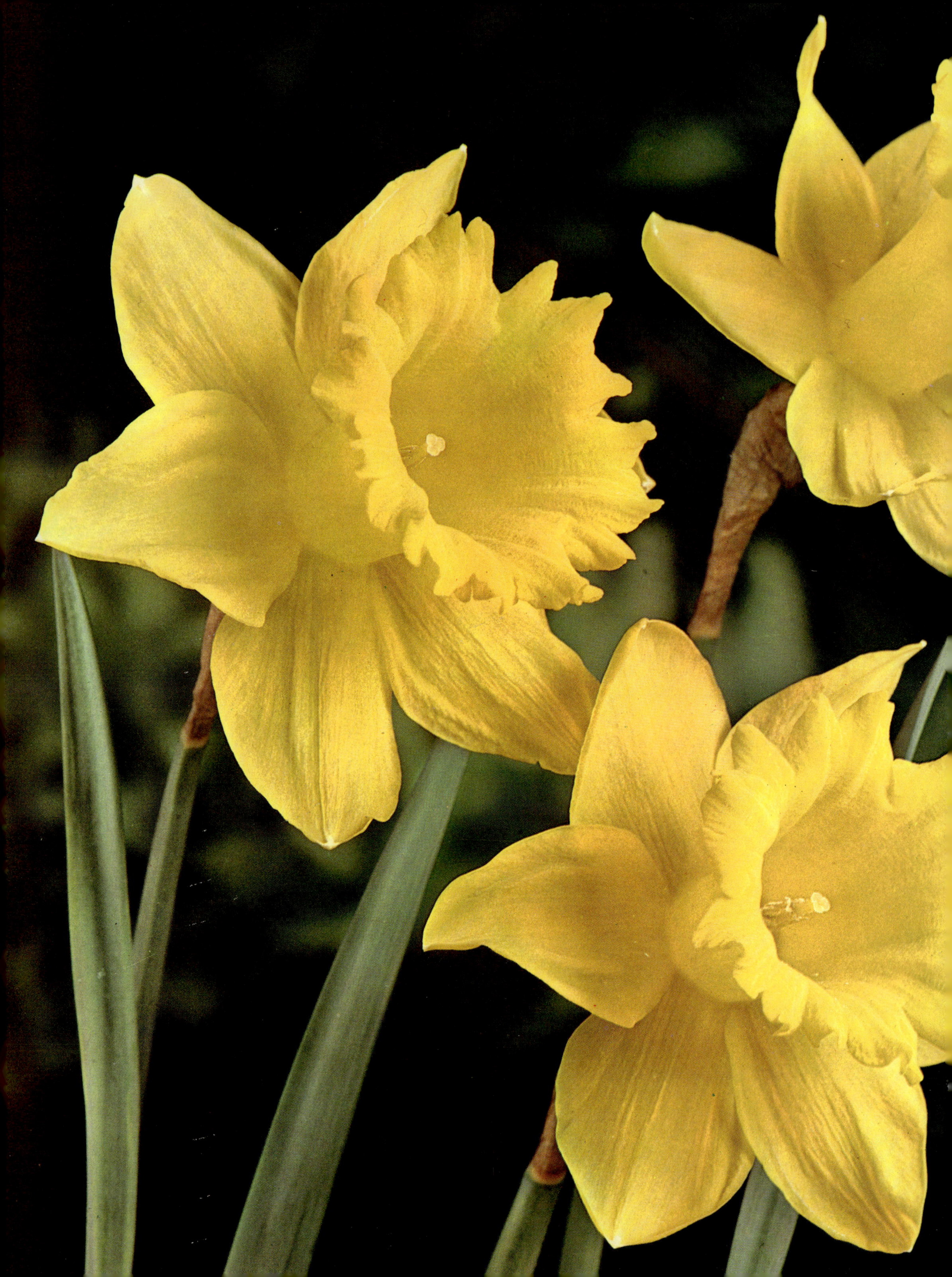

ica. Although they may bloom the first year, they soon disappear. The solitary flowers are green-tipped bells on short stems, opening just as the foliage is pushing up.

In North Carolina it is unusual for the spring star-flower (*Brodiaea uniflora*, better known as a triteleia) to bloom in January. It usually comes in February or early March, a little later in northern gardens and not until early May in Massachusetts, where it usually needs light protection. This bulb from the Argentine grows north of Philadelphia, and it is definitely hardy in New York City. The six-pointed stars are typically white with violet stripes, and there is a form with pale bluish-violet flowers.

Narcissus 'Bambi' is not the only small early daffodil, though it is one of the most dependable. A small form of *N. pseudo-narcissus* called *pumilus* (it may be listed as *N. nanus* or *N. minor*), produces drooping, bright yellow flowers in February. An even smaller form of *pseudo-narcissus* called *N. minimus* is the tiniest of all, and blooms in January or February in mild climates, late February or March in the North.

The brilliant purple, violet-scented flowers of *Iris reticulata* open in my garden at the end of February or early in March, and even as far north as Boston they bloom in March or April. The blue flowers of the cultivar 'Cantab' are earlier still, and in some gardens the cultivar is more permanent than the species. Both will bloom in part shade, but they are better off in full sun.

North or South, the glory-of-the-snow blooms in March. The large forms of *Chionodoxa luciliae* are the handsomest. The flowers of the variety *gigantea* are pale blue-violet; those of *gigantea alba* are pure white. 'Pink Giant' is pale amaranth-pink. *C. sardensis*, said to be earlier, has never proved so with me. It is smaller, but the color is an intense gentian-blue. Chionodoxas should be planted in full sun, though they will bloom in part shade, and they should be planted in quantity—hundreds, not dozens.

Grape-hyacinths (*Muscari*) have so much unattractive foliage, early and late, that they are scarcely worthy of garden room, even though the spikes of the variety 'Heavenly Blue' are the color of chicory. Much better is the bulb listed as Muscari azureum or Hyacinthus azureus (correctly *Hyacinthus ciliatus*). It puts up tiny conical spikes of sailor blue in February, and these bloom on into April. The true hyacinth leaves, usually two to a bulb, remain neat.

Dutch hyacinths are to the early garden what tulips are to mid-spring. After the first year they produce more foliage than flowers, and, if you want big flowers, it is best to plant new bulbs each fall. My favorite kinds are two early ones—the massive white 'Arentine Arendsen' and the pale blue-violet 'Myosotis.' Two fine late ones are rose-pink 'Lady Derby' and, most beautiful of all, 'Chestnut Flower,' which is a double pink as delicate as a seashell.

A Host of Golden Daffodils

The early daffodils are most welcome. 'February Gold' lives up to its name in my garden, and has even bloomed in January. In Ohio it sometimes blooms at the end of February and even where there are no daffodils before St. Patrick's Day, its pale flowers, like a splash of early sunshine, are ahead of most of the garden varieties. As for trumpets, 'Forerunner'—a larger flower of cool yellow with a heavily frilled crown—blooms here in February, often before the middle of the month. 'Winter Gold,' 'Christmas Glory,' 'Sun Chariot' and 'Helios'—a very early large-cupped variety—should never be allowed to disappear from the growers' lists.

At the other end of the season, 'Lights Out,' a charming poet's narcissus (*N. poeticus*) blooms early in April in North Carolina, and a month later in Pennsylvania. *N. gracilis*, a pale yellow, blooms here in North Carolina in the middle of April, in Pennsylvania the last of April and in Massachusetts so late in May that it often blooms on into June. This year, 'Frigid,' silvery-white except for the green eye of the small cup, bloomed in my garden on the 19th of April along with *N. biflorus*, 'Elfhorn' (a tiny hoopskirt daffodil) and 'Lintie.' These were the last to bloom.

The following are among the most beautiful, durable and trouble-free daffodils in the various divisions (I omit the miniatures, for they are too difficult to sum up briefly). These are popular and garden-worthy in all parts of the country.

Trumpet daffodils. 'Golden Harvest' is clear yellow without being brassy, large without being coarse, and is early. 'Lord Wellington' is the general favorite among the very large ones. And the magnificent 'Kingscourt' has now come down to a gardener's price. 'Music Hall' may be the best all-around bicolor trumpet. The bicolor 'Foresight,' a sizable and shapely flower with a flat ivory perianth, has a bright primrose trumpet. Of the really white trumpets, 'Beersheba' is the only one that is permanent in my

The daffodil is the most loved of the many spring-flowering bulbs. A member of the *Narcissus* genus, the daffodil is available in varieties and species that bloom early or late and in many shades and combinations of white and gold. Generally trouble free, small burrowing pests don't eat them and few insects trouble them. They naturalize quickly in almost any location and thrive for years.

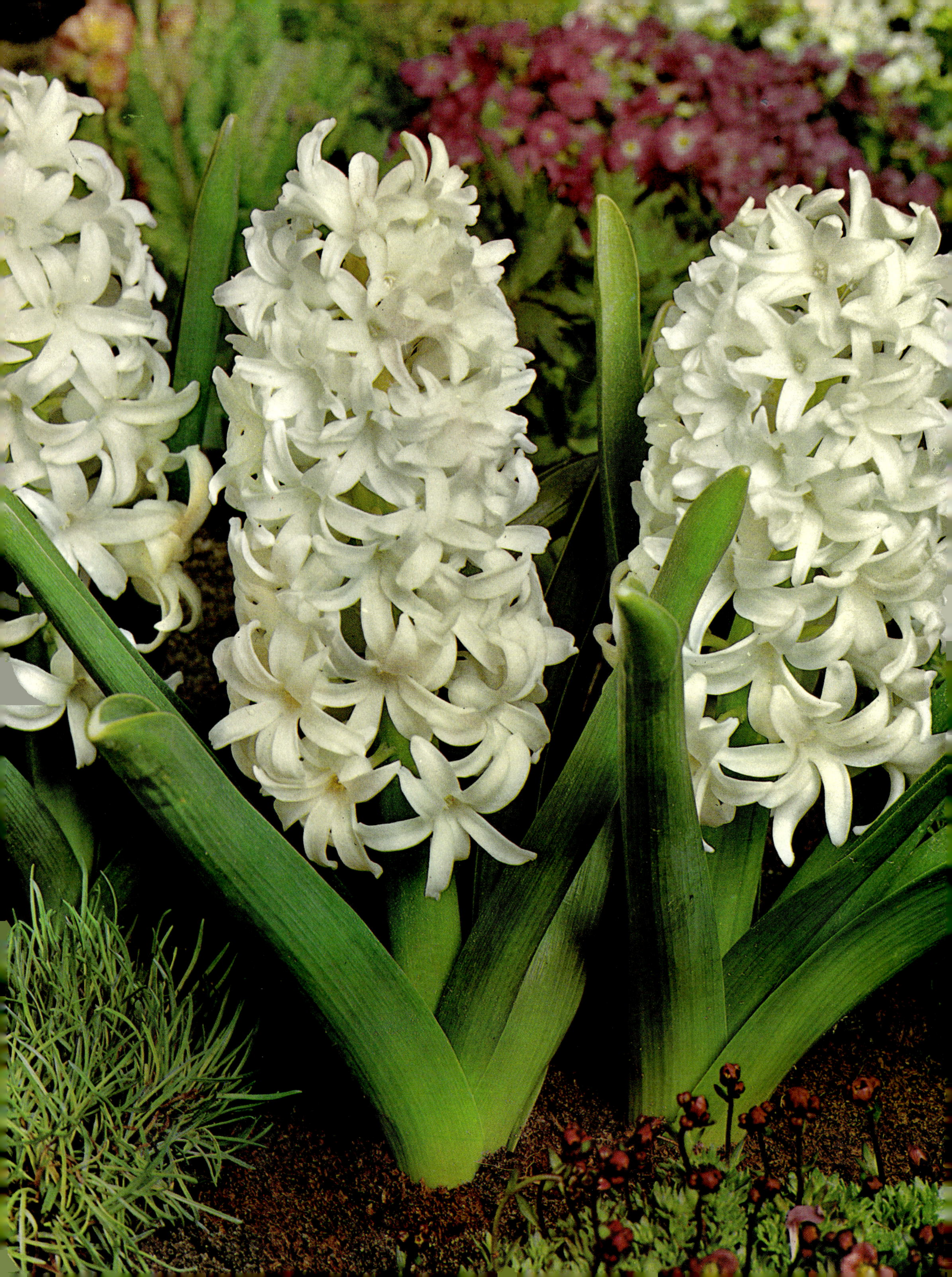

garden, and I have had none that I like better. 'Mount Hood' is much larger, but not so white. 'Broughshane' is larger still; 'Rosy Trumpet' is one of the pinkest, as well as a dependable garden variety.

Large-cup daffodils. 'Carlton' is a fine, early, lemon-yellow, deliciously fragrant variety. 'Fortune' sometimes blooms here at the end of February; in Pennsylvania it comes early in April. Though the crown is described as a vivid orange, it seldom has more than a slight orange flush. 'Quirinus' is really brilliant, with its wide yellow perianth and fiery cup. 'Scarlet Leader' is another with a striking contrast between the creamy-yellow perianth and the almost flat cup of flame-scarlet. For contrast between a bright yellow cup and a white perianth, 'Bodilly' has qualities that make it outstanding among daffodils of all types. The large, frilly cup of 'Gertie Millar' is such a pale yellow, and becomes white so quickly, that the effect is that of a pure-white trumpet. 'White Duchess' is another frosty one. It has a delicately frilled, dainty cup that is called lemon but turns a silvery-white almost at once. If beauty is all that is wanted, 'Ludlow' will fill the bill. As for daffodils with red cups and white perianths, two of the best are the very early 'Gerda' and the rather late 'Redbird.' For pink cups, none is lovelier than 'Mrs. R. O. Backhouse,' but this does not always prosper. 'Rose of Tralee' colors well some seasons and is always charming.

Small-cup daffodils. 'Mangosteen' is a reliable variety with clear yellow petals and an orange cup. 'Merry Market' is similar to it. 'Shantallow,' sparkling white, has a moss-green cup as it opens, then turns to a lemon-white. The real beauties are those with white petals and red cups, such as 'La Riante' and 'St. Louis.' 'Pomona' is pale and early; it looks fragile but endures. I have never seen 'La Beauté' outside of my own garden, but I would not be without it. It does not increase (though it does not dwindle either) but blooms in perfection year after year, a round white flower with a delicately marked cup. The all-white daffodils of this class bloom late. 'Cushendall,' 'Silvermine' and 'Polar Ice' have green eyes, which make the whiteness of the petals even more sparkling in contrast.

Double-flowered daffodils. There is great variety in double daffodils. 'Inglescombe' is like a double yellow rose; 'Hollandia,' a combination of yellow and orange; 'Mary Copeland,' white and orange. 'Daphne' is a double poet's narcissus, white and fragrant. 'Cheerfulness' is a double white poetaz, and 'Yellow Cheerfulness' the same thing in pale citron-yellow. 'Snowsprite' is one of the latest daffodils in bloom.

Triandrus hybrids. There are several very similar to the silvery-white 'Thalia' but none lovelier, and none that blooms and increases so prolifically. 'Stoke' has the same airy form, but it is a pale yellow. 'Silver Chimes,' with its cluster of ivory and citron flowers, is somewhat tender, although it sometimes blooms in very cold gardens. (In the North it may need to be mulched each year.)

OPPOSITE: The most fragrant of all the bulbs, spring-flowering hyacinth can be grown out-of-doors as far north as New England if mulched through the winter.
RIGHT: Triandrus hybrid white daffodil, in the named variety 'Thalia.' A prolific producer of airy blooms, it increases rapidly in naturalized situations.

BULB

Cyclamineus hybrids. These are the most graceful of all daffodils. This same grace is inherent in 'February Gold,' in 'March Sunshine' (which nearly always blooms in February for me and lives up to its name even in cold gardens) and in 'Beryl,' which looks like a fragile poet's narcissus with tilted petals. To those who like bold flowers, 'Peeping Tom,' with its long stem, exaggerated trumpet and brassy color, will be welcome.

Jonquilla hybrids. 'Trevithian' is the general favorite among the early, short-cup jonquil hybrids. It blooms early in March for me, and early in April in the North. The later 'Golden Perfection' has also two or three flowers to a stem, but the flowers are larger. The larger single flower of 'Golden Goblet' is like a trumpet daffodil. All of these have the characteristic jonquil fragrance and clear yellow color. 'Cherie' is a small, charming, white jonquil with a cup that in some seasons has a shell-pink flush.

Tazettas. 'Cragford' and 'Geranium' are colorful, prolific and free-flowering, with white petals and orange cups. 'Cragford' is early, 'Geranium' later—with larger flowers. The flowers of 'Martha Washington' are larger still and come only two to a stem. The cups are yellow with an orange rim. 'Red Guard' is a distinct tazetta with a sharp contrast between the pale yellow petals and the scarlet cup.

Poet's daffodils. 'Actaea' is by far the largest poeticus variety and has an excellent flower. 'Smyrna' is smaller but of better substance. I like to keep a corner for "pheasant eye," *N. poeticus recurvus*, because it blooms so late.

Tulips for a Long Bloom Season

Every fall I buy as many tulips as I have time to plant and can afford, and in the spring I dig them up as soon as the flowers fade and usually throw them away. Sometimes a friend who cannot bear such willful waste comes along and gathers up the outcasts. She heels them in until the foliage dies down,

OPPOSITE, TOP LEFT: *Narcissus poeticus* is the poet's narcissus. One of the most fragrant, the cup has wavy edges usually rimmed with a sienna or burnt-orange shade of red.
OPPOSITE, LEFT: Close-up of the poet's narcissus. 'Actaea,' the cultivar shown, is one of the largest of this type.
OPPOSITE, TOP RIGHT: The named variety 'Peeping Tom' is one of the *cyclamineus* hybrid narcissus. A native of Portugal, it has a long stem, an exaggerated trumpet and a bright brassy color. *Narcissus cyclamineus* is considered to be the most graceful of all the narcissus species cultivated.
OPPOSITE, RIGHT: A brilliant display of bulbs naturalized in drifts. Greigii hybrid tulips in the foreground are backed by golden daffodils, grape-hyacinth in two shades of blue, the white of massed *Anemone blanda*. Hybrid tulips and daffodils repeat the pattern as far as the eye can see. Tall flowers in the distance are crown imperial fritillaria.
ABOVE: The tulip hybrid x *fosteriana* named variety 'Red Emperor,' *Anemone blanda* and grape-hyacinth massed in a growing bouquet of red, white and blue. They bloom at about the same time and have similar soil and culture requirements.

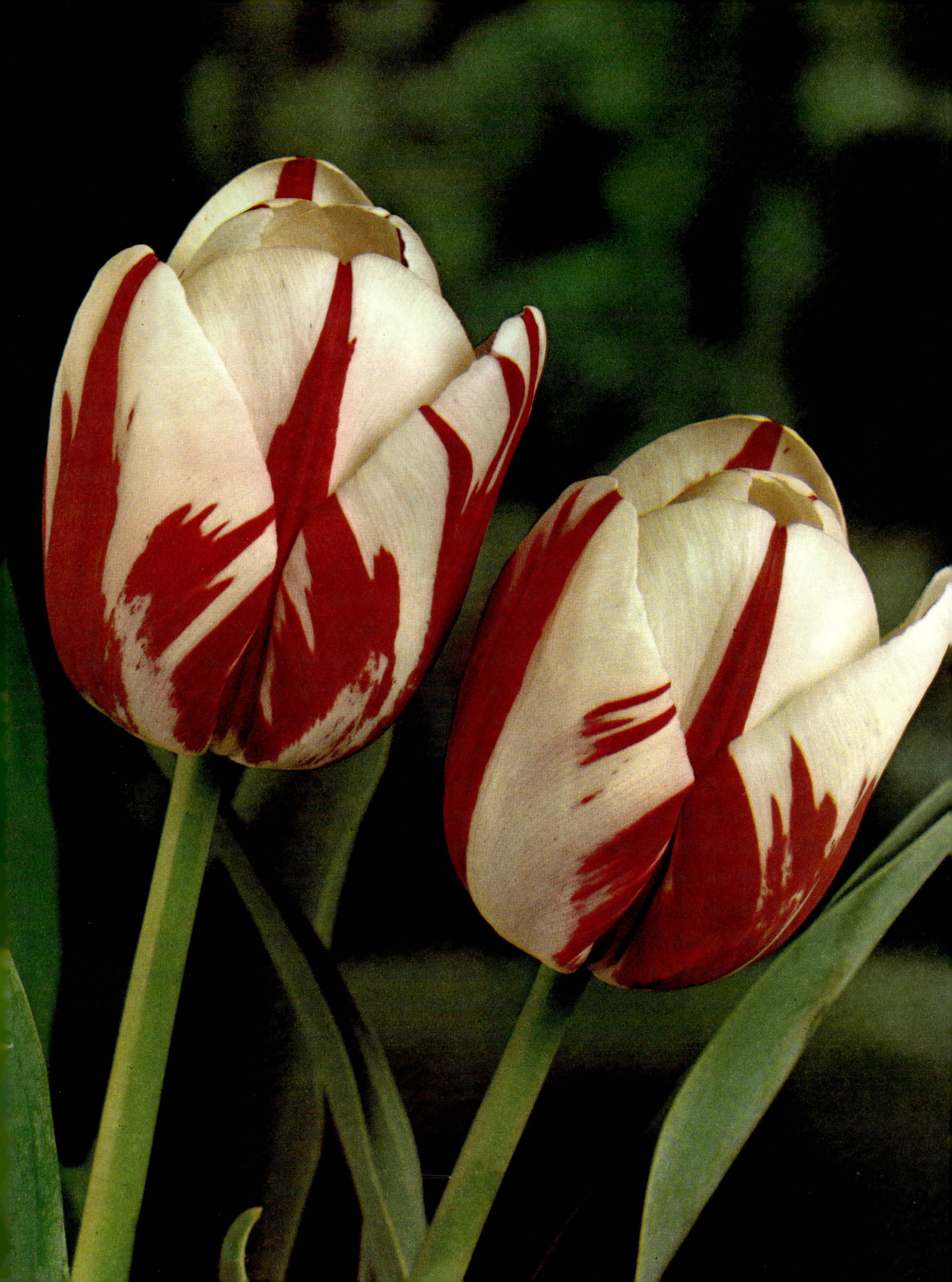

then cures the bulbs and plants them in the fall. She says they bloom beautifully the next spring. Some of the old varieties like 'Clara Butt' and 'Mrs. Moon' can be left in the ground, and they will bloom for years if they are planted deep (at least 10 inches) in poor soil, but the flowers will not be large.

Tulips are among the last bulbs to go into the ground. They should not be planted until November in the North, and late November or early December in the South. If they are to be taken up in the spring, they need not be planted more than 5 inches deep. Put a handful of bone meal under each clump and in early spring, a sprinkling of commercial fertilizer should be worked among the plants.

The most effective tulips in the garden are the Multifloras. 'Monsieur Mottet,' a creamy Cottage variety with four or five flowers to a stem and more than one stem to each bulb, turns a dark rose color as it fades. This and two others, 'Rose Mist,' a pink flower that darkens as it matures, and 'Wallflower,' which is maroon, are usually available.

Tulips bloom over a period of several weeks, beginning (in my garden) early in March and lasting into May. Even as far north as Boston the water-lily tulip (*Tulipa kaufmanniana*) is in bloom by the middle of March if the season is an early one. The single early tulips come soon afterward. Too little appreciated, these include some charming varieties, such as 'Red Signal,' the snowy 'Diana,' rosy 'Proserpine' and 'Madame Gevers,' with globe-shaped flowers that look like cups of lemon sherbet.

Some of the Darwin cultivars bloom very early too—'Blanca' and 'Demeter' far ahead of the rest, and then 'Niphetos' and 'Glacier.' 'Niphetos' opens lemon-yellow and pales to ivory. It has a delightful lemon fragrance. The enormous flowers of 'Demeter' are a brilliant purple. 'Aristocrat,' a classic Darwin in form and a soft rose in color, is another early one. These early Darwins are followed by 'Mamasa,' a clear bright yellow; 'Sweet Harmony,' pale yellow petals edged with white; 'Scarlett O'Hara,' a brilliant Oriental red; and 'Smiling Queen,' a clear pink. 'Blanca,' 'Glacier' and 'White City' bloom in succession and keep white in the border for more than a month. And don't forget the "black" tulips; 'Queen-of-night' is the darkest of all; its maroon petals are almost black. It blooms early and lasts a long time.

'Advance' is a very early Cottage tulip of brilliant coloring, a fiery red tinged with violet. The flowers of 'Rosy Wings' are the clearest pink of any tulip I know; when they open wide, the aptness of their name is apparent. 'Zomerschoon' has been blooming in gardens since 1620. The flowers are carmine with creamy-white feathering. Three good late yellows are 'Mrs. F. E. Dixon,' a pale one that becomes ivory with a rosy flush as it ages; the lemon-colored 'Mongolia' and 'Zina,' the darkest yellow of any tulip I know.

The Breeder tulips that I have liked are 'Papago,' a scarlet flower with a yellow base; the carmine 'Chappaqua' and the coral-red 'Dillenburg.' 'Dillenburg' and 'Southern Cross,' a lemon-colored flower with a bronze sheen, are very late. In my garden they come

OPPOSITE: The dramatic feathered coloring of a "broken" tulip is caused by a virus disease. Some are called the Rembrandt tulips and the striated and striped effects are very beautiful. This named variety is 'Mount Beauty of Volendam.'
RIGHT: Brilliant red of just-opening lily-flowered cottage tulips shows the pointed segments that characterize this variety. Cottage tulips are generally lower growing than the Darwins.

BULB

at the end of April and bloom on into May, stretching the tulip season to nearly two months.

The Parrot tulips, like the long-stemmed Breeders, bloom at the end of the season, but, unlike them, are not effective in the garden, for their stems are not stiff enough to support the heavy-headed flowers. They are delightful for cutting, however, and show great variety in color and pattern. 'Black Parrot,' 'White Parrot,' 'Discovery' (a pale lilac flower with silver-edged petals), 'Fantasy' (a soft rose with apple-green feathering), 'Orange Parrot' and 'Parrot Wonder' (an enormous cerise flower)—all of these are beautiful. Then there are the fringed tulips. The petals of these are edged with fine fringe and lack the deep slashing of the Parrots.

Four good doubles are 'Peach Blossom' and the lovely white 'Schoonoord' (early), the rose 'Eros' and snowy 'Mount Tacoma' (late).

I have read that "broken" tulips should never be planted in a garden where lilies grow, as the virus that gives them their flames and flakes and feathers is the one that is fatal to lilies. Most gardeners would choose the lilies without hesitation, but I find the patterned tulips very hard to part with. The Rembrandt tulips are broken Darwin and are white with markings of red and violet; the "bizarre" type, broken Breeders, are yellow with featherings of scarlet, orange, brown, bronze and garnet. The bijbloemen (biblooms) have flames of rose or violet on a white ground.

Tulip species may be hard to bloom all through the season. Some are difficult, some are easy. Some bloom in one garden and not in another. Here are a few that are generally satisfactory:

I have known *Tulipa kaufmanniana* to be in full bloom the first week in March. Louise Beebe Wilder said that it sometimes bloomed for her by the end of the month, and I have read that it may bloom near Boston by the end of March. In all climates it varies greatly with the season. The wide, short-stemmed, water-lily flowers are typically pink and white, but there are yellow forms and red ones, and hybrids in myriads of colors and patterns.

T. tarda (sometimes known as T. dasystemon) occasionally blooms *too* early in North Carolina, and the buds are nipped by cold. But it is generally a reliable species. It is a small Multiflora type with several gold-centered white flowers to a stem. *T. biflora turkestanica*, another little white-and-gold Multiflora, persists and multiplies.

The peppermint-striped flowers of *T. clusiana*, with stems to 18 inches tall, usually bloom for me soon after the middle of March, although in New York they may not open until early May. This is the best of all species for the South, and I find it offered by a

Massachusetts grower without any hint of winter tenderness, but some people consider it uncertain in New York.

T. batalinii that I've had for several years has never increased, but it produces regularly, the first week in April, two perfect urn-shaped, pale yellow flowers. It is planted on a terrace wall in my garden, where it gets the spring sunshine, the summer baking and the sharp drainage that all of the tulip species need. As the wall has been raised several inches since the little bulb was put there, it is now very deep, which may account for its not having increased. The yellow-flowered *T. chrysantha,* and *T. linifolia*—vivid red even to the stems and the margins of the narrow leaves—come at the same time. In the North all these usually bloom in May. *T. hageri* is a most dependable species, but the short-stemmed terra-cotta flowers need just the right companions—flowers in pale yellow or related tones of burnt orange—otherwise they will seem dull when they open out in the sun.

T. patens (T. persica) and *T. sprengeri* end the season. The delicate flowers of the Persian tulip, golden within and burnished red on the outside, bloom here in April. The handsome and rather large *T. sprengeri* comes at the end of the month and blooms on into May. In the North, both bloom at the end of May and last well into June.

Other Late Spring Bulbs

When the first flush of spring bloom is over, the Dutch irises are the bulbs that make a show. They are so small and the foliage is so scant that they can be tucked in among other plants without being in the way when they are out of bloom. I never take my bulbs up. Sometimes they bloom for several years, and occasionally a few become established. I plant new ones from time to time to replace those that gradually disappear. In the South the bulbs are planted late, at the end of November or early in December. In the North they should be planted early in the fall and the ground mulched with a light cover. There are a great many varieties, but the white ones are by far the most beautiful. By planting several kinds I managed to have them in bloom for several weeks. 'White Excelsior' is a good early one, opening here before the middle of April. 'Joan of Arc,' also very early, has a large creamy flower with a wide yellow spot on each petal. 'White Pearl' and 'White Perfection' are later. 'Wedgwood,' the best blue, is early. 'Golden Harvest,' with its large, brassy yellow flower, comes at the very end of the season. Many of the blues are dingy, and the bronze and two-toned varieties are not really effective out-of-doors. In New York the Dutch irises bloom late in May.

I never plant Spanish iris because they are small and insignificant; nor the English, because they are notoriously difficult, and I, for one, have no success with them.

In cold gardens the summer snowflake (*Leucojum aestivum*) blooms in May. Where I live, it often blooms in January, and usually lasts until the second week in April, but the late form, 'Gravety Giant,' doesn't begin to bloom until the middle of March. The stout stems of the snowflakes are short when they begin to bloom, but they stretch until they reach 20 inches or more, with sprays of green-trimmed bells at the tips. The wide, dark, glossy leaves are about the same length as the stems. Snowflakes will grow in any part of the garden, even in deep shade. They increase abundantly, but it is not necessary to divide them unless you want to start additional colonies.

Scilla amethystina blooms early in April, a blue-violet mist of tiny flowers. Spanish hyacinth (now listed as *Endymion hispanica*) blooms about the same time, some of the white ones coming late in March and the variety 'Skyblue' in the middle of April. There are several other blue varieties, but they all look alike to me—wisteria violet. The pinks are all the same, too, really a somewhat grayed lilac. "White Triumphator" is large and handsome, an improvement on *E. hispanica alba.* These squills, like the early ones, do well in the open, but they endure shade and will even bloom under pine trees. When left to themselves, the spikes improve in both height and size. In northern gardens they bloom in late May.

The nodding star-of-Bethlehem (*Ornithogalum nutans*) is another bulb that thrives on neglect and is found in old, untended gardens. It blooms well in part shade, but better in full sun. The fragrant bells, grape-green satin without, silvery-white within, are hung along one side of the 12-inch scape. They appear in late April in New York, in March here.

OPPOSITE, TOP: Other late spring bulbs are the Dutch irises.
OPPOSITE, CENTER: Combined color and unusual form belong to the *Tulipa* species known both as *tarda* and as *dasystemon,* an early bloomer.
OPPOSITE, BOTTOM: *Leucojum,* the snowflake, a small bulb.
BELOW: The peppermint-striped flowers of *Tulipa clusiana.*

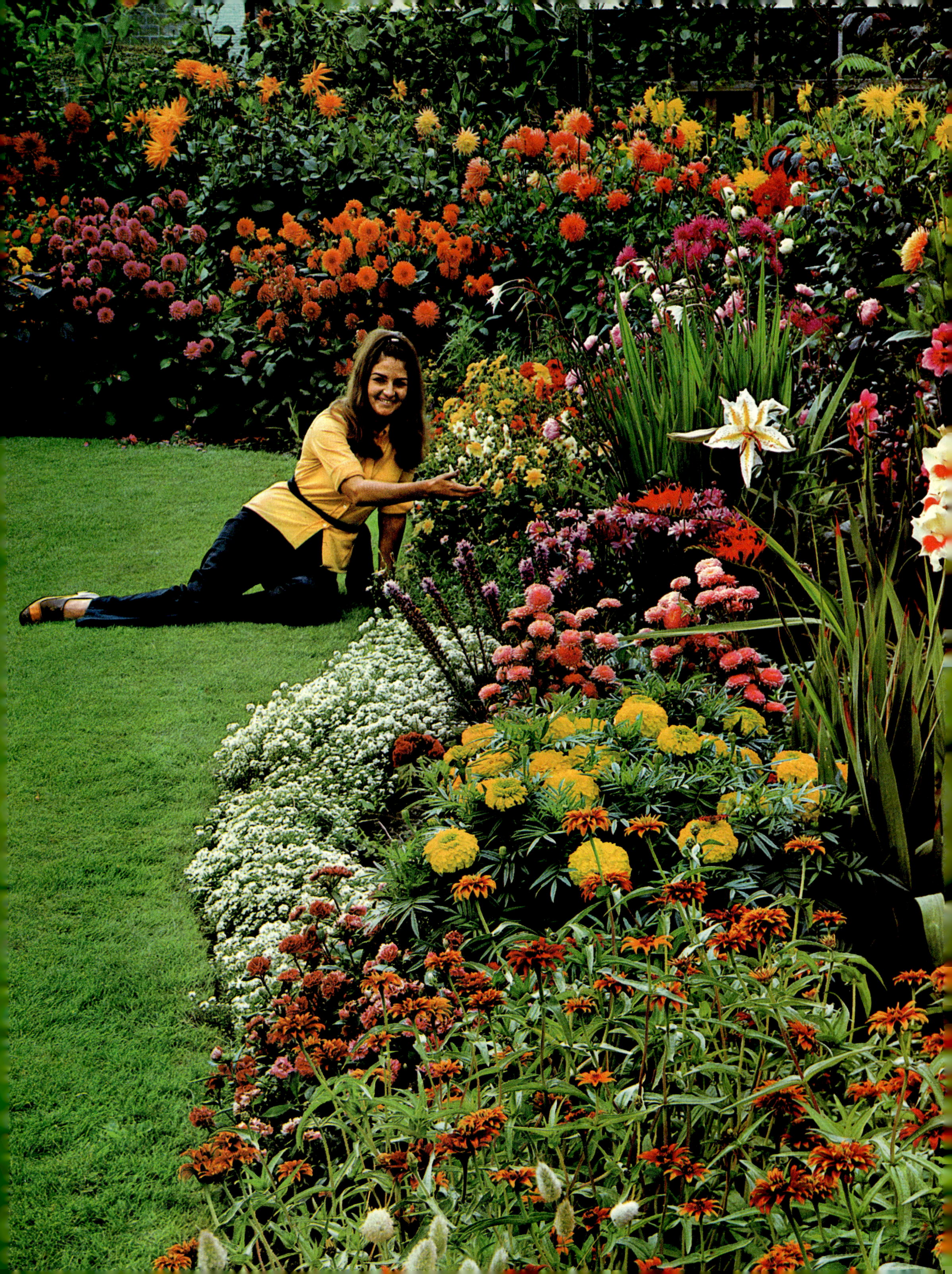

Camassias also bloom indefinitely if they are left undisturbed, and will thrive in much wetter, heavier soil than most bulbs can put up with, but they will not tolerate much shade. The large flowers of *C. leichtlinii* have widely separated petals of hyssop-violet flushed with pink. The even lovelier white form blooms a little later. The flowers of *C. cusickii* are small, pale blue, and close together on the scape. These two species are the best, and both grow to a height of 3 feet. They begin to bloom early in April (May in the North) and sometimes last for a month.

Brodiaea is a western bulb that is difficult to grow in eastern gardens. Some of the species are short-lived, but several are lifetime possessions. *B. coronaria* is hardy and dependable. The large flowers open wide umbels on 10-inch scapes. This is the harvest brodiaea, which blooms late, from mid-May to mid-June, according to the latitude. The bulbs must be planted in full sun, and perferably in heavy soil. *B. bridgesii* comes ahead of the others, blooming here in April. Its pale flowers are lilac or lavender, according to the eye of the beholder. The anthers are blue. This one grows in a shady place.

The western fritillarias have never prospered in my garden, but *F. meleagris*, the checkered-lily, will bloom for several seasons. It is so charming and costs so little that I am glad to renew it occasionally. The named varieties are superior to the type, and the loveliest of these is 'Aphrodite,' a tall, silvery-white flower that lacks the checks. The other forms are checkered in violet and purple on a gray background. I have read that fritillarias respond to lime, and perhaps this is the secret of keeping them. The bulbs should be planted, if they can be obtained early enough, in July and August, in soil that is very well drained and rich in humus.

Hardy Summer Bulbs

Alliums. Earliest of these relatives of the onion, *A. giganteum*, blooms for me in late spring, and I once found it just coming into bloom in the New York Botanical Garden on the last day of May. But July is the usual month for the bright lilac globes that tower above the lesser perennials and give character to the flower border even after their colors fade. I always cut the flower heads before the seeds ripen, and save

Annual marigolds, zinnias, alyssum and asters splash color through a border of summer-flowering bulbs. In the background red, yellow, purple and orange dahlias color-keyed to the low-growing yellow and white dahlias beyond the alyssum. On the right can be seen crocosmia, butterfly gladiolus, the gold-streaked white cup of an 'Imperial Gold' lily and, behind it, acidanthera.

them for friends who like to make dried arrangements.

A. tuberosum, sometimes offered as *A. album*, can be troublesome if allowed to go to seed. If the stalks are cut as soon as the flowers fade, seedlings will be avoided, and the borders will be tidier. The clumps increase slowly, and bloom better every year, a cool green and white for August.

One of the nicest small bulbs for shady places is *A. triquetrum*, which spreads itself freely, though the seedlings never seem to be too numerous. I plant the bulbs under trees where they can be left to themselves and forgotten until early April, when sprays of frosty white bells, trimmed with hairlines of bright green, hang from the tips of the triangular stems. Although this is a Mediterranean species, so far as I know, it is hardy. *A. moly*, the golden garlic, blooms here early in May, though in the New York Botanical Garden I have found it in full bloom during the last part of April. It is much finer there than in my garden. If I lived north of the Mason-Dixon line, I think it would be my first choice among the alliums. It is usually at its best in full sun, but in the South I have found that it demands a little shade. The spectacular *A. albopilosum* blooms in April for me and in June where the seasons are later. As many as 80 metallic, violet stars, on stiff, 4-inch pedicels, form a huge sphere at the tip of a 10-inch scape. If the flower heads are cut before they go to seed, they last forever. *Tulbaghia violacea*, called society-garlic, looks and smells and tastes like an allium (I often use the leaves in salad), but the violet flowers have a pleasant, sweet fragrance, are prettier than those of any allium that I know, and have a longer season, blooming from June into October. I always thought of this as a very tender bulb, but it is hardy against a south wall in New York City if heavily mulched in winter. Like the alliums, it blooms best in full sun, and is not particular as to soil.

Lilies. In the North the lily season begins in June, but in the South it begins in early May with two species small enough to fit into the rock garden. The fragrant, pale-pink trumpets of *Lilium rubellum* come first, and a few days later the shining scarlet flowers of the miniature Turk's-cap (*L. pumilum*). The bulbs of the former are planted 6 inches deep in part shade, and those of the latter, 4 inches deep in full sun.

Provided I plant new bulbs every season, the madonna lily (*L. candidum*) usually blooms in my garden about the middle of May. But I have never been able to keep it, though established clumps bloom for years in country gardens. Bulbs of this and the lovely apricot-flowered Nankeen lily (*L. testaceum*) must be planted very early (preferably in

August but not later than September) and covered with only 2 or 3 inches of soil. Both are sun lovers and, unlike most lilies, do not like an acid soil.

The meadow lily (*L. canadense*) makes itself at home in gardens more readily than any other American species and is quite as lovely as any of the hybrids, though the maroon-spotted, yellow flowers are not large. It blooms early in June in my region. This species grows naturally in wet meadows, but while it needs more moisture than most lilies, good drainage is still essential. Plant it 6 inches deep in partial shade. The European Turk's-cap, *L. martagon*, blooms about the same time, and its lovely white variety, *album*, comes a little earlier. The typical purple-flowered form grows in sun or shade, the white one in shade only. Plant the bulbs four inches deep. Another species for shade, *L. hansoni*, blooms in my garden early in June. The flowers are a soft orange-yellow, sprinkled toward the center with mahogany dots. Plant these bulbs 8 inches deep.

The estate lily, a tall form of the Easter lily (*L. longiflorum*) is widely planted in the South, where it blooms about the middle of June. A dwarf form with very large flowers called the 'Croft Lily,' and offered by Southern nurserymen, is not hardy where winters are severe. I plant the bulbs 6 inches deep in a sunny place.

The wonderful strains that the hybridizers have developed in recent years have brought lilies into many more gardens than ever before, making summer an entirely new affair. The Bellingham hybrids, based on American lilies, have a history of years of experimentation. They vary in the flower shape, some being funnel-form, some recurved and some bell-like, in color from palest yellow to deepest red and in both height and season. Their garden value is increased by the lasting quality of the flowers; the first to open is still fresh when the last one comes out. Two of the Griffith cultivars, 'Shuksan' and 'Kulsan,' have bloomed in the test garden of the Garden Club of Virginia during the first half of June. Plant bulbs 6 inches deep in porous soil, in part shade or light woodland.

The Olympic hybrids, based on *L. leucanthum chloraster* (*L. centifolium*) and other trumpet species, come into bloom in my garden early in June and last into July. The stems are tall, up to 5 feet or more, and the flowers vary in form. In color they are white, pale pink, yellow or green, with a wash of green, brown or wine on the outside. Plant the bulbs 6 inches deep in full sun or a light shade.

The Mid-Century hybrids—from a cross between *L. umbellatum*, which blooms in these parts at the end of May, and *L. tigrinum*, which blooms about the middle of July—follow one another through the early and middle summer. The colors range from yellow to red; the flowers are upstanding or outfacing; the plant is from 2 to 4 feet in height. 'Enchantment,' a rather late variety with flowers the color of red nasturtiums, is outstanding. Plant these lilies 5 inches deep, in full sun.

L. henryi blooms in my garden in mid-July, sometimes earlier. It is a handsome, healthy and easygoing lily, but the stems will not stand up unless they are staked. This fault has been overcome in its offspring, the Aurelian hybrids, a strain that bears cream or pale yellow flowers on strong, stiff stems, and in the Sunburst hybrid strain with Turk's-cap flowers in a series of pastels from almost white to orange. The Fiesta hybrids, based on *L. davidii* and related species, also have recurved petals. Their colors range from yellow and orange to dark red.

Two late species are the most sumptuous lilies of all. When the great creamy flowers of *L. auratum*, the goldband lily of Japan, are open, the garden is filled, day and night, with fragrance. The crimson-spotted flowers are up to 12 inches across. I have had as many as ten to a stalk in bloom from the 4th of July into the second week of August. They seemed unmindful of the hottest summer sun although they are supposed to need part shade. They were planted 8 inches deep. *L. speciosum rubrum*, blooming here in late July and all through August, is just as striking in its own way. The graceful stalks bend just enough to show the rose-dotted flowers to advantage. I think the frosted white form is even more beautiful, but I find it practically impossible to grow. Some of the late forms bloom in September. The bulbs are planted 10 inches deep, in part shade. *L. formosanum* blooms in August here; September flowering is not unusual in the North. It is supposedly a sun-loving species, but grows best in my garden in light shade under a pine tree. The long slender trumpets come at the tips of tall stems that never need staking. Price's variety is a dwarf, early-flowering form, and Wilson's variety is one of the last of my lilies to bloom. Plant the bulbs 6 inches deep.

Unfortunately, these three late-flowering species (*L. auratum*, *L. speciosum* and *L. formosanum*) are particularly susceptible to mosaic disease. Watch carefully for pale streaks, mottling or yellow stripes on the foliage, as well as for stunted, deformed plants. Dig the bulbs out and destroy them in a hurry. Also watch for aphids that pass the virus on to other

This cultivar named 'Destiny' is typical of the showy blooms of the Mid-Century hybrid lilies. Completely hardy, they bloom from late spring through July, following each other in a progression of bloom from early to midsummer. Colors range from yellow to red and darkest maroon shades.

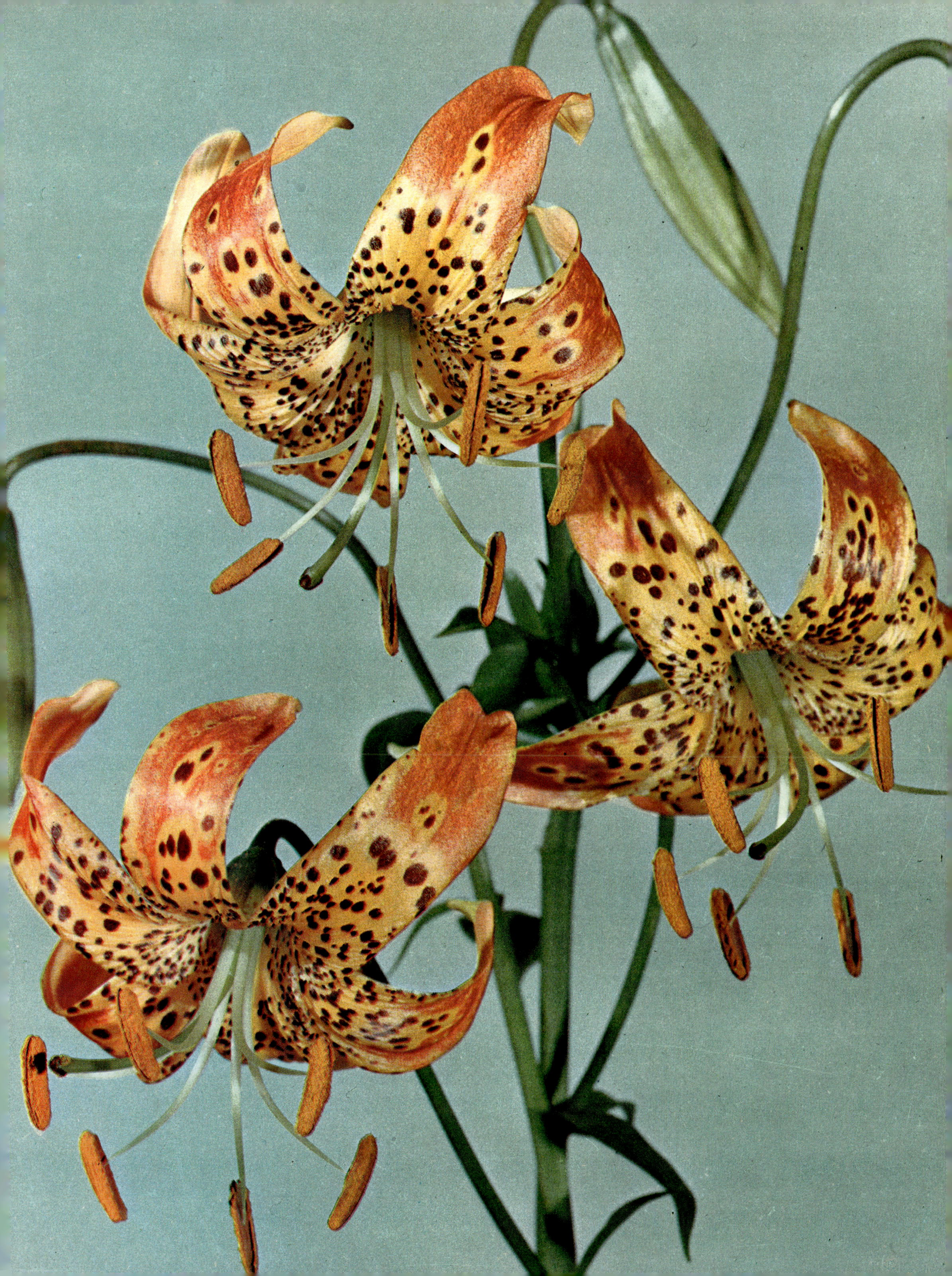

BULB

plants. Best cure is prevention: Try to buy from reliable sources and see to it that no diseased bulbs come into your garden. Isolate, too, such species as *L. tigrinum* that are latent carriers of the virus.

Order your lilies early and plant them as soon as they come. It is most important to plant the bulbs as soon as they become dormant. If they are shipped in sealed polyethylene bags, they can be kept for a while. Late-flowering kinds that have been properly stored can be planted in the spring, if it is not possible to set them out in the fall.

Good drainage is an essential condition for successful lilies. Dig the soil to a depth of 18 inches and supply it with leafmold or peat moss. No manure should be used, but bone meal or superphosphate can be mixed in when the bulbs are planted, and a sprinkling of bone meal, cottonseed meal and wood ashes worked in over them in the spring. Do not allow your garden lilies to go to seed. If you cut the flowers, leave at least half of the stem. Mulches are helpful in hot weather, as are low-growing plants that shade the ground over the lily roots.

Lycoris. The various species of *Lycoris* that are hardy in my garden bloom from the middle of July through the first week in October. The first one, *L. squamigera*, lasts for about three weeks; where more lavishly planted, for more than a month. The naked scapes spring from the ground and stretch up to 3 feet almost overnight. Then a circle of six or seven rose-lilac trumpets bursts into bloom. Some days later, *L. incarnata* follows with smaller, paler flowers. At the end of August the still smaller, blue-tinged, daphne-pink flowers of *L. sprengeri* appear. All bloom without foliage, which comes up about the middle of January in my garden and two or three months later in the North. All bloom well in anything from shade to full sun.

The first two species are hardy in Ohio, where a gardener I know grows them by the acre under the beeches and maples in his woods. They get no attention except that the woods are mowed before the scapes break through the ground. After about ten years the clumps are divided. As soon as the flowers have faded, the bulbs are dug and separated carefully, so that the roots are not cut, and planted again the same day. Dry, rootless bulbs will not bloom for several years. Growers are beginning to realize this and to ship them, like lilies, with live roots attached. The bulbs will often bloom better when they are planted with only an inch of soil on top of them. *L. squamigera* is said to be hardy in Michigan and Maine, and *L. sprengeri* in Nashville, Tennessee, where the temperature may sometimes drop to zero.

Scilla chinensis. Early in August I begin to watch for the small spikes of *S. chinensis* to come up between the two or three narrow leaves that appear earlier in the summer. When they are about 6 inches tall, the blue-green buds begin to break open into fuzzy, pale pink flowers. This squill, unlike the spring-blooming kinds, does best in sun, though I have a planting that does very well at the foot of a tall pine tree. It is a charming bulb for the rock garden and is easily grown, although it does not increase very rapidly.

Summer Bulbs for Spring Planting

Crinum. When I had a big garden, I grew more than 40 kinds of crinums. Now that I have a small one I grow only a few, for most of them take up a great deal of room, and many have few flowers in proportion to the foliage. Two of the hardiest are two of the best: *C. x powellii album* and 'Cecil Houdyshel,' both hybrids of *C. moorei* and *C. longiflorum*. *C. x powellii album* blooms from late May into July. When the clumps are well established, up to 30 umbels of pure-white flowers (even the anthers are white) bloom in a rush. Scapes nearly 4 feet tall hold the flowers well above the fountain of wide, tapering leaves. It is hardy in New York City with protection. The pink-flowered 'Cecil Houdyshel' blooms over a long period, from late May until the end of August, with sometimes as many as ten scapes in bloom at once. Mr. Houdyshel once told me that his namesake was hardy as far north as Independence, Missouri, and that it had been wintered twice in Brooklyn. In northern Texas it has survived 12 degrees below zero—under shallow wooden boxes placed over the bulbs after the first hard freeze.

Crinum kirkii, one of the best, has large creamy flowers with a wine-colored stripe on each petal. It blooms at intervals all through the summer. This species is perfectly hardy in North Carolina, but I haven't any data on its performance farther north. *C. moorei* is a dwarf species with large pink flowers in August. The others are at their best in full sun, but this one must have shade.

In the South, crinums are planted with part of the bulb above the ground, but in the North, the bottom of the bulb should be 8 inches below the surface. Bulbs should be planted against a wall and heavily mulched. Once planted, they should be left alone, for they improve with age, and if they are given water and lots of well-rotted or dried cow manure, they will bloom better every year.

Dahlias. Dahlias need sun, perfect drainage, a rich soil and an abundance of water. Plant tubers 8 inches

Today's easy-to-grow dahlia tubers are increasingly used to bring summer color to the border. This beauty, 'High Society,' belongs to the informal decorative class.

deep, with a handful of bone meal to each tuber, putting the eye toward the stake, which should have been set beforehand. Plant early for garden effect, late for exhibition. Remember that dahlias are cool-weather plants and that if they are planted too early, their best bloom will be over before cool weather comes. Mulch the roots heavily in the South and cut the tops back to the ground after the first hard frost. Lift the clumps in late spring; divide and replant. In the North, lift the tubers after frost and store them upside down in sand or vermiculite in a cool place. The clumps can be most safely divided in the spring when the "eyes" are evident. Discard all roots without eyes. Productive shoots develop only from roots with eyes.

These are what I consider some of the best types and varieties for the average gardener:

CACTUS

'Autumn Leaves'—amber-orange
'Border Princess'—salmon-rose-yellow
'Park Jewel'—rose
'Park Princess'—rose
'Salmon Perfection'—salmon-red

DECORATIVE

'David Howard'—orange-yellow
'New Drakestyn'—cerise
'Park Beauty'—flame-colored
'Park Delight'—white
'Rocquencourt'—red

MIGNON

'G. F. Hemerick'—orange
'Irene Van Der Zwet'—soft yellow
'Nelly Geerlings'—red

POMPON

'Albino'—white
'Apropo'—yellow
'Stolze von Berlin'—lavender-pink
'Zonnegoud'—dark yellow

Galtonia candicans. South of Philadelphia, where winter and spring are mild, the summer-hyacinth is counted hardy, but it is not really a good bulb where summers are likely to be wet. Bulbs planted in April may bloom in July or they may rot before they can bloom. Still, I plant more from time to time for the pleasure of the spires of cool white bells in the midsummer heat. I like to plant them so that each spire stands alone—the beauty of form is lost when they are planted in clumps. In northern gardens, the summer-hyacinth does well when the bulbs are planted 6 inches deep on a cushion of sand that is in rich, moist soil in full sun. Plant them in the spring and take the bulbs up and store them in the fall.

Gladiolus. In summer I depend upon clumps of gladiolus to augment the bloom in the perennial border, and to furnish spires to relieve the monotony of phlox and daylilies. I find it more effective to use only white varieties, and 'White Gold' has proved to be a good one. In our part of the country the corms can be left in the ground. They bloom beautifully for several seasons; then, when the clumps become crowded, I lift them and replant the largest corms and throw away the rest. Since all corms left in the ground bloom during the early summer, I plant a few new ones each year in June and July to carry bloom on until frost. In northern areas the corms should be taken up after the leaves turn brown and before freezing weather. Cut off the tops, remove the spent corms and store the new corms in shallow, screen-bottomed trays or old nylon stockings in a frostproof place.

If gladiolus are grown in quantities, the only place for them is the cutting garden, where they can be planted in rows. For succession of bloom from early summer until frost, the corms can be planted at intervals of one or two weeks from early February to early August in the South, and from early March (or whenever the ground is workable) to early July in the North. Plant them 6 inches deep, preferably in full sun and in light soil. Good drainage is essential. Since too much nitrogen makes the stems and flowers weak, the fertilizer should be high in potassium. Use bone meal and superphosphate when planting, and a complete fertilizer when the leaves are a few inches high. A sprinkling of wood ashes makes sturdy stems and flowers of good substance. Water generously in dry weather.

This list may help you choose varieties for cutting and for the garden: white 'Sierra Snow,' cream 'Lorelei,' light yellow 'Prospector,' dark yellow 'Catherine Beath,' buff 'Patrol,' orange 'Regina,' light salmon 'Polynesia,' dark salmon 'Salmon Queen,' scarlet 'Red Wing,' light pink 'Ethereal,' medium pink 'Tivoli,' dark pink 'Spic and Span,' light red 'Royal Stewart,' dark red 'Harrisburger,' black-red 'Negus,' light rose 'Traveler,' medium rose 'Rosita,' dark rose 'Burma, lavender 'Princess,' purple 'King David,' light lavender 'Violet Charm,' dark violet 'Salman's Sensation,' smoky tan 'Glow,' blend 'Buckeye Bronze.' Some other good standard varieties are: 'Blue Beauty,' 'Elizabeth-the-Queen,' 'Evangeline,' 'Picardy,' 'Spotlight,' 'Sunspot'; good white-flowered varieties: 'Florence Nightingale,' 'Leading Lady,' 'Maid-of-Orleans,' 'Snowdrift,' 'White Gem' and 'White Gold.'

The cultivar 'Atom' seems to stand alone among

Clumps of gladiolus add color to the perennial border and provide cut flowers. For a succession of bloom, plant corms at two-week intervals from early spring to summer. Excellent for cutting are 'Sierra Snow,' white; 'Prospector,' yellow; 'Negus,' a dark red; 'Patrol,' buff and 'Polynesia,' a light salmon. 'Red Wing' is a good scarlet.

the miniatures. Its flowers are vermilion with silver edges, and there are more on a stalk than is usual in this class. Other good ones are 'Orange Butterfly,' 'Little Gold,' 'Pink Ribbon,' 'Snow Baby' and 'The Orchid.'

Corms of early-flowering gladiolus should be planted 4 inches deep very early in spring. Where I live, they bloom late in spring; in cold climates they open just before the large-flowered varieties. 'Peach Blossom' and 'The Bride' are favorites. 'Spitfire' is a brilliant red and 'Charm' is purple. *G. byzantinus* blooms in May in my garden. It is the same thing as, or similar to, a form that has grown for generations in gardens throughout the South, where it is known as Jacob's-ladder. Though you may not like its brilliant red-violet color, you will find it a most useful little bulb for accent in borders, and it goes on blooming for years.

Similar to the gladiolus is *Acidanthera bicolor*, which blooms in August and September. The corms should be planted as early in the spring as possible because of the plant's long growing season, and should be taken up in the fall even where they are hardy, since plants soon run to a clump of foliage without flowers if they are left in the ground. The flower is like a graceful, starry gladiolus (to 2 inches across), white with a dark wine center, and wonderfully fragrant.

Montbretias, which are now called *Crocosmia*, are more like gladiolus to me. They begin to bloom early in July and makes a splash of bright orange in the borders for at least a month. This is seldom offered by most dealers, but the handsome hybrids appear in the spring catalogs and, if they are planted early and in variety, will bloom all summer and well into the fall. The earliest hybrid is 'George Davison,' a golden-flowered variety that comes into bloom about the middle of July. The majority begin to bloom at the end of July and early in August. The scarlet flower of 'E. A. Bowles' has a zone of Brazil red and a pale yellow center. The large flowers of 'Star of East' are pale orange with a lemon eye, and scarlet on the outside. 'Lady Wilson' is bright yellow with an orange sheen. 'His Majesty' is yellow, shading to scarlet. At the end of August, three late varieties come into bloom: 'Hereward,' pale orange-yellow; 'James Coey,' scarlet with a yellow center and a zone of red; and 'Comet,' a very flat, dark orange flower with a scarlet zone, which blooms for two months. 'Comet' and 'James Coey' are short-stemmed, not over 2 feet, but the others are tall, to 30 inches and more.

Montbretias may prove hardy around Philadelphia and even farther north with a heavy winter mulch. Unlike gladiolus, montbretia corms must not be allowed to dry out in storage but should be covered with soil that is barely moist. Therefore it is essential to buy them from a reliable dealer and plant them at once. They can be planted in April or May, 3 inches deep, in soil that is rich in humus but without manure. Full sun and plenty of water at all times are important.

In cold climates it is well worthwhile starting montbretias in a cold frame or greenhouse in early spring, being careful not to disturb their roots when they are set out in May. They are heavy feeders and, as soon as their leaves are a few inches above ground, they should be fertilized with liquid manure in a regular feeding program.

In the South, lift and divide the corms every third spring. When the leaves die back and the plants go dormant, cut them back and use the leaves as a mulch. They also like a winter mulch of weathered ash. In the North, before storing, allow the corms to air-dry for two or three days.

Ismenes. *Hymenocallis calathina*, the Peruvian-daffodil, is commonly called by its old name, ismene. The fragrant, white crystalline flower has a flaring cup with bright green stripes and six narrow, slightly curled segments. There are six or seven flowers on a stout, 30-in. scape, blooming in June and July. The leaves are as exotic as the flowers, 2 inches wide and 2 feet long and appearing dark and shining in two ranks.

In the North the bulbs should be planted the latter half of May and taken up about the middle of October. The tops should be cut off, if this chore has not already been done by frost, and the bulbs dried and stored in a cool place in paper bags. The temperature must not fall below 55 degrees. The bulbs are surprisingly hardy, but the buds are killed by low temperatures. Some North Carolina gardeners think that ismenes are better left in the garden all winter, but I find that they bloom better when they are taken up. They can be planted again as early as April, and I have on occasion kept them out of the ground safely as late as the middle of July. Those planted early bloom the first part of June; those planted later bloom almost at once and bloom just as well. I use no fertilizer, but well-rotted manure and bone meal can be recommended. Plenty of water is essential for ismenes, and full sun is preferred, though they will bloom well in part shade. While a light soil is supposedly best, mine thrive in stiff clay.

The variety 'Sulfur Queen' is almost more beautiful than the parent plant. The flowers are a pale, sparkling yellow. I have a single bulb which has bloomed faithfully for 20 years, but has never increased. No wonder it is so rare. This one has always wintered outdoors in the garden.

'Festalis,' a cross between *H. calathina* and *Elisena longipetala*, is hardier than the Peruvian-daffodil. Its delicate, pure-white flowers have more slender crowns and narrower petals than those of the ismene. I leave the bulbs in the ground, and they bloom very well each year.

The variety 'Olympia' is magnificent. Its very large flowers open pale yellow and turn white as they mature.

St. James-lily (*Sprekelia formosissima*) is hardy in North Carolina but not in northern Virginia. Even where hardy, it is uncertain as to bloom. One theory is that the bulbs bloom better if they are taken up and dried out each year; another that they must not be disturbed because they do not bloom well until they become crowded. My theory is that it is a difficult bulb in any garden. But it takes up little space, and the red flowers, like delicately carved fleur-de-lis, are so beautiful that I keep a few bulbs and leave them to sulk or bloom as they choose. They bloom, when they bloom, in late May or early June. Full sun and poor soil are their preferences.

Tigridias are tropical bulbs originating on the high plateaus of Mexico. They do not like hot nights and bloom better in northern gardens than in the South. Even where the bulbs are hardy, it is better to take them up in the fall and keep them dry in the winter. Dig them before frost, and do not divide the clusters until they are replanted—in April in the South, May in the North. Plant them 4 inches deep, and water well when they are coming into bloom. They need a rich, light soil. The flowers of *T. pavonia* are brilliant. Their three broad outer petals form a heavily spotted cup with a flaring brim. There is a pure-white form. Others are white with rose spots, rose with white spots, creamy-yellow with bright red spots, scarlet with white spots and so on in endless variety. They bloom in late July and August.

Tuberoses (*Polianthes tuberosa*) bloom in my garden from late July until frost. When frost comes late, they bloom on into November. Here, the bulbs stay in the ground and are never disturbed except when I dig some to give away. The clumps bloom better every year. Where they will not winter out-of-doors, the bulbs can be taken up before heavy frost and stored in a dry place. In the spring they should be planted (preferably without dividing the clumps) 3 inches deep, in April or May outdoors, or in February in pots to be set in the borders in June. (Bulbs planted as late as the 1st of July have bloomed in September.) Plant them in a sunny place. The single form called 'Mexican Everblooming' is the one that I have. Its slender, 3½ ft. wands are tipped with spikes of wax-white, perfumed flowers. I think it is hardier than the dwarf double form, 'The Pearl.'

BULB

Zephyranthes, Habranthus and Cooperia bloom in the South from early spring until frost, popping up whenever showers invite a new crop of buds. *Zephyranthes atamasco* is sometimes in bloom by the end of March. The fragrant white flowers are 3 inches long, and I have known them to have 12-inch stems. The raspberry-pink flowers of *Z. grandiflora* sometimes appear in May, but more often in early June. They come at intervals all summer, and even in September. The white flowers of *Z. candida* are as small as crocuses, but on taller stems. From early June or July the clumps of shining, slender foliage are crowded with buds and flowers. They bloom on until hard frost, and, when frost comes late, I have even found a few the first week in November. It is not necessary to worry about drainage with any of these three; they like wet ground. But they will grow in dry places too. They need humus in the soil but not fertilizer. *Z. grandiflora* blooms better in full sun, but the other two do just as well even in deep shade.

Habranthus robustus is like the atamasco-lily except that flowers are tinged with pink. It blooms off and on during the summer, and is somewhat tender; after a hard winter it may not bloom at all. Plant zephyranthes and habranthus 2 or 3 inches deep, and the long-necked bulbs of *Cooperia pedunculata* a little deeper. The red buds of the cooperia open at twilight into white flowers that shine in the darkness and perfume the night. In the South these bulbs can be left in the ground indefinitely, dug only if you want to give some away or increase your planting. In gardens where they are not hardy, they can be lifted in the fall and stored in dry sand.

Fall-flowering Bulbs

Amaryllids. Some members of the Amaryllis Family have a pleasant habit of flowering after summer flowers are gone, bringing a sudden freshness to the autumn garden. The hardiest of these is *Sternbergia lutea*. Its flower of shining buttercup-yellow that looks like a large, long-stemmed crocus is most welcome in September. The leaves come up with the flowers and die down in the spring. The bulbs should be planted, or transplanted, during the summer dormant period, and not later than August. Three inches deep is about right, as they need a summer baking. For the same reason, they are supposed to demand full sun, but I have seen great patches in bloom under a large oak tree; and the best clump in my garden is on the south side of a pine where the soil is poor and very dry.

Hippeastrum advenum, the oxblood-lily, is hardy at least as far north as Maryland, perhaps farther. The bulbs must be planted deep enough for the long

UPPER: The corm of *Tigridia pavonia* produces large, colorful irislike flowers in summer. The colors shade from yellow through orange and purple, usually spotted, and 3 to 5 inches across. Culture is similar to that required by the undemanding gladiolus.
LOWER: 'Festalis' is a cross between Hymnocallis calathina, which used to be called ismene, and Elisena longipetala. It is hardier than the ismene it resembles and has more delicate flowers, slender crowns and narrow petals. The ismenes bloom from bulbs and are hardy enough to leave in the garden through the winter in North Carolina.

necks to be completely underground. They grow in any soil, in sun or part shade, and multiply rapidly. The flowers are cardinal-red bells, six or eight on a short, stout scape that appears before the masses of narrow leaves. I sometimes find them in bloom in the middle of August and often there are still a few early in October. The rare pink form does not bloom as freely, and it increases very slowly, but to me it is one of the most beautiful fall bulbs.

Lycoris radiata, the red spider-lily, is almost as hardy as the oxblood-lily. Cover these bulbs with only an inch or so of soil, even in cold climates; otherwise they will not bloom until they have worked their way up by producing one bulb on top of another. The jasper-red flowers open in a circle at the tip of the tapered scape. They bloom as well in sun as in shade and require no special attention.

The white lycoris (*L. radiata alba*), which blooms about the same time, is less hardy than the red one, but I think it is dependable in the southern part of the country. The flowers are a little larger and the foliage a little broader, but the general effect is much the same. The flowers are pale coral as they open, gradually changing to creamy-white. If the bulbs are allowed to dry out, they will take several seasons to settle down and bloom. Where they are not hardy, they can be wintered in pots; but the roots must not be disturbed when plants are set out in the spring, and repotted in the fall.

x **Amarcrinum howardii** I think could be grown as far north as New York, as one parent is *Crinum moorei* and the other the fairly hardy *Amaryllis belladonna*. The pink, vanilla-scented flowers are much like those of crinum 'Cecil Houdyshel,' but on shorter scapes and rising from a lower, much neater clump of foliage. They come into bloom just before or just after the first of August and sometimes bloom until the end of October. Another *Amarcrinum*, called 'Delkin's Find,' is much the same except that the flowers and foliage are a little smaller. It blooms at the same time. Both do well in sun or part shade and bloom more freely if they are heavily fed and given lots of water when the buds begin to appear.

Colchicum and crocus. Colchicums begin to bloom in early fall, often at the end of August or even earlier. They are often called by the pretty name of meadow-saffron and also, no more accurately, autumn-crocus (they belong to the lily family and crocuses do not). The real autumn crocuses, which belong to the genus *Crocus* and the Iris Family, come into bloom later, but the colchicum and crocus seasons overlap, so that they keep the garden in flowers of white or varying tones of violet, from the end of summer to the beginning of spring.

Colchicum speciosum and its varieties start the

season. The large, well-shaped, wide-petaled flowers are pure white in the rare and difficult and extremely beautiful variety *C. speciosum album*; otherwise they are some shade or tint of violet with a white throat. The leaves are 3 or 4 inches wide and more than a foot long. When they first come up, in the spring, they look very pretty, but they are not so welcome when they grow large and turn yellow. This is to be remembered at planting time. Of the named varieties, 'Autumn Queen' is likely to bloom first, in a burst of purple. The flowers of 'The Giant' are like lilac tulips and the largest of all; spread out flat, they may measure 8 inches across. This and the pansy-violet 'Violet Queen' bloom early in September.

The flowers of *Colchicum autumnale* are smaller, but they make up for their size by profusion of bloom. The variety *C. a. majus* is usually first to bloom; then the silvery-white *C. a. album*, which comes along at the end of September. Early in October the two exquisite double forms appear, one violet and one white. The leaves of this species are narrow, 2 inches wide or less, and therefore not so bothersome in spring.

Colchicums need some shade and will bloom even in deep shade. All they require in order to live and grow and bloom is a soil that is not too dry and is well supplied with leafmold. It is important to plant the bulbs as soon after midsummer as possible. They will bloom even if they are left out of the ground, but they bloom better if they are planted before the end of August. Although the bulbs are large, plant them only 3 or 4 inches deep.

The true autumn crocuses bloom in shade too, but they can also be planted in full sun. The earliest, *Crocus zonatus*, is easily established, and once it is settled, seedlings appear in all directions. This is delightful in October, when the pale lilac flowers come in crowds, but bear in mind the prospect of abundant spring foliage with untidy, narrow leaves up to a foot long.

This species is followed by *C. speciosus*, the most popular fall-flowering crocus. It is extremely variable. Though it is called "blue," all of the kinds that I have had have been in tones of pure violet. The handsomest is 'Cassiope,' a selected seedling, with a very large flower of wisteria-violet delicately veined in a darker tone. The variety *C. speciosus albus* is pure white with a bright scarlet stigma. Two more easily grown species bloom in November. *C. longiflorus* is small and dark, a slender mauve flower with dark violet veining. The flowers of *C. ochroleucus* are also small, but creamy-white.

The prettiest of all, *C. laevigatus fontenayi*, begins to bloom around the first of December and continues to flower, at mild intervals, until the middle of January. Full sun and a protected corner are needed.

Hardy cyclamen. I used to think that the hardy cyclamen would be too difficult for me to grow, and so for years I didn't have the pleasure of watching this most delightful of all little bulbs come into bloom at the very time that bloom is most wanted.

Cyclamen europaeum is really a summer bulb with me. It blooms here in July, though in colder regions it comes along in late summer and fall. The round, dark, silver-marked leaves come first, and then little rose-colored flowers, about the size of a violet and as delicately scented. When the plant is satisfactorily grown, the leaves are evergreen, the old ones disappearing just before the new ones come along. *C. europaeum*, a native of the mountains of southern and central Europe, might be expected to be one of the hardiest cyclamens, but it is surprising to find that *C. neapolitanum* is the other. These two survive severe weather, though when temperatures approach zero their foliage needs a light mulching.

Even in northern gardens the tubers must be planted very shallow, with only ½ in. of soil on top and a sprinkling of peat moss. A top-dressing of bone meal and leafmold in late spring is the only supplement they need, but the soil should never be allowed to dry out. They must have part shade and will bloom in almost full shade. The tubers can be planted at any time if the leaves and roots are not allowed to dry.

C. neapolitanum is one of the most adaptable of garden bulbs; its one peculiarity is that its roots, along with the leaves and flowers, grow out of the top of the tuber, which must be planted with the smooth side down. Flowers of the faintest pink, marked at the base of the petals with a bright spot of magenta, begin to open in early fall, sometimes by the end of August and once on the 4th of July (flowering at odd times seems to be characteristic of cyclamen). The flowers are unbelievably frostproof, and they bloom on into December. Marbled leaves, each with a different silver pattern, begin to unfurl in October, making a green-and-silver carpet for winter and spring. In summer the ground is bare, and must be left so.

UPPER: The hardy garden cyclamen here, *Cyclamen europaeum*, has silver-marked leaves and produces small, fragrant bright red- or cyclamen-colored blossoms. It is a summer bulb in warm regions, a fall-flowering bulb farther north, where it gets off to a slower start in spring.
LOWER: Fall-blooming *Crocus zonatus*.
Flowers are rose-lilac spotted inside with orange.

Elizabeth Lawrence, author of a classic gardening book called The Little Bulbs, *is widely read and respected because her excellent writings are based on expertise gained over many years of experience.*

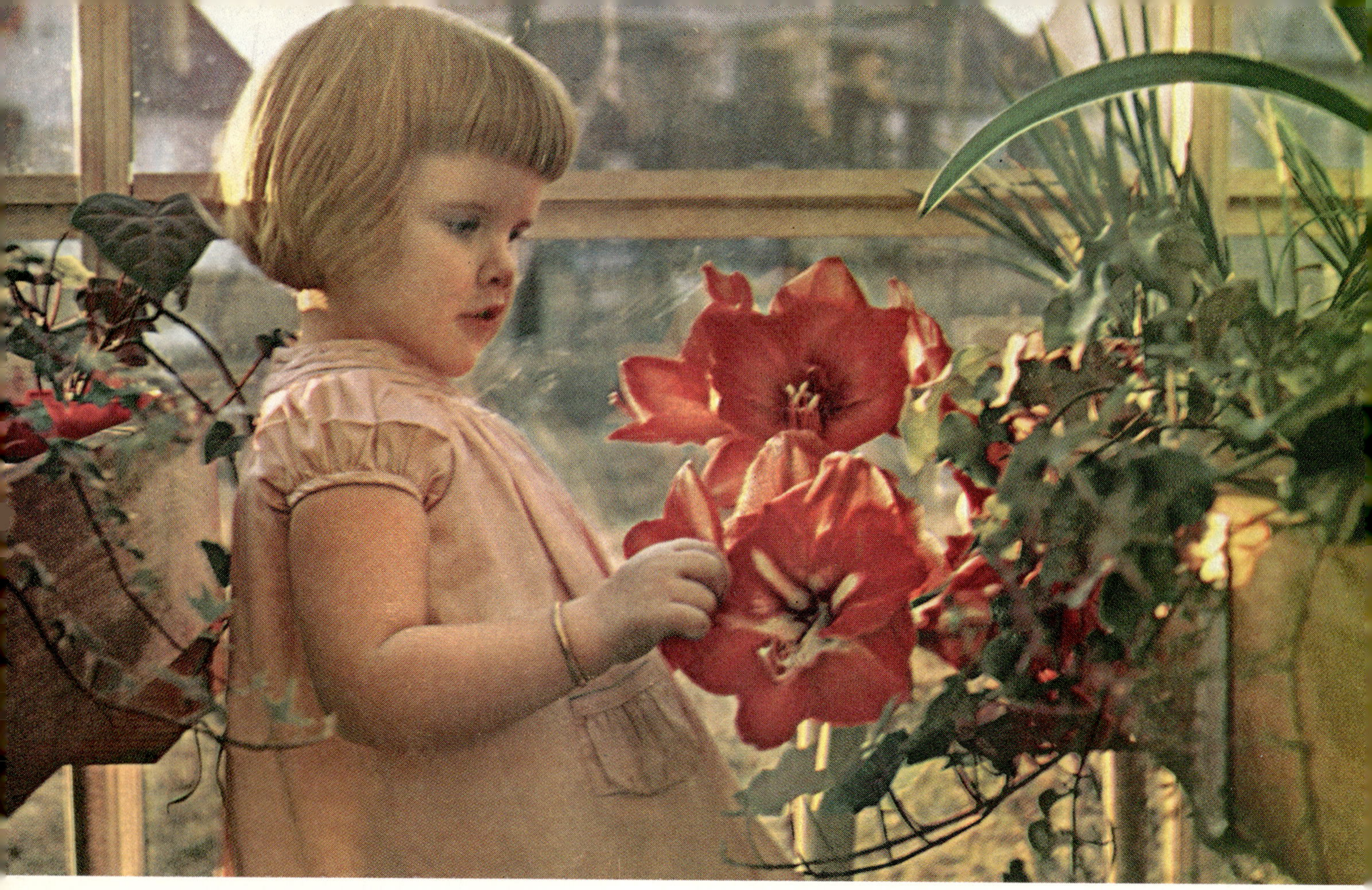
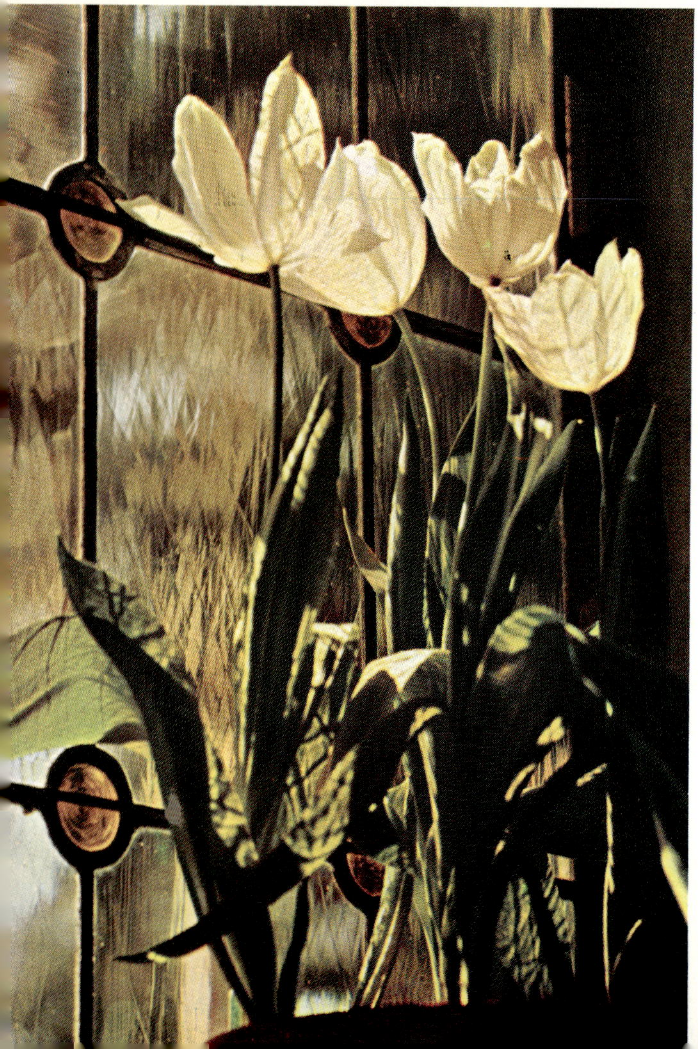
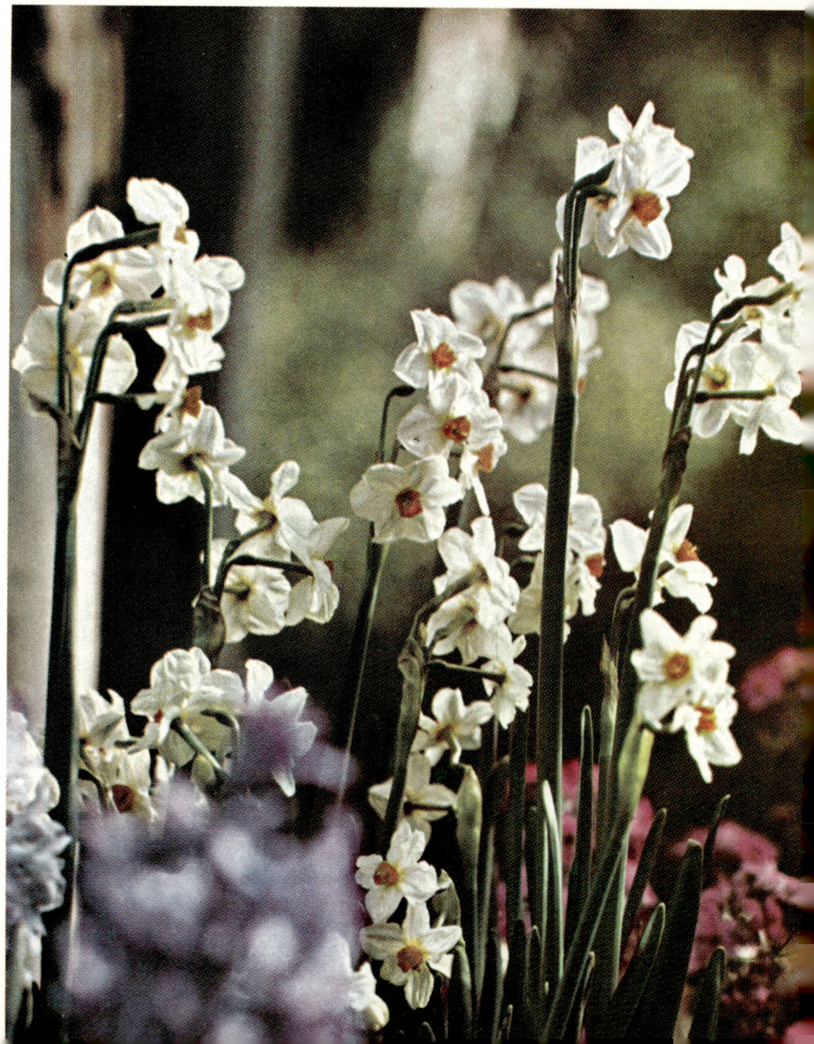

Bulbs To Force

The bulb is nature's well-wrapped marvel, a perfect holiday package. Late October or early November is the time to start the growth cycle that first sends down roots into moist soil or pebbles, then sends up fresh greening leaves, buds furling jewel colors and, finally, flowers as fragrant as spring. The best kinds to plant for flowering gifts and decorating the house in December are the tender narcissus (paperwhite, golden Soleil d'Or and Chinese sacred lily), amaryllis, hyacinths and precooled early tulips.

To grow narcissus, all you need is water, pebbles, the bulbs and a bowl or flowerpot at least 2 inches deep and large enough to hold three to twelve of them. Fill the container half full of pebbles. Set the bulbs on this surface, allowing about a half-inch of space between. Pour in more pebbles until a third of each bulb is in the gravel. Add water until it touches the bulbs and place the planting in a dark, cool place (60 to 70°) for about two weeks to encourage root growth. After this time bring the planter to a sunny, warm place. Keep moist at all times, and avoid hot, dry drafts.

Hybrid amaryllis in white, pink, rose and red, or patterned reds and whites, send up splendid scapes of flowers two to eight weeks after planting. Plant in commercially prepared potting soil (or in a mixture of equal parts garden loam, peat moss and sand), allowing about an inch of space between bulb and pot, and leaving at least one-third of the bulb above the surface. Keep evenly moist at all times, but water more freely when growth becomes active. Amaryllis need a well-lighted, warm place until buds begin to open; then they may be moved to a cooler, shaded interior where the blooms will last longer.

Roman Hyacinths

Fragrant Dutch and French Roman hyacinths force into bloom easily in eight to ten weeks. Colors range from palest yellow to orange, from red to rose and pink, and through all the blues to delicate lavender. Plant the bulbs in the same kind of soil recommended for amaryllis, positioning them so that the tips are near the surface, even protruding slightly. Moisten well. Keep cool (less than 60°, if possible), moist and dark for two weeks, then move to a warmer place (about 70°), but continue to keep in the dark until leaves are 4 or 5 inches tall. After this period, provide abundant light.

Precooled early tulips can also be forced to bloom by Christmas. Plant and care for as hyacinths, except keep tulips cool, moist and dark for three weeks, then move to a sunny, warm place to finish the growth cycle.

Other bulbs that may be planted and treated as tulips for flowers in late December and January include ixia, ornithogalum, sparaxis, freesia, ranunculus, *Iris reticulata* and *I. danfordiae*. While lily-of-the-valley is not considered a bulb, its sweet-smelling flowers may be enjoyed any time after Thanksgiving by planting pips that have been specially prepared for forcing into bloom in 21 days.

OPPOSITE, TOP: Jeannene McDonald feels the petals of hybrid amaryllis. FAR LEFT: Creamy-white tulips forced into early bloom. LEFT: Fragrant Chinese sacred lilies and hyacinths bring an early spring indoors.
ABOVE RIGHT: Transparent wrapping provides brief protection from the cold for a paperwhite narcissus holiday gift.

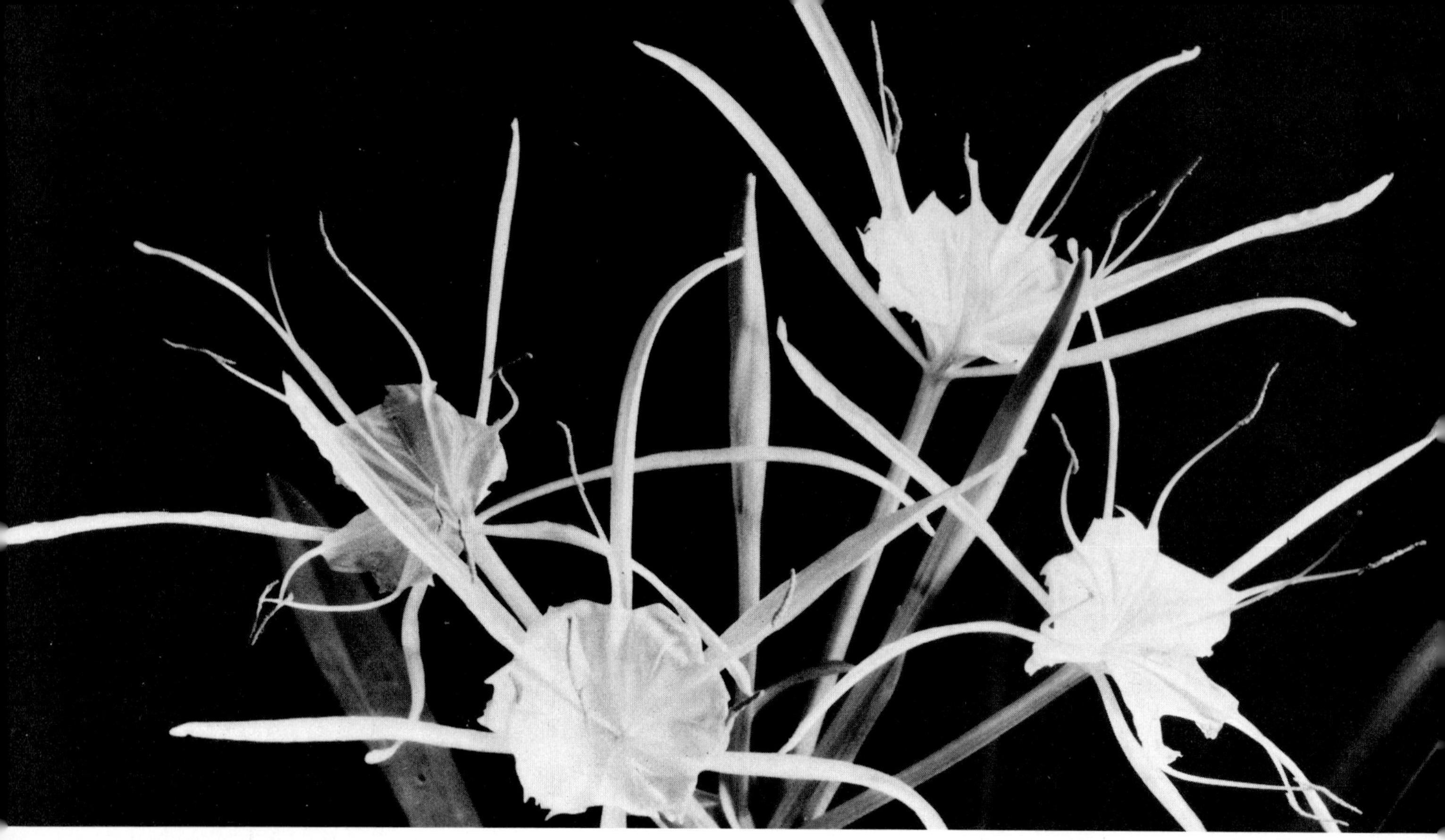

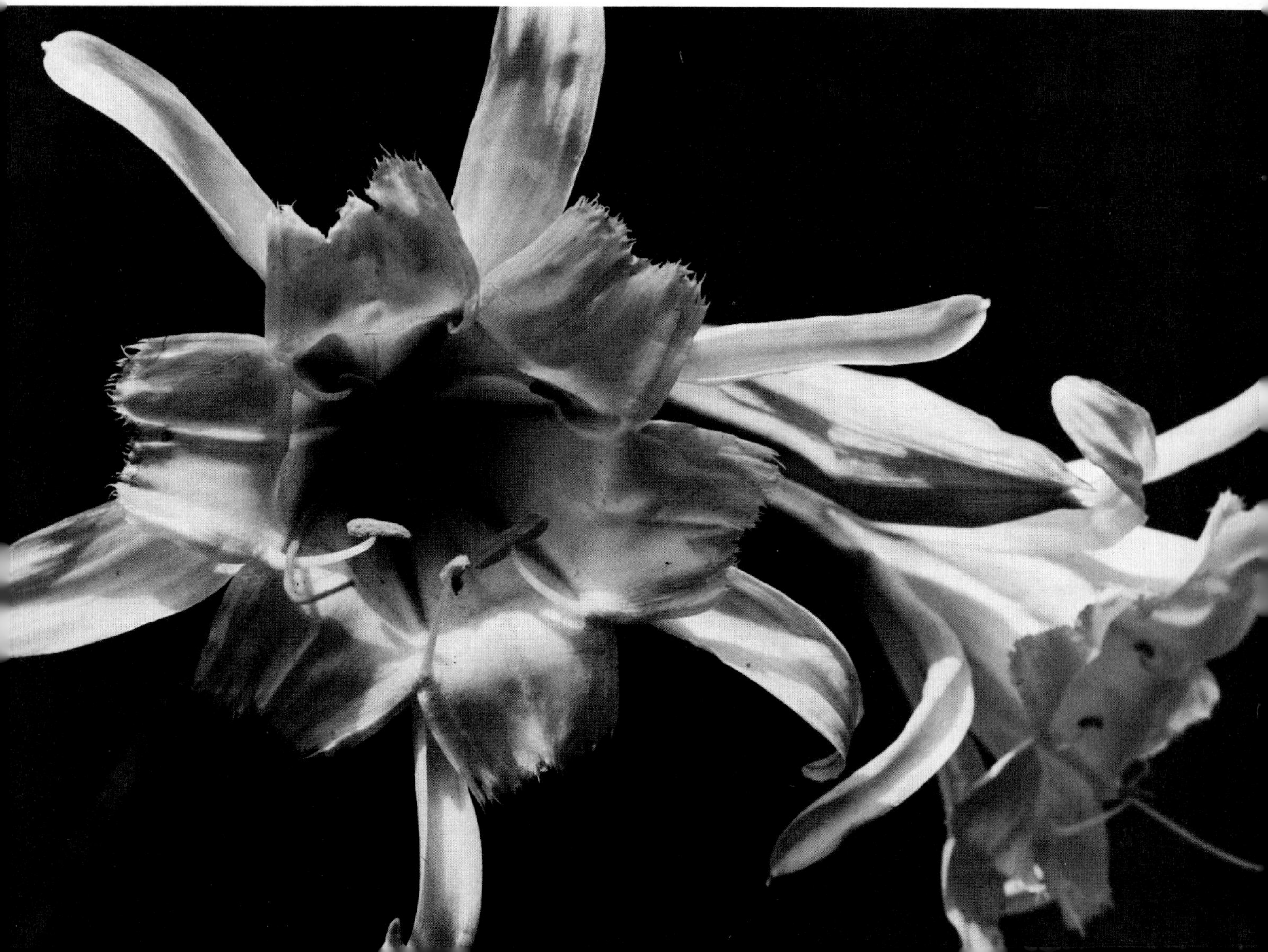

Hot Weather Bulbs To Accent the Summer

By JEAN LAWSON

Some plants are so reliable, so spectacular, they're worth using over and over to provide color in the most important parts of the garden. Azaleas are in this category. So are daylilies, geraniums and petunias. Handled skillfully, these flowers deserve great credit as garden mainstays.

But as spring becomes summer and then fall, a garden with only the popular, proved plants may lose appeal, especially to those who have gardened before. Good plants become common—not because they are seen too much, but because they are seen in the same combinations and to the exclusion of other noteworthy but lesser-known or forgotten materials.

In contrast, a single handsome, offbeat plant can make a garden come alive, can make everything in it seem more beautiful. The plant becomes an accessory, an unusual detail giving distinction to the total garden picture. Used indiscriminately, massed or spotted here and there, the effect would be lost. But in an appropriate setting where every aspect of its beauty is seen and appreciated, the plant is like a jewel on the costume of a well-dressed, beautiful woman. Such a garden with choice flowers enlivens periods of summer lethargy when interest in ordinary gardens may lag.

Consequently, the more plants a person knows, the more rewarding his garden is likely to be. He can draw upon a mental reservoir of plant potentialities for just the right varieties to give the effect he wants. His garden can be a personal expression of lighthearted fun or solemn dignity, of sophisticated understatement or simple charm. Because it is so individual, he enjoys his garden and so do all who share it with him.

For such highlighting of the summer garden, no group of plants offers more appealing choices than the flowering bulbs.

Like many of our most wonderful perennials, the summer bulbs as a group passed out of the everyday gardening picture when publicity was concentrated on a few all-purpose, grow-anywhere plants. But like the perennials, they are available to those who appreciate their great beauty. These bulbs are sturdy and reliable enough so that they might well be used in quantity, especially in warm climates where it is not necessary to dig the bulbs for storage at the end of the season. Even in colder regions where they must be dug in fall they are worth the effort required.

Ismene Blooms First

If whiteness were its only distinction, ismene would somehow find its way into good gardens. For this is a white flower with substance, its petals long and heavy, attracting attention even from a distance.

Add to this the exotic, unfamiliar form of the flowers, their happy habit of clustering in twos or threes or fours, thus increasing their visual impact, and you have an asset for any garden. An added value is the sweetly irresistible scent of the white flowers.

Ismenes have a lilylike quality, but they're more graceful than most lilies and easier to use in small plantings. The 2-foot scapes or flower stems are sturdy without being stiff, holding each crown of flowers well above the long, shiny, dark green leaves.

Useful in a perennial border, yet able to stand alone in an important position, ismenes are appropriate with broadleaf evergreens and spectacular as pot plants. Imagine them, too, with a collection of polished white rocks, or reflected in the tranquil water of a garden pool. Ismenes need space to be appreciated—don't crowd them in with lesser plants.

You'll find these bulbs also called spider lilies, basket flowers, even Peruvian or sea daffodils, and in proper botanical circles, various species of *Hymenocallis*.

The most common kind is *Hymenocallis calathina* and its varieties 'Advance' and 'Olympia.' 'Olympia' varies from the type in that its flowers are cream-colored. The hybrid 'Festalis' is white, with narrow, wildly curled petals. There is also a yellow hybrid, 'Sulfur Queen.'

UPPER: *Hymenocallis calathina* is the spider lily. A bulb, and one of the loveliest of all for hot-weather bloom. In the South it can be grown out-of-doors, but in cooler regions should be brought indoors in winter and stored with roots attached in dry soil at temperatures of about 60°.
LOWER: Another *Hymenocallis*, species *occidentalis*, is called the inland spider lily. A perennial bulbous plant, it produces large white flowers. In marshes and streams from Indiana to the Gulf it grows wild and farther north can be grown in the bog garden with some protection. The hymenocallis somewhat resemble the *Amaryllis*, and general cultural instructions are similar. In some areas they bloom as early as mid-June.

Precocious as compared to the other summer bulbs, ismenes bloom early—in mid-June in the Northeast. The bulbs should be planted four or five inches deep, eight to ten inches apart when consistently warm weather seems certain, or early May in the New York City area. The flowers usually open about six weeks after planting, but bulbs have been known to send up buds within a week after planting.

Soil for ismenes should be rich and well drained, the location sunny. If there is little rain, you can help things along by supplying extra water from the time the buds first appear. In addition to increasing flower size, watering will help keep the foliage at its attractive best all summer.

In fall, before frost, lift the bulbs carefully, damaging the roots as little as possible. Let them dry off inside in an inverted position and then store over the winter, with the soil around the roots, where the temperature is 60°. Since the bulbs produce numerous offsets, be sure to separate them before replanting in spring. If fed occasionally, as you would other plants, the offset will reach blooming size in a year or two adding to your border display.

The Tigridias

Whether you know them as tiger flowers or shell flowers or by the Latin *Tigridia*, you're not apt to forget these floral fireworks. Flamboyant, with a brilliance not often found in flowers, the blossoms open wide to display an extravagant pattern of dots and dashes centering solid-color petals. Most spectacular are the scarlet, orange and yellow varieties, but there are also rose, wine-red, and white marked with red varieties. The triangular flowers measure three to six inches from corner to corner, and although they last but a day, they are produced in such quantity that a good display can be counted on from July until frost. To make the most of the flowers, and since the grassy foliage is rather meager, set bulbs close—four to six inches apart—and in clumps of a single color. The effect will be that of big plants. Important: Insist upon selected colors or varieties, not mixtures, and then plant in groups of a single color. If you don't, your garden will have an Indian war dance appearance.

If your summers are relatively cool, full sun is satisfactory for tigridias. In hot weather, however, light shade is preferable to prevent fading of the flowers. Give the bulbs rich soil, moist, but well drained. Plant them about four inches deep when the ground is warm. When the plants are several inches high, a mulch can be spread between them to conserve moisture and keep the sun from heating the soil. Tigridias are also successful as pot plants if kept from drying out. Use shallow containers such as bulb pans and a loose, water-retentive soil. When falls comes, just move the containers indoors for storage.

Dig bulbs in the garden before frost, as you would gladiolus, and store dry where the temperature is about 50°. Or, if your winters are mild, leave bulbs in the ground and cover with a thick mulch. Tigridias *have* survived winters as far north as New York and Boston but it's risky and not guaranteed to be successful by any horticultural experts.

Fairy Lilies

In sharp contrast to the fun and fury of the antic tigridias, the gentle fairy or zephyr lily is like a whisper, soft and hesitant. Whether you choose the rosy-pink summer blossoms of *Zephyranthes grandiflora* or the white autumn flowers of *Z. candida*, the effect is gay, but subtle. There is also a rare yellow species, *Z. longifolia*. The fairy lilies flower freely, above grassy, graceful foliage from 6 to 8 inches high.

Like the tigridias, there is a tendency in *Zephyranthes* toward hardiness, especially in *Z. candida*, but it is safest to dig the bulbs before frost. Plant in a sunny location when the soil is warm, 2 inches apart and with the tips of the bulbs just below the surface. Or, plant about six to a five-inch bulb pan, and move the bulbs and pan, all undisturbed, indoors when cold weather comes. Let the bulbs dry off and store at 50°. It would be a simple matter to plant a few pots of bulbs for the terrace, enjoy them all summer, then simply move them indoors in fall. Amazing heirloom plants 50 to 100 years old and filling dishpans have been tenderly cared for in just this simple manner.

Consider, too, the light, dancing effect of fairy lilies against a dark green ground cover, say of ivy or pachysandra. Unless the area is large, use just one color, or choose bulbs which bloom at different times. Fairy lilies are ideal for extending the color of spring bulbs into the summer months. Remember, though, that by the time fairy lilies bloom, any nearby trees will be clothed in leaves, so don't forget to plant these bulbs where they can get some summer sunshine to guarantee full blooms next season.

The Exuberant Cannas

Do you still associate cannas with traffic circles or iron horses and stiff geometrical flower beds? If these outdated and ill-conceived uses of cannas have conditioned you against this clan, step back a moment and consider them anew as the flowers are now, not as you remember them.

First, today's cannas have new flower colors.

BULB

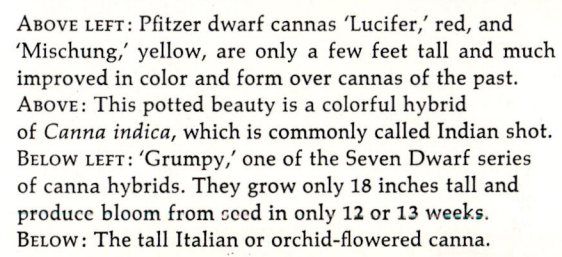

ABOVE LEFT: Pfitzer dwarf cannas 'Lucifer,' red, and 'Mischung,' yellow, are only a few feet tall and much improved in color and form over cannas of the past.
ABOVE: This potted beauty is a colorful hybrid of *Canna indica*, which is commonly called Indian shot.
BELOW LEFT: 'Grumpy,' one of the Seven Dwarf series of canna hybrids. They grow only 18 inches tall and produce bloom from seed in only 12 or 13 weeks.
BELOW: The tall Italian or orchid-flowered canna.

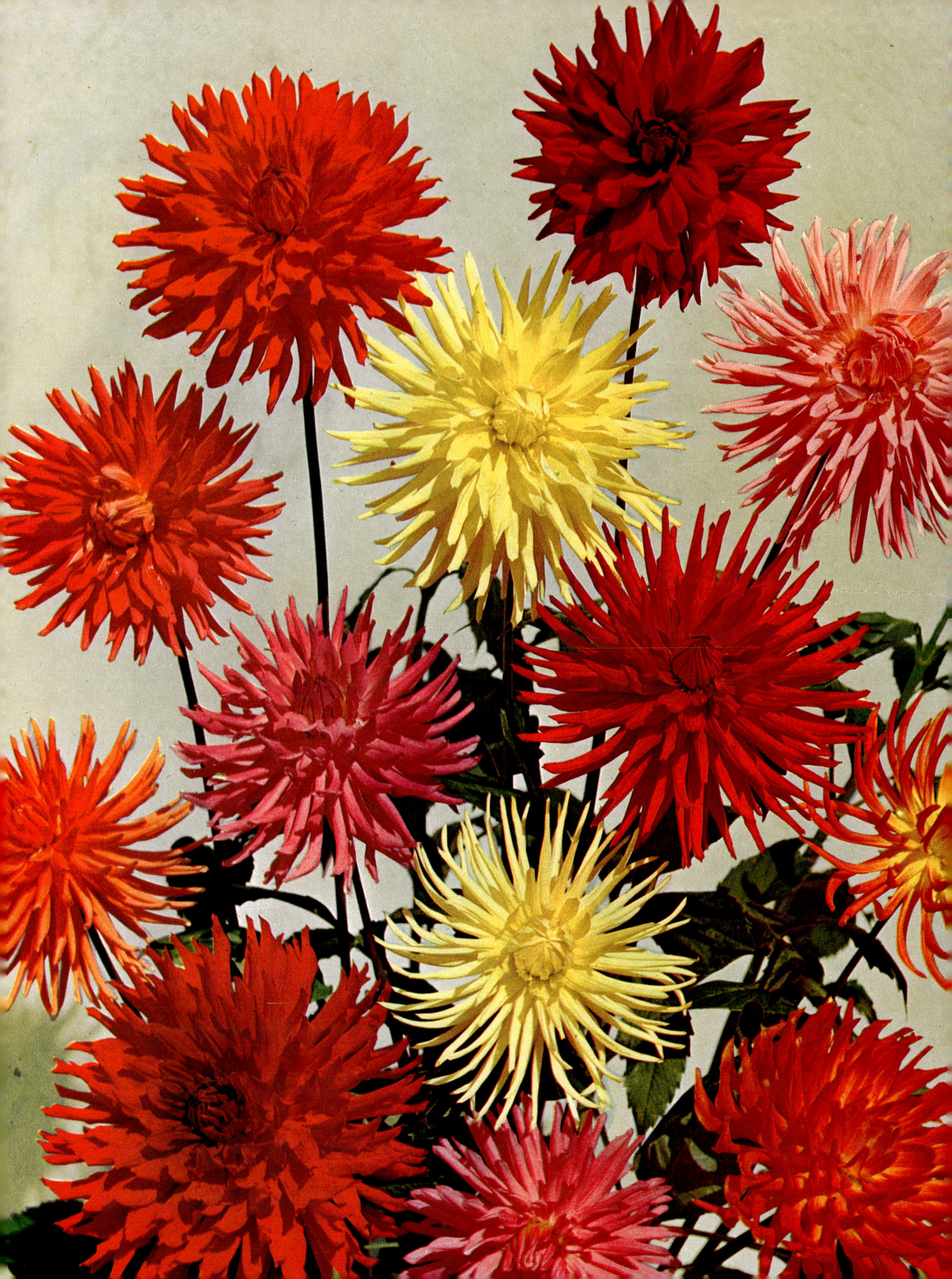

They're softer, subtler, without the old-time harshness. Now you can select varieties in peach, pink, rose, terra-cotta and yellow blends or in glowing scarlet, yellow and deep red. Individual blossoms are larger, too, sometimes measuring 6 to 8 inches.

Canna foliage is luxuriant, sometimes glossy green, sometimes bronze, depending upon the variety. Ultimate height, too, depends upon the variety, from the newer dwarf Pfitzer varieties which are about 30 inches high to the truly magnificent (and difficult to use) kinds eight feet tall. Choose your plants according to your purpose.

Keep in mind that even the dwarf varieties are large-scale plants—their leaves may be 20 times the size of foliage on any other plants you grow, comparable in effect to the larger water-lily pads. For that reason, cannas are best grown apart, their scale contrasted with larger objects—lawn or paving, perhaps the house or trees. They needn't always be planted in masses but cannas are seldom at their best standing alone; arrange them in clumps of at least three. The dwarf kinds are ideal for big containers, just right for an antique tub or a big redwood box.

Many plants tolerate hot weather; cannas thrive on it, blooming through the worst heat spells. In fact, long periods of foggy drizzle may cause them to sulk. If you plant them directly in the garden, dig the soil deep—at least 12 inches—and work in plant food and peat, leafmold, or compost. If you garden in the North, you'll get flowers sooner if you start the tubers indoors in peat or sandy soil as you would tuberous begonias, about four weeks before the date of your last spring frost. At least one mail-order firm sells the dwarf varieties as growing plants in pots, shipping them at the proper planting date. With warmth and moisture, these will bloom in no time.

Canna tubers should be planted 2 to 4 inches deep and 1½ to 2 feet apart, depending upon the mature size of the varieties. When the vigorous upward growth begins, feed and water the plants liberally.

Let frost kill the foliage in the fall, then cut plants back to within 6 inches of the roots, dig and proceed as you would with ismenes. Those who garden in warm climates can leave cannas in the ground the year around.

When you buy cannas insist upon the newer named varieties. Look for the new dwarfs and the pastel Grand Opera series. Many are not yet widely available except through specialists' catalogs. A series named the Seven Dwarfs is offered by some of the most popular seed houses.

A Dahlia for Everyone

Dahlias today are so diverse in character and quality, entire catalogs are devoted to their descriptions. In color, form and size, dahlias vary widely, serving almost any conceivable purpose in late summer and fall gardens.

Most useful are the small-flowered types: single, anemone, peony, cactus, pompon, bedding and miniature.

The miniatures are small editions of the big—really giant—varieties. The plants are bushy, the tallest about four feet high. Flowers vary from 2 to 4 inches in size and are profuse, opening over a long period.

Pompon dahlias seem to bloom by the bushel, producing a multitude of small, 1- to 2-inch globular flowers on spreading plants much like chrysanthemums.

Bedding dahlias differ from the others in that they reach maturity so quickly they can be started from seed outdoors (rather than tubers) and still bloom in late summer and fall. Naturally, you can get earlier bloom by starting the seeds indoors, as you might zinnias or marigolds.

The tallest bedding dahlia, Mignon, is about 2 feet. Other smaller favorites are Coltness Single and the Unwin Hybrids. The latter has semidouble blooms and is practically foolproof. Colors are varied —choose those you like best and at the end of the season, before severe frost, dig and keep the tubers.

Dahlias must have full sun and moist soil, plus abundant plant food to keep them growing. Once the plants have hardened off, due to lack of food or water, they are through flowering for the season. If a drought in July does set your plants on strike, try cutting the plants back to a new shoot near the base of the plant. This, followed by liberal watering, may encourage new growth and more flowers in fall. Feed plants when they are set out and then at two- to four-week intervals until flowers have begun to open. You can buy roots, or started plants, but don't set either out until all danger of frost is past. When the plant has developed three sets of leaves, pinch out the top to encourage strong, bushy growth.

After frost, lift tubers and store as you would the other bulbs.

A bouquet of cactus dahlias in a brilliant array of colors. Dahlias are considered among the best bulbs for color after the heat of midsummer and today are so diverse in shape and shade that whole catalogs are devoted to them. Among the most decorative are cactus dahlias. Colors range widely, are generally bright and clear. Flowers vary in size and in effect. Some are starlike, others fluffy. The largest are as wide as 10 inches across. Dahlias require full sun and a moist soil well supplied with humus. The small-flowered dahlias are useful for the front of the border.
Tallest bedding varieties are the mignon class, 24 inches.

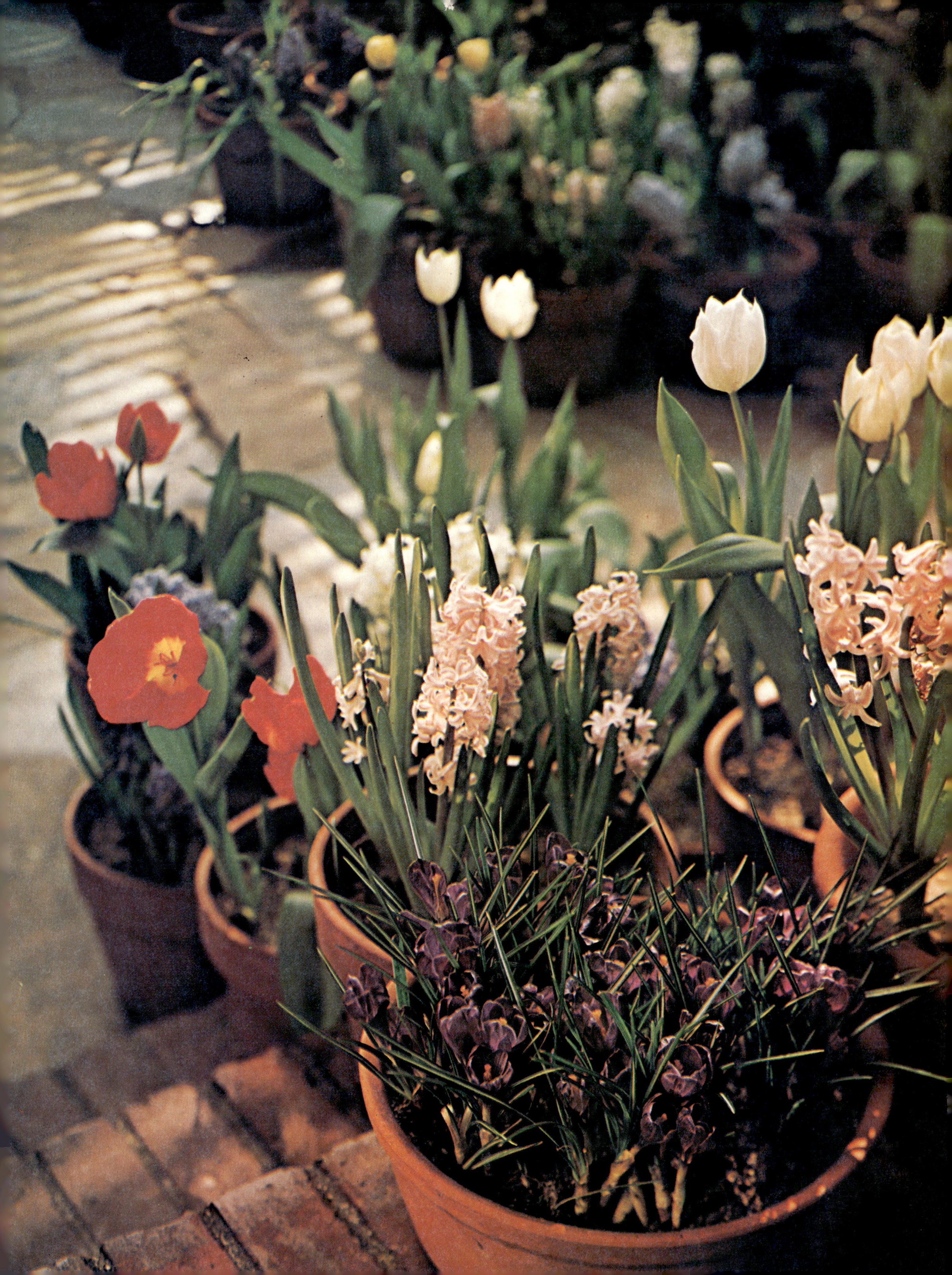

Potted Bulbs

By C. JACQUES HAHN

Colorful drifts of bulbs in the full glory of bloom are to me the essence of springtime beauty. And the easiest way I know to enjoy them—and eliminate the problems they bring—is to grow them in pots.

Let's face it, bulbs do bring problems. After they bloom and begin to die down, the yellowing foliage gives the garden an unfortunate look of neglect—just when you'd like it to look its best. You can lift the bulbs and heel them in to harden off somewhere out of sight, but this is a lot of extra work.

Also, if you grow them in beds, you have only bare earth to look at from fall until they begin to bloom in spring. Some of them can be naturalized and grown in a lawn or ground cover, but this limits the kinds you can have. Another problem, although no fault of the bulbs, is that gophers and mice love them.

The way to solve all these problems at once is to grow the bulbs in pots. You can keep them out of sight while they are developing, and move them front and center when they are at their absolute best. You can take them away as they begin to fade. And they are completely safe from underground thieves. The portability of potted bulbs is also a great advantage in arranging color combinations.

There is another dividend, too. When your bulbs are planted in pots, you can move some of them inside and "force" the bloom to bring an authentic touch of spring to your breakfast table or living room a full month or more ahead of their flowering time.

When you are after a strong show of bloom, the place to put the bulbs is right up close, where you can enjoy all they have to offer. This means you should buy the biggest, healthiest specimens of the showiest varieties you can find. The big bulbs may cost more, but you can get more effect for your money.

How To Choose Bulbs

Don't be misled by their size. Bulbs of some varieties are naturally larger than those of other varieties. However, size within the variety *is* important. The largest daffodil and tulip bulbs are called *top size*. The best hyacinths are called *exhibition size*, the next grade is called *first size*. These large specimens are best for growing in pots. Some of the large daffodil bulbs are double-nosed and produce two flowering stalks. I prefer these. When you choose bulbs, pick out the largest, firmest, heaviest ones with no bruises, cuts or obvious damage.

The Right Soil and Containers

Bulbs will grow in almost any garden soil, but I think it is worthwhile to pot them in soil they really thrive in. The ideal bulb soil is a rich sandy loam. If your best garden soil is not good enough, you can make an ideal bulb mixture with these ingredients: About 2 parts peat moss (to retain water), 2 parts sifted loam (for its organic content), 1 part sand (for good drainage), ½ part dehydrated cow manure, or a 5-10-5 fertilizer (to feed the bulb).

I use 8-inch bulb pans, which are not as deep as pots, for the tulips and smaller daffodils. For 'King Alfred' daffodils and hyacinths I use 5-inch pots with one bulb in each.

How To Pot Them

Except for the one-to-a-pot bulbs, leave about a half-inch between bulbs and put as many in the containers as you can.

If you use new pots, soak them for a few days in water. A dry pot will pull moisture right out of the soil and increase your watering chores. Dirty pots may harbor disease. So wash old pots well.

Put pieces of broken pots or crushed gravel over the drainage hole. Then add enough soil to bring the top of the bulbs almost level with the edge of the pot. Firm the soil and level it so the tips of the bulbs just show. Water thoroughly.

Winter Care

Here in California the potted hyacinths and tulips must be set in a dark place for the winter. Daffodils may be left in filtered light. In colder climates they should all be kept in a cool, dark place, such as a cool shed or cellar, or outside under a mulch. One way to handle them outdoors is to group the pots in a shaded place, fill in around them with peat moss, water well, and cover with about a foot of peat, salt hay, straw, or leaves mixed with soil. Where gophers or mice are a problem, put a covering of hardware cloth over the pots before you add the top mulch. If you need a cover to hold it down, use a porous material like burlap. Fall rain will keep the soil moist. If you store them under cover, you have to water them. In areas where there is snow, the snow will act as a protective blanket to keep them safe from the worst frosts.

Most of the bulbs make excellent container plants which can be used indoors or out for an early display of color. Here crocuses, hyacinths and tulips bloom in clay pots.

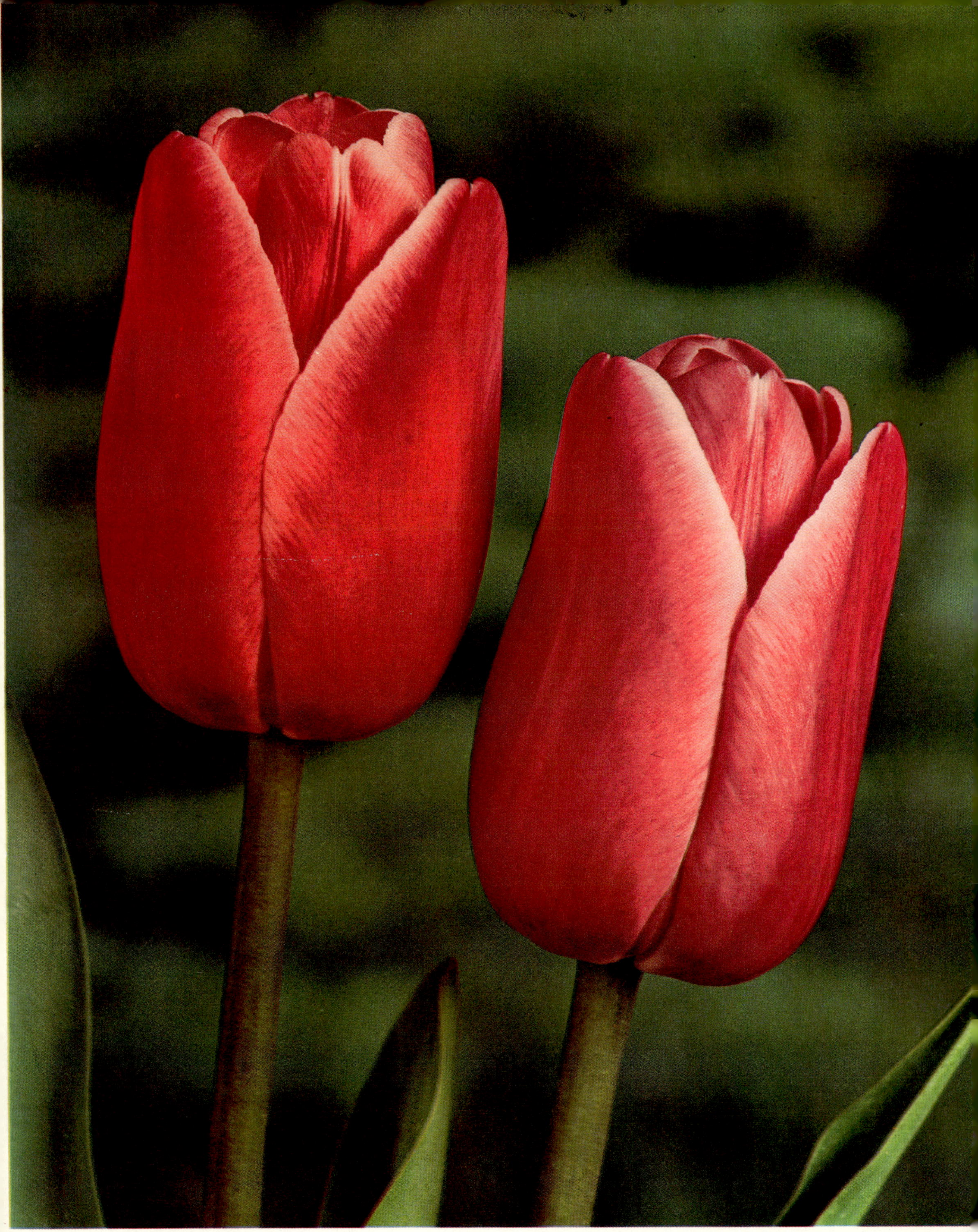

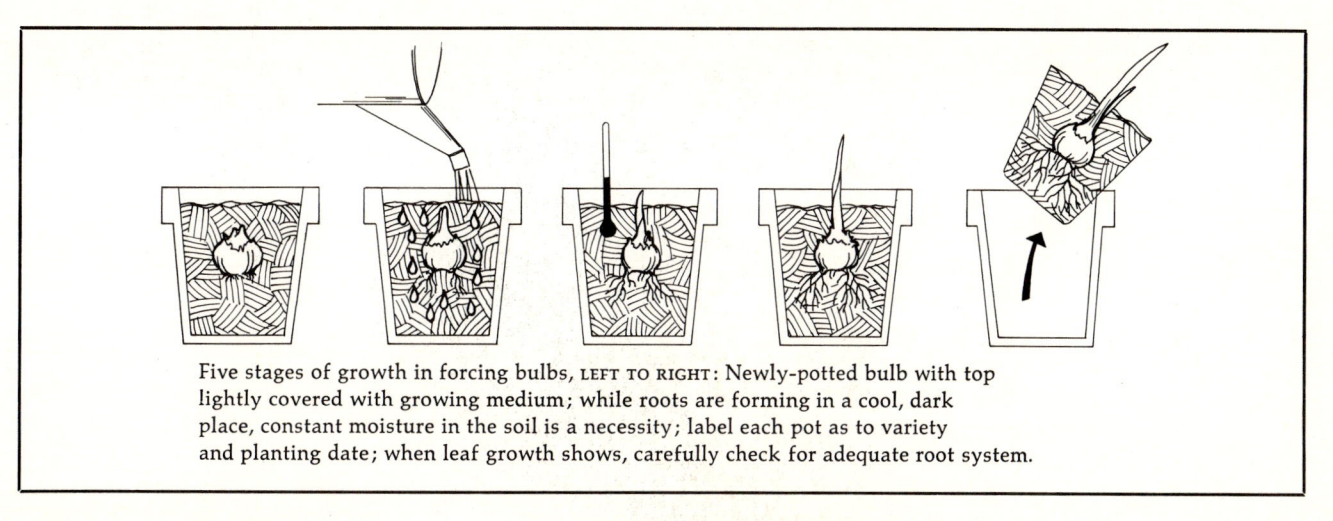

Five stages of growth in forcing bulbs, LEFT TO RIGHT: Newly-potted bulb with top lightly covered with growing medium; while roots are forming in a cool, dark place, constant moisture in the soil is a necessity; label each pot as to variety and planting date; when leaf growth shows, carefully check for adequate root system.

What To Do in the Spring

After a bulb has formed a good mass of roots, it will start its top growth and cycle of bloom as soon as it is brought into the light. If you want them to bloom out-of-doors at their normal season, remove the top mulch, or bring them out of cold storage, when danger of frost is past in the spring and before the sprouting tops get tall and spindly. Water them as they need it. Feed with liquid 5–10–5 fertilizer about every two weeks until after bloom.

I don't put them on the terrace until they are far enough along to make a real show of color. And I move them out just as soon as they begin to fade.

Forcing Bloom Indoors

You can bring the bulbs into bloom a month or so before their normal season if you move them into the house as soon as they have developed a strong root system. To check on the roots, moisten the soil so it will not crumble, invert the pot and tap it so the soil will come out in one piece. If you can see a network of roots all around the soil, the bulb is ready to start.

When you bring bulbs indoors, put them first in a rather cool place (about 55°) out of direct light. When the tulip or daffodil buds begin to show, put the pots in direct light by a window. The hyacinths are ready for the increased light and temperature when the leaves are a healthy green and about 6 inches long. Keep pots away from direct sunlight or they may get too warm. A temperature of 65° F. is ideal in the flowering stage.

A formal Darwin tulip will bloom indoors as well as out planted in rich sandy loam and kept in a dark cool place for the winter. Plant several to a pot and bring indoors a month before blooms are desired.

After-bloom Care

As soon as the last flowers have faded, give the bulbs a final feeding with liquid fertilizer, water well, and put them in an out-of-the-way place while they harden off. Leave the foliage on until it is yellow and dead, then cut it off. In the fall take bulbs out of the pots, knock off the soil, put them in ventilated bags and hang them up to dry. You can plant the bulbs again in the fall and they will repeat the cycle, but they aren't as dependable the second year.

bulbiferus (bulb-*iff*-er-us), **-a, -um.** Bulb-bearing.

| BULBS PREFERRED FOR POTTING |||
DAFFODILS	HYACINTHS	TULIPS
King Alfred Huge, all-yellow flowers	*City of Haarlem* Soft lemon-yellow	*Golden Harvest* Large, golden-yellow
Fortune Yellow and golden-orange	*L'innocence* Immaculate white	*White City* Sturdy white flowers
Mrs. E. H. Krelage Cream and white, tall, long-stemmed	*Pink Pearl* Rosy-pink	*Pride of Zwanenburg* Salmon-pink, tall
	Lady Derby Soft clear pinks	
Diana Kasner Cream, yellow and red	*Myosotis* Soft sky-blue, large	*Spring Song* Red-orange, very large
Beersheba Magnificent pure-white	*King of the Blues* Fine dark blue	*Insurpassable* Lavender, very large
Thalia Pure-white flower clusters		*Aristocrat* Orchid pink, fine quality

Daffodils bloom first, then hyacinths and tulips. Varieties are listed in approximate order of bloom, the earliest at the top.

bulbil. A small bulb borne above ground either in the leaf axils, as in the tiger lily, or in the flowers, as in some onions.

Bulbil lily. See *Lilium bulbiferum*.

bulblet. A small or immature bulb produced below the ground by and around a mature bulb.

Bulblet bladder-fern. See *Cystopteris bulbifera*.

BULBOCODIUM (bulb-oh-*koh*-dee-um). SPRING MEADOW-SAFFRON. Lily Family (*Liliaceae*). The only species is a crocuslike spring bulb, native in Europe and Asia and closely related to *Colchicum*. It is characterized by narrow, grasslike leaves and large flowers. The bulbs multiply so rapidly that the offsets must be dug up and divided every second or third year. It is particularly good for rock gardens and should be planted in the fall for early spring bloom. It can be propagated readily from offsets. Zone 4.

B. vernum (*vern*-um). Grows about 6 in. high. The violet-purple, funnel-shaped flowers bloom in very early spring. The leaves appear after the flowers have died and persist for several months.

BULBOPHYLLUM (bul-bow-*fill*-um). Orchid Family (*Orchidaceae*). Widely distributed, much varied tropical and subtropical epiphytes comprising the largest genus in the Orchid Family. Nearly 2,000 species are recognized although some taxonomists divide certain species into the genus *Cirrhopetalum*. The most popular bulbophyllums are tropical species grown for bizarre flowers, some of which have unpleasant odors. (Naturally, pleasantly perfumed species are preferred by all but bulbophyllum specialists, who may tolerate the stench of an especially rare variety.) Generally the cultivated species are under 10 in. in height and a good many are true miniatures with creeping rhizomes and pseudobulbs 4 to 5 in. tall. These thrive on slabs of tree fern or in tightly packed mixtures of bark and sphagnum moss. Since most bulbophyllums have elongated rhizomes, though the plants may be short, they quickly outgrow pots. Better luck is had by growing them on rafts, slabs, poles and logs of tree fern. Keep the fine roots evenly moist during formation of new growths. (Species from areas where there is a distinct dry season, Burma, Himalayas and parts of subtropical China, should be given several weeks of dry resting period after new growth is completed.) Popular species from tropical Africa and Asia grow and bloom satisfactorily when kept evenly moist at all times. Provide humidity of 60 to 80 per cent and bright diffuse light. Direct sun will burn foliage and many species thrive in the same low light levels favored by paphiopedilums. Repot or remount plants as soon as the medium begins to deteriorate. Provide sharp drainage in containers. The cultivated sorts thrive with intermediate to warm nights (60 to 70°). Propagate by dividing clumps of pseudobulbs.

B. dearei (*deer*-ee-eye). Pseudobulbs about 2 in. tall, single leaves to 6 in. long. Flowers 1½ to 3 in. across, long-lasting, pleasantly fragrant, sepals buff-yellow spotted with red-purple, lip white to yellow. Native to the Philippines and Borneo.

B. medusae (me-*doo*-sye). Delightful dwarf under 3 in. tall with flower spikes to 8 in., bearing, in the fall, several long-sepaled yellow to cream-colored flowers which are spotted red. Overall effect is like a Medusa head. A warm-growing species from Malaya, Sumatra and Borneo.

B. umbellatum (um-bel-*lay*-tum). Under 8 in. tall with umbel or cluster of 1½-in. flowers on upright stalks, yellow sepals spotted with red, white lip, blooms mainly in fall.

bulb pan. A clay pot wider than it is deep. For instance, a pan 9 in. in diameter is 4½ in. deep; a pan 12 in. in diameter is 5⅝ in. deep. Used for growing bulbs or other shallow-rooted plants, it is suitable for rooting cuttings or for raising seedlings.

bulgaricus (bul-*gay*-rik-us), **-a, -um.** From Bulgaria.

bullatus (bul-*lay*-tus), **-a, -um.** Swelling, puckered, convex, hence bullate.

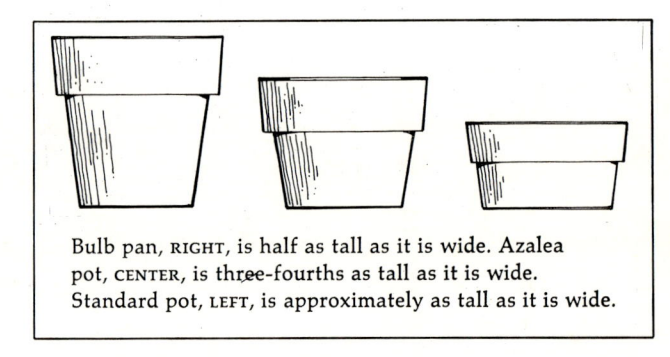

Bulb pan, RIGHT, is half as tall as it is wide. Azalea pot, CENTER, is three-fourths as tall as it is wide. Standard pot, LEFT, is approximately as tall as it is wide.

OPPOSITE, LEFT: This unusual member of the Orchid Family is the *Bulbophyllum* species *medusae*, a delightful dwarf under 3 inches tall which in the fall bears yellow or cream-colored flowers spotted with red.
OPPOSITE, TOP RIGHT: The genus *Bulbophyllum* includes some 2,000 species with an unusual variety of forms. This is *B. mastersianum*.
OPPOSITE, CENTER RIGHT: *B. porphyroglossum* produces tiny flowers on a gracefully arching stalk.
OPPOSITE, BOTTOM: *B. umbellatum* is less than 8 inches tall and bears a cluster of small flowers that are pale yellow spotted with red, with a white lip. It blooms mainly in the fall and comes from Nepal and the Himalayas. It thrives in high humidity and prefers the intermediate temperature ranges.

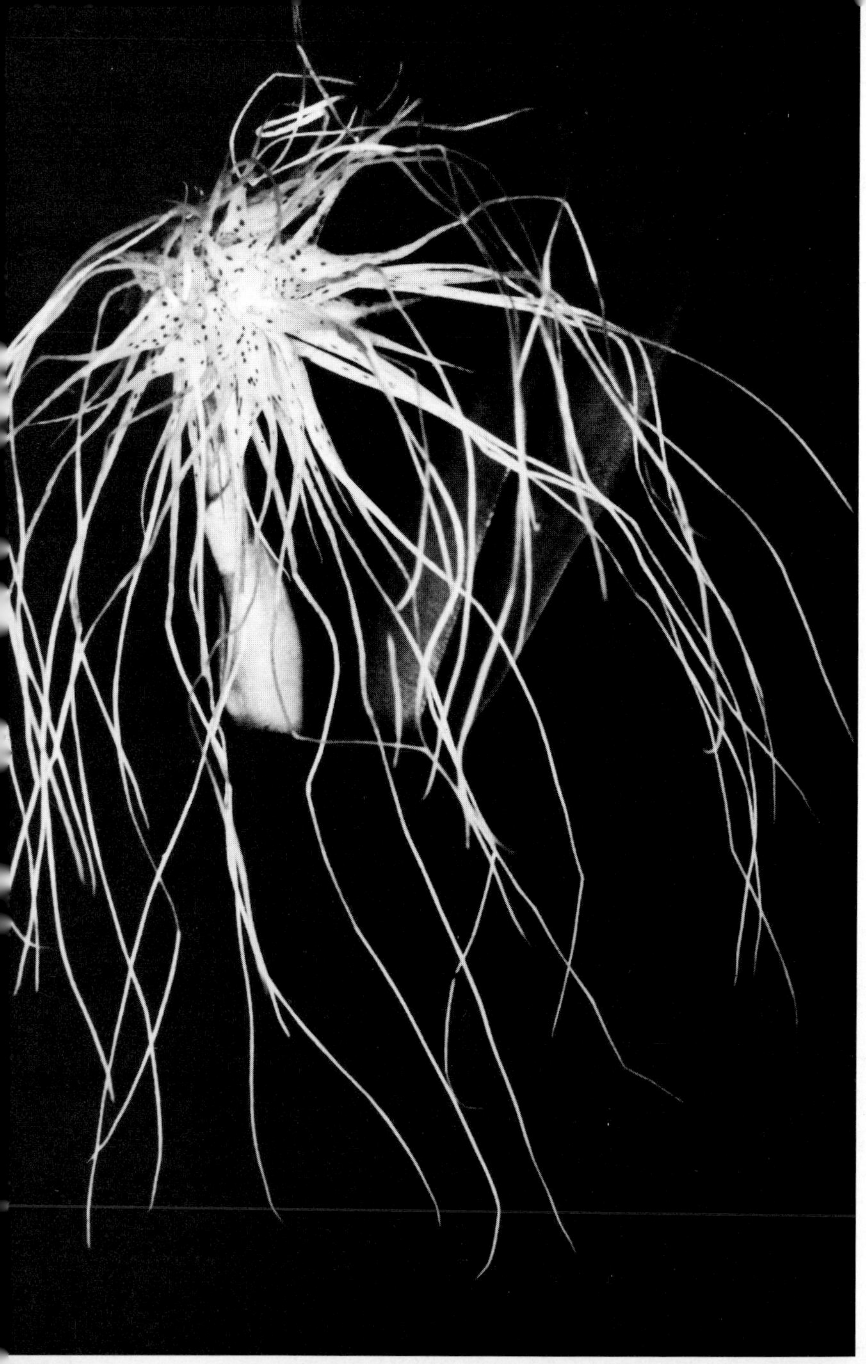
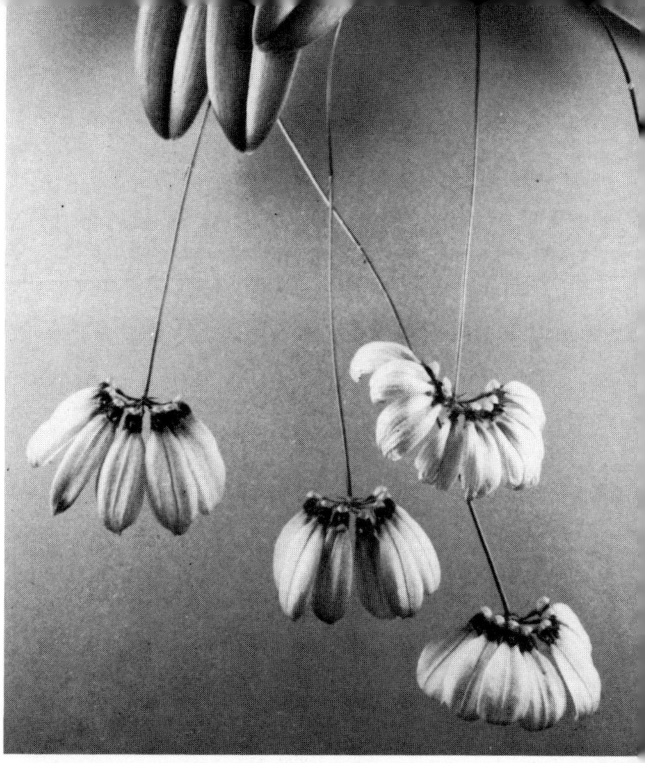
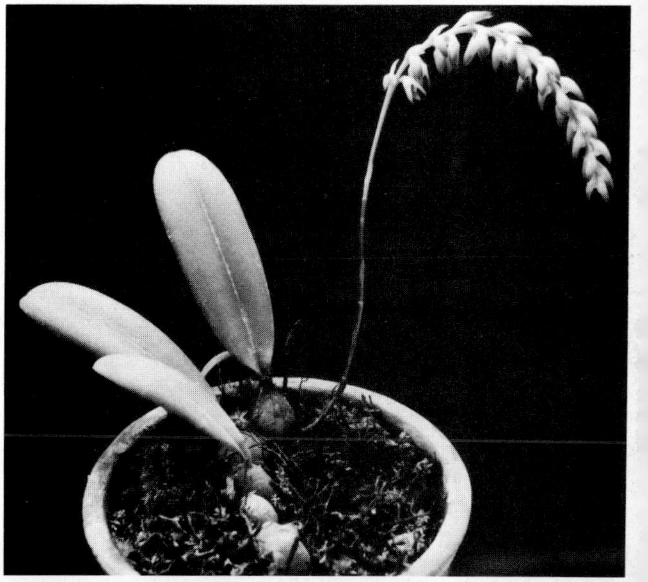
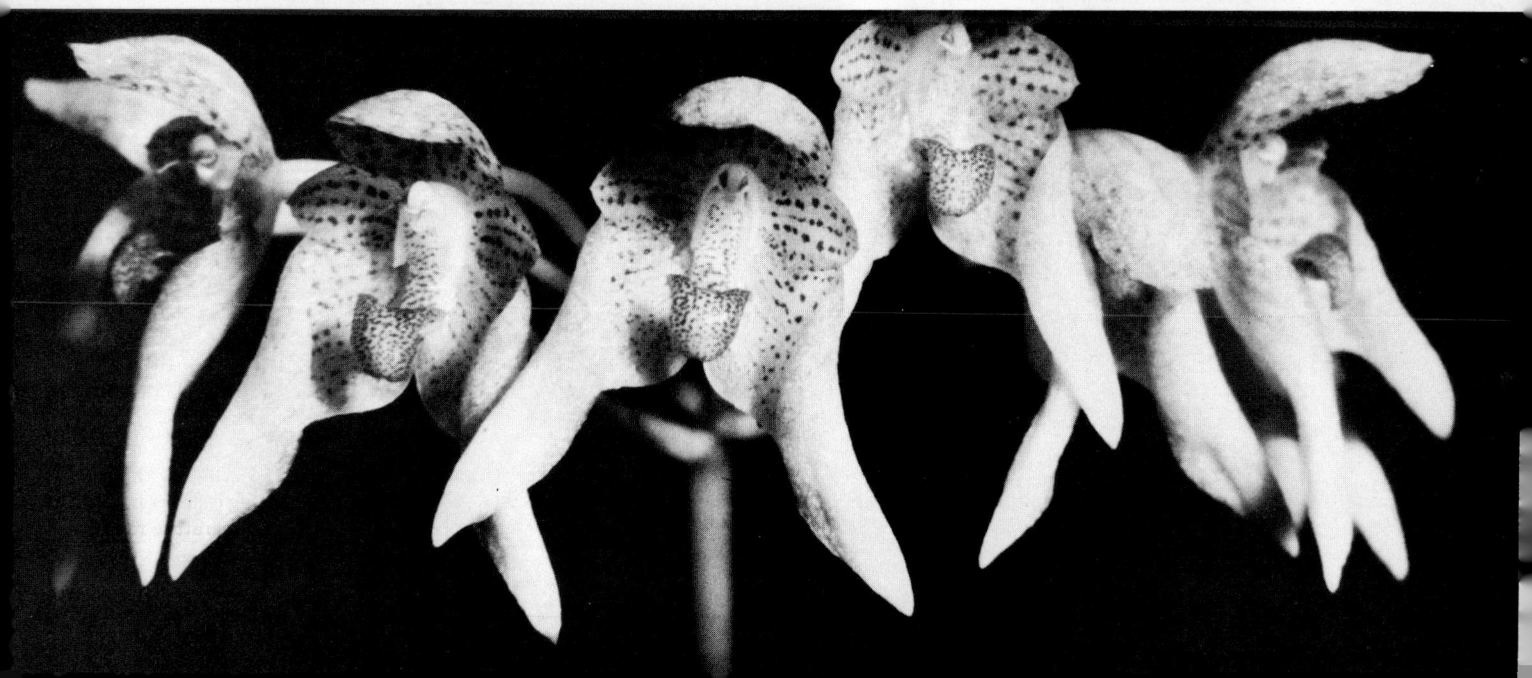

BULL-BAY

Bull-bay. See *Magnolia grandiflora*.

Bullock's-heart. See *Annona reticulata*.

BUMELIA (bew-*mee*-lee-uh). Sapodilla Family (*Sapotaceae*). Evergreen or deciduous trees, native to south and middle U.S. They have very hard wood, thorns and, in July, small green or greenish-white flowers that are intensely fragrant. Easily propagated from seed sown as soon as it is ripe. Besides the species discussed below, *B. lycoides* and variety *virginiana* and *B. swallii* are worthy of consideration wherever a small-stature tree with sweet-smelling flowers is needed. *B. lanuginosa* and *B. lycoides* have proven hardy in sheltered positions at the Arnold Arboretum in Boston, Mass. Most species grow naturally on dry, rocky or sandy soil and are particularly useful in such situations.

B. lanuginosa (lan-yew-jin-*noh*-suh). CHITTAMWOOD. Sometimes called false buckthorn. A deciduous tree that reaches 55 ft., with alternate leaves 2 to 3 in. long that stay on late into the fall. The greenish-white flowers are followed by small black fruit, 1/3 in. long. The variety *oblongifolia* is also recommended.

Bunchberry. See *Cornus canadensis*.

Bunchflower. See MELANTHIUM.

-bundus. Suffix meaning abundant.

Bunya-bunya. See *Araucaria bidwillii*.

bur. The spiny, prickly covering of a fruit such as the chestnut. Also, any plant that bears burs.

Burkwood daphne. See *Daphne* x *burkwoodii*.

burl. An enlarged woody excrescence on a tree trunk. Burls are common to only a few trees, notably the redwood. If a redwood burl is cut off and placed in water, it will very quickly produce green sprouts— but roots will seldom be produced.

Redwood burl, which resembles a knot in wood, will sprout green shoots when placed in water, and will live from several months to four or five years. Transferred to soil, and kept perpetually moist, it sometimes produces roots. To sprout a burl place it on a layer of moss, cut side down. Add one-quarter inch of water and keep the water at this level, rinsing away any scum as it forms. Set the dish in a light place at normal room temperature. The first sprouts of ferny green foliage should appear in two to four weeks. Burls offered commercially are cut from the giant redwoods of California and generally are the size of a man's hand.

How To Sprout a Redwood Burl

If you want a unique gardening experience, start a redwood burl cut from the giant redwoods of California. A burl is closely akin to what we know commonly as a knot in wood. References give various definitions for the word "burl." The dictionary defines burl as: "A burl is a kind of knot on some tree trunks," or, "veneer made from wood with burls in it."

Professor Emanuel Fritz of the University of California School of Forestry writes: "A burl may be any unnatural wartlike protuberance on a tree. Burls may be irregular growths resulting from injury, or they may be natural growths made up of dormant buds. In the redwood region only the second type is recognized as burl, the former being known simply as overgrowth."

Professor Fritz continues: "Redwood burls develop from a bud which originates at the pith. This original bud for some unknown reason remains dormant instead of growing into a branch. It divides and redivides as the tree grows older to form additional buds, each of them increasing in length each year just enough to keep up with the tree's diameter growth or just a trifle ahead of it. If the buds increase in length just a trifle more each year than the trunk increases in diameter, the mass of buds will form a wartlike lump on the trunk, limb or base of the tree."

Two basic types of burls are of commercial importance. One is taken from the base or trunk of the tree and varies in weight from several hundred pounds to more than ten tons. From this type burl are made such novelties as ashtrays, vases, bon-bon dishes, salad bowls, tabletops and bookends. The color of the wood may be in any shade from light pink to a rich, dark red. The second type burl is of chief interest.

Sprouting burls are sawed from trees because chopping or knocking them off separates the bark from the wood and makes growth impossible. When a burl is properly sawed from the tree, no injury occurs to the burl and very little to the tree. The wound heals and usually forms another burl, this one more unusual than the first. Burl hunting is definitely for professionals, and is, in fact, illegal in parks. Trespassing on private lands for burls is a punishable offense.

After being sawed from the tree, each burl is packed in damp moss, which provides sufficient moisture for about two weeks. Thus, it is possible to ship the burls anywhere. To sprout a burl, all you do is keep it moist. Step by step, here's how: (1) Place the burl, cut side down, on a layer of moss, unmilled sphagnum, for example. (2) Add one-fourth inch water. Replenish daily. Rinse away any scum that may form. (3) Kept properly moist in a light place with a temperature range comfortable for you, the first sprouts of ferny green redwood foliage will be apparent in two to four weeks. By means of water culture as described here, the burl will last from six months to four or five years.

After sprouting a burl in water, it is possible also to transplant it to a pot of humusy soil (equal parts garden loam, peat moss and sand) for a more promising future. When the sprouts are 8 to 10 inches long, place the burl in soil so that the top half of the stems shows above the surface. Keep evenly moist, and rooting will occur eventually.

Bur-marigold. See BIDENS.

burn. Plants are said to burn when the leaves shrivel or become discolored slightly, as when they are exposed to too much intense sun or prolonged drying wind. Young leaves and plants are more likely to be affected by such conditions than mature or thoroughly seasoned ones. Protect young plants from the sun by shading; from the wind with a screen of boards or brush, or by means of other plants. Keep the soil well watered. What is commonly referred to as fertilizer burn is caused by excessive applications of fertilizers that become toxic to the plant and cause wilting or foliage discoloration.

Burnet. See *Sanguisorba officinalis;* also *Poterium sanguisorba,* salad burnet.

Burning-bush. See *Euonymus europaeus atropurpureus.*

Bur oak. See *Quercus macrocarpa.*

Burro-tail. See *Sedum morganianum.*

bush. A shrub or woody plant that naturally produces multiple stems rather than a single trunk. Also, uncultivated land with shrubby vegetation. For information on shrubs and woody plants to use in the landscape, see articles following the discussion of "trees."

Bush-anemone. See CARPENTERIA. Sometimes called tree-anemone.

Bush-clover. See LESPEDEZA.

bushel. A dry measure equaling 4 pecks, or 32 qts., or approximately 1¼ cu. ft. The weight of a bushel of grain, fruit or vegetables varies widely between about 30 and 60 lbs.

bush fruit. Any one of the fruit-bearing shrubs, such as blueberry, currant or gooseberry. See Small Fruit Plants for the Home Garden, following *fruit* where the subject of bush fruits is discussed at length.

Bush-honeysuckle. See DIERVILLA.

Bushman's poison. See *Acokanthera venenata.*

Bush morning-glory. See *Ipomoea leptophylla.*

Bush-poppy. See *Dendromecon rigida.* Also called tree-poppy.

Bush red pepper. See *Capsicum annuum.*

Busy Lizzie. See IMPATIENS.

Butcher's-broom. See *Ruscus aculeatus.*

BUTEA (*bew-tee-*uh). Pea Family (*Leguminosae*). A group of trees and shrubby vines having pealike flowers. From Asia. Zone 10.
B. frondosa: *B. monosperma.*
B. monosperma (mon-oh-*sperm*-uh). FLAME-OF-THE-FOREST. A tropical tree, reaching a height of 50 ft., that drops its leathery leaves in Feb., and then produces a mass of orange-red flowers in clusters. Individual flowers are 1 in. long, the racemes 6 in. long. The blossoms are used to produce a red dye. Native of India and Burma, it is grown in southern U.S.

BUTIA (*bew-tee-*uh). YATAY PALM. Palm Family (*Palmae*). These palms, natives of tropical America, grow only 3 to 15 ft. high and are used almost as shrubs in southern Calif., along the Gulf Coast and on the East Coast as far north as N. C.
B. capitata (cap-ih-*tay*-tuh). The long, gracefully

ABOVE: The flowering head of *Butia capitata* emerges from the wooden spathe which sheathed its frothy fronds from view.
UPPER LEFT: A full view of the gracefully arching branches of *Butia capitata* with its stout trunk marked by old leaf scars.
LOWER LEFT: *Butomus umbellatus*, flowering rush, is a valuable addition to the bog garden or for the edges of a natural pool since it will hold its delicate rose-colored flowers high all summer even while standing in up to a foot of water.

curving, feathery leaves of this palm form a fountain from the top of a short trunk, making it popular as a landscape plant in the South. It is also grown as a tub plant. The fruits, grown in clusters, are sometimes used in making jellies. Zone 10.

Butomaceae. See Butomus Family.

BUTOMUS (*bew*-toh-mus). Butomus Family (*Butomaceae*). An aquatic herb, native to Europe and Asia, with but a single species. Zone 3.
B. umbellatus (um-bell-*lay*-tus). FLOWERING RUSH. Narrow leaves, 20 to 30 in. long, give this plant a rushlike appearance. It grows at the edge of ponds or in swamps and is very colorful with its rose-pink blossoms borne in long racemes on scapes as much as 4 ft. tall. Easy to propagate by division.

Butomus Family. Aquatic perennial herbs with basal leaves and bisexual flowers consisting of four genera. Sometimes the genera are placed in the Alismaceae Family. *Butomus*, *Hydrocleys* and *Limnocharis* are suitable for ponds and aquariums.

Butter-and-eggs. See *Linaria vulgaris*.

Buttercup. See RANUNCULUS.

Buttercup Family (*Ranunculaceae*). Also called the Crowfoot, Peony or Hepatica Family. A large group of plants containing some of our most beloved garden flowers. Almost all are poisonous. Mostly herbaceous perennials (with some annuals) from cool parts of the North Temperate Zone, these plants are characterized by alternate or opposite leaves and varied flowers, many large and showy. A few of the better-known genera are *Aconitum, Actaea, Adonis, Anemone, Aquilegia* (columbine), *Clematis, Delphinium, Helleborus, Hepatica, Paeonia* (peony), *Ranunculus* and *Thalictrum*.

Buttercup-tree. See *Cochlospermum vitifolium*.

Butterfly bauhinia. See *Bauhinia monandra*.

Butterfly-bush. See BUDDLEIA.

Butterfly-flower. See *Bauhinia monandra*; also *Schizanthus pinnatus*.

Butterfly iris. See *Iris spuria*.

Butterfly orchid. See *Oncidium papilio*.

Butterfly-pea. See CENTROSEMA; CLITORIA.

Butterfly plants. Butterflies, those graceful, enchanting bits of darting color, give a garden a final fillip of charm. Since they feed on nectar, they will live in a garden where they find food that pleases them. If they also find plants of the sorts on which they lay their eggs, and on which the caterpillars feed, butterflies will settle down and stay, claiming the garden as their own.

Adult butterflies are especially fond of the following plants: *Alyssum, Arabis, Aubrieta,* butterfly-bush (*Buddleia*), butterfly-weed (*Asclepias tuberosa*),

TOP RIGHT: One of the plants guaranteed to be of interest to Monarch butterflies is the milkweed. Here a Monarch caterpillar enjoys a prime lunch of succulent milkweed leaf.
SECOND FROM TOP: Having stuffed himself for his long sleep (9 to 15 days), he attaches himself to a twig by spinning a silken band and molts his skin, which becomes his chrysalis. This is a bower fit for the King of the Butterflies—jade green studded with gold dots.
THIRD FROM TOP: Later the chrysalis shows almost black as the folded, nearly mature wings appear through the shell.
BOTTOM: Finally the triumphant Monarch clings to his empty and now useless home as he rests before setting off.

BUTTERFLY PLANTS

candytuft (*Iberis*), daisy (all single forms), *Gaillardia*, goldenrod (*Solidago*), *Lantana*, lavender (*Lavandula*), mignonette (*Reseda odorata*), *Phlox*, primrose (*Primula*), rosemary (*Rosmarinus*), *Scabiosa*, sweet rocket (*Hesperis matronalis*) and *Sedum spectabile*.

Butterflies choose carefully the plants on which to lay their eggs, selecting those the caterpillars, which eat green leaves, find tasty and nourishing. Such plants include: butterfly-weed (*Asclepias tuberosa*), Queen Anne's-lace (*Daucus carota*), spicebush (*Lindera benzoin*), thistle (*Cirsium*), violet (*Viola*) and white clover (*Melilotus alba*).

Butterfly vine. See STIGMAPHYLLON.

Butterfly violet. See *Viola papilionaceae*.

Butterfly-weed. See *Asclepias tuberosa*.

Butternut. See *Juglans cinerea*.

Butterwort. See PINGUICULA.

Buttonbush. See CEPHALANTHUS.

Button-fern. See *Tectaria cicutaria*.

Button pink. See *Dianthus latifolius*.

Buttonwood. See *Platanus occidentalis*.

Buxaceae. See Box Family.

BUXUS (*bux*-us). Box. Boxwood. Box Family (*Buxaceae*). Traditionally popular, densely branched, evergreen shrubs, native to Europe and Asia. They have small opposite leaves, with clusters of tiny flowers without petals, which bloom in spring. Slow-growing plants that grow best in well-drained soil, they can tolerate partial shade. One of the most valuable plants for hedges and edgings, box stands shearing and shaping very well. Prune in late spring after new growth has formed. When established, the plants thrive for years. To control leaf miners, which frequently cause blisters in the leaves, spray with malathion when the adult orange flies are seen. Clean out dead leaves and twigs from the inside every spring. Eating even small quantities of leaves has caused death of animals. Propagate by cuttings in late summer; the dwarf form is popular for edgings and is propagated by division in spring.

The American Boxwood Society was founded in

BELOW: A charming formal garden makes full use of *Buxus sempervirens* in traditional, perfectly clipped geometric hedges. Anyone lucky enough to live in a climate where boxwood likes to grow should trim this tidy evergreen in April and May to hold it to its formal shape.
OPPOSITE: A brick walk leads through this garden in Colonial Williamsburg. This shrub's tolerance for drastic clipping is amply shown by the topiary shapes here.

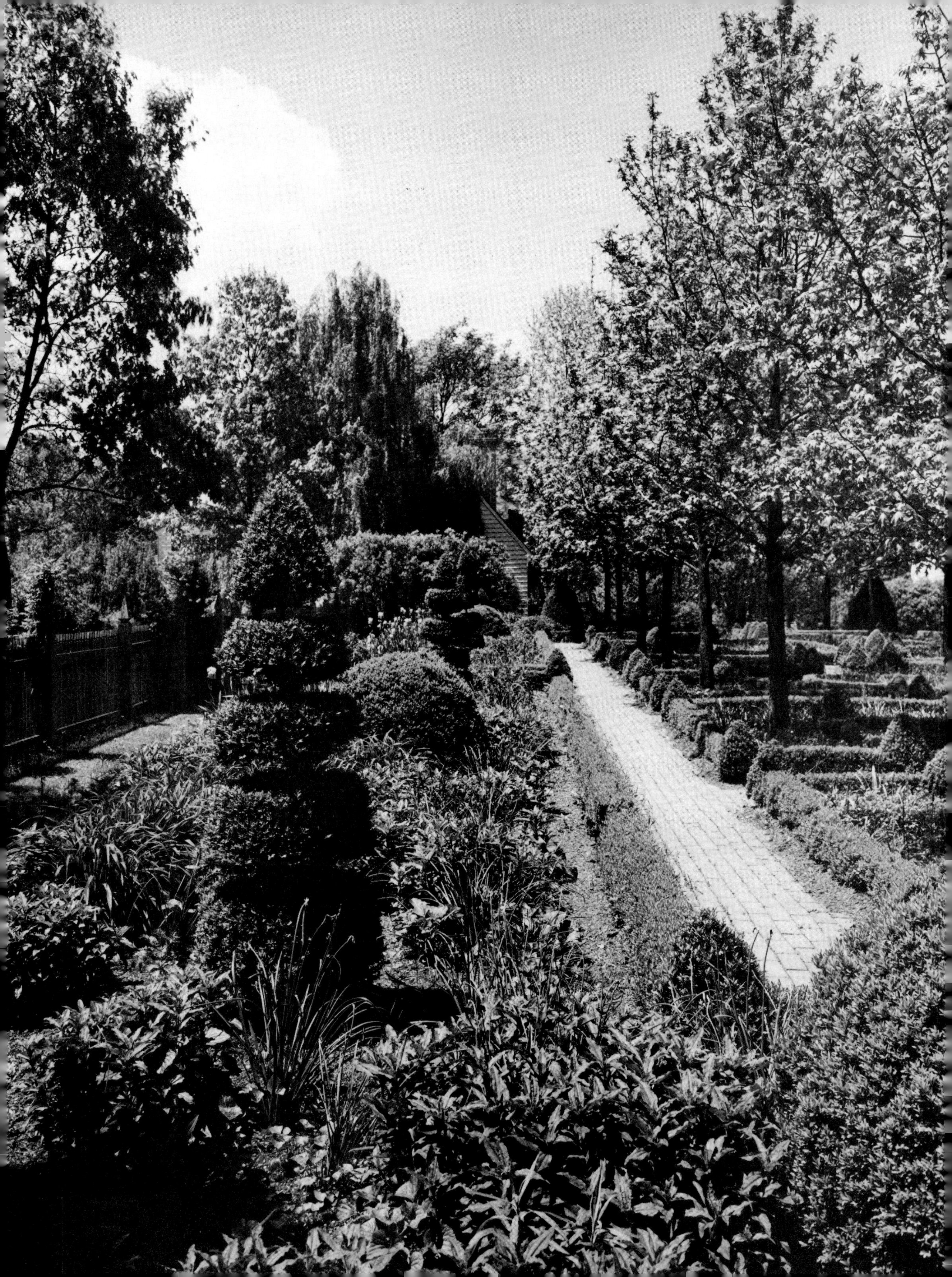

BUXUS

ABOVE: Common boxwood (*Buxus sempervirens*), the largest representing many decades of growth in this Virginia garden, is exceedingly handsome when left to grow to its natural billowy form without any special pruning. Strolling into a mature boxwood maze on a hot summer day, and feeling the lowered temperature and smelling the refreshing odor is a delightful experience.

LEFT: Japanese box (*Buxus microphylla*), especially the variety *koreana*, is an excellent substitute for other boxwoods where the winter climate is harsh. Boxwood in matching terra-cotta containers is used here on either side of a garden gate. When potted, constant watering is mandatory. If soil dries out even one time the plants may be lost. The dwarf form of common box, *B. sempervirens suffruticosa*, is also excellent as a container plant, and is sometimes bonsai-trained. Where winters are severe, container-grown box needs to be carried over in a cold frame or cold greenhouse.

1961 and is chartered as a nonprofit educational institution. The Society provides information on the care and culture of boxwood, aids in scientific study and classification and is International Registration Authority for boxwood names. It supports two thriving collections of rare boxwood specimens. (One is Heronwood in Upperville, Va., on the estate of Admiral Phillips, and may be seen by appointment; the other is at the Blandy Experiment Farm, U. of Va., Charlottesville, Va., open Mon.–Fri.). Annual membership dues includes the quarterly *The Boxwood Bulletin*. Address The American Boxwood Society at Box 85, Boyce, Va., 22620. Members share experiences in growing boxwood in various climates.

• **B. microphylla** (mye-kroh-*fill*-uh). JAPANESE BOX. Attractive, compact shrub, growing to 3 ft., tolerant of both sun and considerable shade. Angled, winged stems, leaves to 1 in. long, broadest above the middle. Zone 4. The form usually known as B. japonica, a 6-ft. shrub, is a variety of this species, and one of the two hardiest boxes (Zone 5). The other is the lower-growing variety *koreana* (kor-ee-*ay*-nuh), which spreads to 4 or 5 ft. but reaches only 18 in. in height. Korean box foliage turns brown in winter, but the plant is a good substitute in regions where other species suffer excessive winter damage. Zone 4.

• **B. sempervirens** (sem-per-*vye*-rens). COMMON BOX. Broad, dense shrub or small tree, common box grows to 25 ft. (in a mild climate). Slower growing than B. microphylla, this is the species that includes the traditional English and American box of historic veneration. Many plants from Colonial days are still flourishing in Va. Dark green, glossy foliage, pale beneath, each leaf is about 1½ in. long, with slightly winged stems. There are many forms in cultivation, notably the dwarf variety *suffruticosa* (suf-frew-tik-*koh*-suh), long prized for garden edgings. A few forms have gold- and silver-variegated foliage. Zone 7–6 with considerable winter protection. Some forms are hardy to Zone 4.

Cabbage. See *Brassica oleracea capitata*.

Cabbage palm. See *Roystonea oleracea*.

Cabbage palmetto. See *Sabal palmetto*.

Cabbage rose. See *Rosa centifolia*.

cabbage worm. A segmented green worm, the larva of a white butterfly that chews on leaves of the crucifers (Mustard Family), nasturtium and several other plants. Spray with methoxychlor, malathion, Sevin or diazinon as soon as insects appear. See article on Pests and Diseases.

CABOMBA (kab-*bom*-buh). FANWORT. WATER-SHIELD. Water-lily Family (*Nymphaeaceae*). Easily grown aquatic plants useful in aquariums or occasionally in subtropical outdoor ponds. The finely divided, submerged leaves give a delicate plumelike effect. There must be some soil in the aquarium or tank for these plants to survive. If your aquarium has sand covering the bottom, plant the cabomba in a pot in rich potting soil and sink the pot beneath the sand. Propagate by seeds, division or cuttings (underwater).

C. caroliniana (ka-rol-in-ee-*ay*-nuh). WASHINGTON PLANT. FISHGRASS. A popular and useful plant in the aquarium since the small, hairlike leaves supply needed oxygen to the water. The tiny white flowers bloom on the surface. It may become a rampant pest in outdoor pools, especially in the far South. Native

BELOW: *Cabomba caroliniana* lets its popular name of fishgrass tip us to its use as an aquarium plant. The graceful hairlike leaves float effortlessly in the water, belying its useful function of supplying oxygen for the fish.

from southern Ill. to Tex. See Aquascaping the Aquarium, under Children's Projects.

CACALIA (kah-*kay*-lee-uh). Composite Family (*Compositae*). Tender annuals and perennials, some of which are attractive ornamentals. Flowers are white, flesh-colored to orange and have a tubular corolla. Most species in cultivation are classed as belonging to the genus *Emilia*, and known as *coccinea*, *lutea* and *aurea*. In this encyclopedia, *coccinea* is listed as *Emilia sagittata*, which see.

Cactaceae. See Cactus Family. The Plant Finder section in Volume 16 lists genera desirable for foliage, for ornamental flowers and for many other uses.

Cactus. The Cactus Family is astonishing for the grotesque form of many species and for the unsurpassed beauty of some of the flowers. Primarily native to N. and S. America, cacti are succulents (see *succulent*) and are generally from deserts and arid regions with notable exceptions. Nature has equipped cacti with a water-storing capacity so that they are able to withstand the long, dry intervals between rainfalls. Most cacti are characterized by odd-shaped, spiny, plant bodies without true leaves (except for *Pereskia*). All the vital plant functions are performed by the green plant body. The spines, if any, arise from small openings called areoles. Cacti vary tremendously in shape and size, from tiny, pebble-shaped plants to massive, treelike forms that may be columnar or barrel-shaped.

As cultivated plants in the house, greenhouse or outdoors in frost-free regions, cacti need plenty of water during their growing period, which is usually summer. Good drainage and an open, friable soil are essential (indoors, use Basic Potting Mixture with double quantity of sand for desert species; regular potting mixtures for the others). Most cacti benefit by a vacation outdoors in the summer if they cannot be grown outdoors throughout the year. An outstanding collection of cacti and other desert plants is located at the Huntington Botanical Garden at San Marino, Calif.

Not all cacti are tender plants. Some species of *Opuntia*—notably *O. polyacantha*, the Plains pricklypear—are cold hardy well below zero, to −35°.

All native species of ball cactus, *Notocactus*, are on the preservation list of Ariz. and Colo. and are protected, that is, not to be picked or dug up. They are ball-like with colorful spines and yellow flowers, and only a few inches tall.

Cactus Family (*Cactaceae*). There are more than 120 genera in this family. A few of the more important ones are: *Aporocactus, Ariocarpus, Astrophytum, Carnegiea* (saguara), *Cereus* (partly divided into other genera such as *Nyctocereus, Selenicereus*), *Echinocactus, Ferocactus, Harrisia, Mammillaria, Opuntia, Pereskia* (the only genus with true leaves), *Rhipsalis* and *Zygocactus*. See *Cactus*, and see Plant Finder section of Volume 16 for genera suited to special purposes.

The Cactus and Succulent Society of America, through its *Cactus and Succulent Journal*, which has been published continuously since 1929, presents material of interest to botanists and enthusiasts of cacti and other succulents throughout the world. The modest membership dues requested include the bimonthly *Journal*, as well as the privilege of attendance at local meetings and biennial conventions, shows, desert trips. For further information write to the Cactus and Succulent Society of America, Box 167, Reseda, Calif. 91335.

Cad-weed. See *Anaphalis margaritacea*.

caeruleus (see-*rew*-lee-us), **-a, -um.** Blue.

CAESALPINIA (sez-al-*pin*-ee-uh). Pea Family (*Leguminosae*). Trees and shrubs, some of them climbing, native to warm regions of both hemispheres. Yellow or red flowers, in clusters, and feathery leaves.

BELOW: Caesalpinias grow vigorously in their native tropics and make eye-catching hedges with red and yellow flowers. Their rampant roots resent pots, so they're not house plants.

Grown in tropical and subtropical areas for their ornamental value. Propagate by seeds. Soak seeds in tepid water overnight before planting to hasten germination. Zone 10.

C. gilliesii (gill-*eez*-ee-eye). PARADISE POINCIANA. Tree to 20 ft., grown extensively in the tropics. The flowers are bright yellow with red stamens and prominent pistils. Formerly listed as Poinciana gilliesii.

C. pulcherrima (pull-*kehr*-im-uh). BARBADOS FLOWER FENCE. BARBADOS PRIDE. A woody shrub with clusters of bright red and yellow flowers—sometimes red petals with yellow edges. Red stamens are long and graceful. Sometimes planted as a hedge. Formerly called Poinciana pulcherrima.

caesius (*see*-see-us), **-a, -um.** Blue-gray.

caespitosus (sess-pit-*toh*-sus), **-a, -um.** Tufted, growing in low clumps or mates; cespitose.

Cafta. See CATHA.

Cajeput tree. See *Melaleuca leucadendron*.

Calabash. Two unrelated plants have been given this common name: *Lagenaria siceraria*, grown for the gourds out of which calabash pipes are made, and *Crescentia cujete*, a tropical tree occasionally grown in Fla. and bearing huge, hard-shelled fruits used for dippers and utensils, especially in the tropics.

CALADIUM (kal-*lay*-dee-um). FANCY-LEAVED CALADIUM. Arum Family (*Araceae*). Tuberous-rooted plants of tropical America, widely grown for their handsome, colorful foliage. The blade of the leaf is shaped like an arrowhead and is held horizontally. The flowers, usually hidden under the leaves, are in the calla-lily form that is typical of this family—a spathe surrounding the upright spike (spadix) that bears the tiny true flowers. Caladiums are stunning foliage plants for moist, shady spots in frost-free regions. In colder climates, they should be grown in pots indoors or in a warm greenhouse. They are excellent plants for massing outdoors in the summer. To get the full effect of the colorful leaves, grow several plants of one variety together, either in individual pots or planted in the open ground. If the bulbs are planted right side up, they will produce large leaves. If planted upside down, they will develop

UPPER AND LOWER RIGHT: Two varieties of caladiums show the color range of these fancy-leaved tubers. Too tender for permanent outdoor planting in the North, they're an ideal pot plant for summer display. Here their needs for partial sunshine and moisture are supplied.

CALADIUM

many more—but smaller—leaves. They need a rich, loam soil and plenty of water during the growing season (summer), but are stored almost completely dry during the winter. For pot plants use Basic Potting Mixture with doubled peat. All caladiums do best in partial shade; full sunlight tends to bleach or burn the leaves unless the plants have been carefully hardened and are kept moist. They are grown in full sun in propagation fields in Fla., where they are given special care. Propagate by division of tubers or by seeds, which germinate readily but produce highly variable offspring. Zone 10.

C. argyrites: C. humboldtii.

● **C. bicolor** (*bye*-kol-or). This species grows to about 2 ft., with straight, smooth, fleshy leaf stalks.

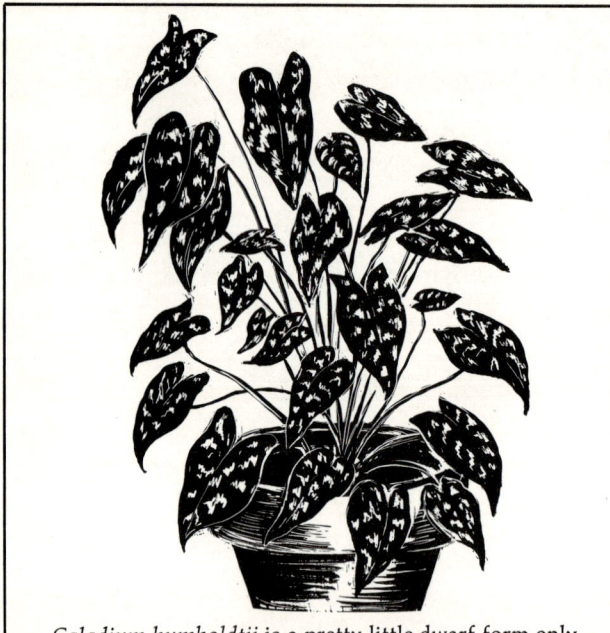

Caladium humboldtii is a pretty little dwarf form only 6 inches high, its fancy leaves green and white.

Long, oval-shaped leaves, deeply notched at the end where the stalk is attached, give the typical arrowhead outline. The leaves are veined, mottled in a great number of patterns and colors, including several shades of green, white, cream, pink, red and purple. An excellent named form is 'Candidum,' which has white leaves with green veins. 'Fannie Munson,' 'Kathleen' and 'Marie Moir' are also exceptionally fine varieties. There are hundreds of others, even a few miniature varieties.

C. esculenta: See *Colocasia esculenta*. (This caladium relative is the popular elephant's ear or taro.)

C. humboldtii (hum-*bolt*-ee-eye). MINIATURE CALADIUM. Green-and-white leaves seldom more than 2 in. long.

Calamint. See *Satureja calamintha*.

Caladium tubers are so happy to grow they'll oblige even if you plant them upside down. They'll have smaller leaves but more of them. Start tubers in flats of peat moss in February or March. When roots show, move them to 4-inch pots. Frequent misting helps develop strong roots. Pot them next in 6-inch pots. At summer's end, decrease watering and store them in their pots in a warm dry place.

Calamondin. See *Citrus mitis*.

CALAMUS (*kal*-am-mus). Palm Family (*Palmae*). A large genus of tropical and subtropical climbing palms. The midrib of the feathery leaves has hooklike spines which enable the plant to climb the tallest tree. Will only grow indoors in this country. Water generously from March to Sept., less the rest of the year. Propagate by seeds and suckers, repot in March in Basic Potting Mixture with added leafmold and sand.

C. rotang (*roh*-tang). This is one of the rattan species; a slender vine with 1½-ft.-long, extremely spiny leaves. Native to India.

CALANDRINIA (kal-an-*drin*-ee-uh). ROCK-PURSLANE. Purslane Family (*Portulacaceae*). These are annuals or perennials, grown mostly as annuals in this country, with alternate fleshy leaves and brightly colored flowers. They are an asset in sunny borders and rock gardens, especially in the West. They vary in size from 6 in. to 1½ ft. Clusters of pink, red, orange or purple flowers bloom all summer. Easily grown from seeds sown where plants are to stand. They like ordinary garden soil and full sun.

C. ciliata (sil-ee-*ay*-tuh). This form grows to 1½ ft.

ABOVE: Fancy-leaved caladiums used as a summer accent display their variegated leaves against a permanent planting.
RIGHT: *Calandrinia ciliata*, variety *menziesii*, is a relative of portulaca and shares its tendency to fold up if the sun is not shining brightly. If you plant it in full sun in the border or rock garden, your reward will be a brilliant display of inch-wide crimson-red flowers all summer long.

and has purplish flowers. More widely grown is the variety *menziesii* (men-zee-see-eye), which is sometimes as tall as 18 in. and has leaves 2 in. long and crimson-red flowers about an inch across. It is effective in borders. Native to western N. America.

C. grandiflora (gran-di-*floh*-ruh). Native to Chile, this is a perennial grown as an annual. About 1 to 3 ft. high, with leaves 6 to 8 in. long and pinkish-purple flowers. It is showy in the border.

C. umbellata (um-bel-*lay*-tuh). Perennial grown as an annual. It is about 6 in. high with narrow leaves growing from the base of the plant. Clusters of dark crimson flowers on trailing stems. It is good in the rock garden. Native to Peru.

CALANTHE (kal-*lanth*-ee). Orchid Family (*Orchidaceae*). Handsome orchids from Asia and Africa, some

CALANTHE

ABOVE LEFT: *Calathea zebrina*, the zebra plant, shows off the velvety green foliage striped with yellowish green that gives it its name. Kept moist, calathea is a fine house plant.
ABOVE: In the same genus, *Calathea picturata argentea* has handsome shimmery silver leaves with wide green bands.

evergreen and some deciduous. All have beautiful flowers in profusion. The broad, plaited leaves are large and the plants need plenty of room. The long-lasting, white, rose or yellow flowers are borne in tight clusters on nodding stems. The sepals and petals are similar, the lip lobed and spurred. These orchids are among the easier ones to grow, provided they are given enough space. As pot plants, they need Basic Potting Mixture, partial shade and perfect drainage. They may be put outdoors in the summer. In the greenhouse, a warm, humid atmosphere is essential. They generally need a rest period after flowering. Propagate by division. Zone 10.

C. furcata (fur-*kay*-tuh). Evergreen, with a rosette of lance-shaped leaves, each up to 2 ft. long. Pure-white flowers to 2 in. across in dense clusters on 3-ft., erect stems.

● **C. vestita** (vess-*tye*-tuh). This is the best-known species, with large, angled pseudobulbs as much as 3 in. long. Broadly lance-shaped leaves to 1½ ft. long and creamy-white flowers 2½ in. across on nodding spikes up to 2½ ft. long. This is a deciduous species, the few leaves dropping before the showy flowers appear. It blooms in late fall and winter in the greenhouse, and does best if divided and repotted annually. From Brazil.

calanthinus (kal-anth-*eye*-nus), **-a, -um.** Basketlike.

July

Water, weeds, and wanderlust are the chief problems; cope with the first two, compromise with the third.
R.B.

CALATHEA (kal-ath-*ee*-uh). Maranta Family (*Marantaceae*). Often listed in catalogs as *Maranta* (which see, also), this is a large genus of handsome foliage plants, mostly from tropical America. The decorative leaves are attractively variegated. The inconspicuous flowers, appearing among the leaves, do not always bloom in cultivation. The plants need high humidity, warmth, moisture, partial shade and well-drained rich loam with added fertilizer to produce the most colorful leaves. They may be grown outdoors in frost-free regions, in a warm greenhouse or as house plants, if a moist atmosphere can be maintained. Propagate by division or leaf cuttings in spring. Zone 10.

C. illustris (il-*luss*-triss). Up to 9 in. high with shining, olive-green leaves about 6 in. long and 5 in. wide, reddish beneath. This is good for terrariums. From Ecuador.

● **C. lietzei** (*leet*-zee-eye). Usually not over 1 ft. high with velvety green leaves to 9 in. long and 2 in. across. The foliage is marked with olive to yellowish green above and is purple-red underneath. Brazil.

● **C. makoyana** (mak-oy-*ay*-nuh). CATHEDRAL WINDOW. PEACOCK PLANT. A handsome plant 2 to 4 ft. high with oblongish, olive-green leaves marked with darker green and red beneath in an incredibly delicate network of veins. Native to Brazil. Unusually fine for bottle gardens while young.

C. medio-picta (meed-ee-oh-*pik*-tuh). Bushy and about 1 ft. high with dark green leaves feathered with white along the midrib.

C. picturata argentea (pik-tew-*ray*-tuh ar-*jen*-tee-uh). Dwarf species, short-stalked silver leaves with a dark green border, maroon beneath.
C. roseo-picta (roh-zee-oh-*pik*-tuh). A dwarf species good for terrariums. Usually not over 8 in. high, with large roundish leaves 9 in. long, 6 in. wide, dark green with a red midrib and red along the edges, purple beneath. Native to Brazil.
C. zebrina (zeb-*rye*-nuh). ZEBRA PLANT. A vigorous and striking plant, growing up to 3 ft., with velvety green leaves, 2 ft. long and 1 ft. wide, banded with yellow- to olive-green and red beneath. The variety *binotii* (bin-*noh*-tee-eye) is slightly larger with darker leaves up to 3 ft. long. Also native to Brazil.

calcareus (kal-*kay*-ree-us), **-a, -um.** Pertaining to lime or growing in calcareous soil. See *calcium*.

CALCEOLARIA (kal-see-oh-*lay*-ree-uh). SLIPPER-WORT. Snapdragon Family (*Scrophulariaceae*). There are both herbaceous and shrubby plants in this group of S. American natives, most of them coming from the area that extends from Mexico to Chile. They are prized for their brilliant slipper-shaped blossoms and are grown in greenhouses and as annuals. Colors range from yellow through orange to red, brown and purple, often spotted.

The annuals grow easily from seed sown in the greenhouse in Feb. and set out in the garden in late May. Seed is very fine and should be sown on top of finely milled sphagnum moss or sifted sandy loam. Water with great care, but do not allow the moss or loam to dry out until the seedlings have started.

The woody types can be propagated by cuttings taken in late summer or early fall or by seed sown indoors in summer.

In the greenhouse, these plants are often infested with red spider mite and white fly. Spray with malathion or diazinon.
C. chelidonioides (kel-id-doh-nee-*oy*-deez). An annual that grows from 1 to 3 ft. tall and has small yellow flowers in summer.
C. crenatiflora (kren-ay-tif-*floh*-ruh). This is the plant grown by florists in greenhouses. A perennial, it has flowers 1 in. long in bright colors ranging from yellow through red to brown, with orange or brown spots. It blooms from early April through May. For greenhouse plants, seed is sown in summer. Zone 10.
C. integrifolia (in-teg-rif-*foh*-lee-uh). A woody plant that grows as much as 6 ft. high, it is used a great

UPPER RIGHT: A calathea, dwarf palm and hoya share a pot and similar needs for moisture and light, make happy pot-mates.
LOWER RIGHT: *Calceolaria multiflora nana*, a form of *C. crenatiflora*, shows the dazzling array of colors in which it blooms.

CALCEOLARIA

deal by gardeners, particularly in Calif. and in Europe. It has ½-in.-long flowers, yellowish to red, unspotted, and is propagated by cuttings as well as seeds. Zone 9.

C. mexicana (mex-ik-*kay*-nuh). A native of Mexico, this annual grows only 1 ft. tall and has yellow flowers ½ in. long in summer.

C. polyrrhiza (pol-lee-*rise*-uh). A dwarf, perennial species with yellow flowers spotted with purple. Hardy as far north as New York if it is given protection. Zone 7.

C. profusa (proh-*few*-suh). An annual, 3 ft. tall, with a profusion of golden-yellow flowers that is an excellent garden plant.

C. scabiosaefolia (skay-bee-*oss*-ee-*fohl*-ee-uh). An annual, to 2 ft., with pale yellow flowers ½ in. long.

calcium (chemical symbol, Ca.). LIME. Chemical element essential to plant life. Also one of the principal soil chemicals involved in the availability of other minerals to plants, by maintaining, or making it possible to establish, the degree of alkalinity in soils that is favorable to good plant growth. Calcium lost by leaching tends to induce an acid imbalance, which may be favorable to some plants (rhododendron and ilex—holly—for example), but unfavorable to others, such as spruce trees and most common vegetable crops. Calcium also has a very important place in the amalgamation of clay particles into the larger units that are essential to the physical texture of a good garden soil. This purely physical function is just as important as the chemical functions calcium performs.

Calcium is always applied to soils, if needed, in the form of compounds derived from a variety of sources. Perhaps the commonest form, and the best for general use, is ground limestone, which yields calcium carbonate ($CaCO_3$). It is relatively slow to act (six months), long-lasting (two to five years), inexpensive and easy to broadcast by hand or in a lawn spreader. Hydrated lime is the fastest, cheapest and probably best for home use, but too expensive for large-scale application, especially in agricultural use. But some forms of the product may be of inferior grade, incapable of doing the job they are supposed to do and sometimes even causing damage to soil or crops. The gardener can usually wait for the slower-acting limestone to work. Lime in any form works best when mixed into the soil by tillage or cultivation.

Calcium is necessary only if the soil pH is below 6 and if the plants in that soil prefer a higher alkaline content. (See *alkalinity*.)

Lime should never be used in soil in which rhododendrons and other members of the Heath Family are growing; near bog plants; in wild-flower gardens (except for those few wild flowers that like an alkaline soil); or around acid-tolerant trees such as oaks and pines. Spruces, however, prefer a strongly alkaline soil.

Calcium is not needed on most lawns, except bluegrass. For most flowers and vegetables, liming is required only if the soil tests below pH 6. The same

BELOW LEFT: Many Calceolarias have distinctive markings. *C. crenatiflora* blooms with bright colors spotted in orange or brown. *C. polyrrhiza* has yellow flowers spotted purple.
BELOW: *C. integrifolia* is a 6-foot woody perennial with unspotted yellow to red blooms.

goes for lawns in decidedly acid soil and for many shrubs and trees.

Before you apply lime anywhere in the garden, analyze the soil; then consider whether your plants require a soil either more or less acid. Assuming that your soil does need lime—and many soils do, especially those not in the limestone regions of the country—apply it sparingly. As a rule, 2 lb. per 100 sq. ft. are adequate, unless a soil test calls for more. Application should be made once a year at most. Apply it in early spring a week before or after—but not at the same time as—you apply manure or a commercial fertilizer.

Lime should never be applied to a compost heap or to manure, lest it cause rapid loss of nitrogen. For further information on soil modification see article under *soils*.

calcium arsenate. A chemical used as an insecticide and, rarely, to kill crabgrass seedlings as they germinate. See article on Pests and Diseases.

calcium cyanamide. A soil sterilant that, upon decomposition, supplies nitrogen to the soil. See article on Pests and Diseases.

calcium nitrate. Chemical used in some fertilizers to supply nitrogen. See *soils*.

Calcutta bamboo. See *Dendrocalamus strictus*.

CALENDULA (kal-*lend*-yew-luh). Composite Family (*Compositae*). These are the "marigolds" of Shakespeare and the ancient herbals, now called pot-marigold to distinguish from the later-introduced *Tagetes*. Annuals and perennials native to the Mediterranean region. The most popular species, described below, is a favorite garden annual, long grown as a herb for its petals, used to flavor and color puddings and cakes. It is excellent in the border for constant bloom all summer and in the herb garden for a brilliant spot of color. On the West Coast and along the Gulf Coast it flowers in winter and early spring. It is hardy enough to withstand light frosts and grows readily from seeds planted early in spring in ordinary garden soil, but does poorly where summers are hot. It needs full sun. In all but the coldest sections it will self-sow year after year, although seedlings of named varieties may not come true a second season. It makes an attractive plant for a cool greenhouse (45° to 55°). Provide soil of equal parts of garden loam, peat moss and sand, and keep it evenly moist. Use a fertilizer low in nitrogen every two or three weeks.

● **C. officinalis** (off-iss-in-*nay*-liss). POT-MARIGOLD. Grows 1 to 2 ft. high, with alternate, blue-green leaves, 3 in. long, on sturdy stalks. Dark orange flowers up to 4 in. Sow seeds in July for Oct. to Jan. bloom; sow in Oct. for bloom in Feb. through the summer; sow in Jan. for bloom starting in May. There are named hybrids in many shades, from palest yellow to darkest orange. Blossoms are long-lasting when cut. *Calendula officinalis* yields petals which in dried form were once used as a potherb to flavor puddings, cakes, salads and meat dishes. Bread pudding can be flavored with two tablespoons of fresh-plucked petals, and one tablespoonful makes a nice addition to cream-cheese dips.

calendulaceus (kal-en-dew-*lay*-see-us), -a, -um. Brilliant yellow-orange (calendulalike).

Calico-bush. See *Kalmia latifolia*.

Calico-flower. See *Aristolochia elegans*.

California bayberry. See *Myrica californica*.

California bleeding-heart. See *Dicentra formosa*.

California bluebell. See *Phacelia whitlavia*.

California buckeye. See *Aesculus californica*.

California fawn-lily. See *Erythronium californicum*.

California fuchsia. See *Zauschneria californica*.

California golden-fern. See *Pityrogramma triangularis*.

BELOW: *Calendula officinalis* is the classic pot-marigold of literature. It is a member of the Daisy Family, but, unlike the daisies it is not a good plant for areas where summers are hot. A bonus: The petals can be used to flavor food.

California laurel. See *Umbellularia californica*.

California live oak. See *Quercus agrifolia*.

California nutmeg. See *Torreya californica*.

California peppertree. See *Schinus molle*.

California pitcher-plant. See *Darlingtonia californica*.

California poppy. See *Eschscholtzia californica*; also *Papaver californicum*.

California privet. See *Ligustrum ovalifolium*.

California redbud. See *Cercis occidentalis*.

California rhododendron. See *Rhododendron macrophyllum*.

California tree-poppy. Also called matilija-poppy and canyon-poppy. See DENDROMECON; also ROMNEYA.

CALLA (*kal*-luh). WILD CALLA. WATER-ARUM. Arum Family (*Araceae*). This is a water-loving plant, which looks somewhat like the tropical calla-lily (*Zantedeschia*) and is closely related to the Jack-in-the-pulpit. It grows from a slender horizontal creeping rhizome and has large, glossy long-stemmed green leaves and clusters of small green flowers on spikes that are protected by large white bracts or spathes. It makes an interesting accent at the edge of pools and bog gardens, requires full sun or light shade and a soil that is rich and acid and constantly moist. Propagate by division or seeds. Zone 2.

C. palustris (pal-*lust*-riss). This is the only species in the genus. Its leaves are heart-shaped, to 6 in. long, and grow on stems that are 5 to 10 in. high. The flowers and the broad white spathes appear in May and are followed by clusters of red berries in late summer. *Calla palustris* is on the preservation lists of Conn., Washington, D.C., Me. and R.I. and is protected, that is, not to be picked or dug up.

Calla-lily. See ZANTEDESCHIA.

CALLIANDRA (kal-lee-*and*-ruh). Pea Family (*Leguminosae*). A large genus of tropical evergreen shrubs and trees. The compound, fernlike leaves have numerous leaflets. There are handsome flowers in heads or clusters, with long, conspicuous, silky stamens. Similar to *Acacia* in appearance and culture.

C. haematocephala (hee-mat-oh-*ceph*-uh-luh). POWDER PUFF. Small tree to 30 ft. with conspicuous, showy

OPPOSITE: *Calliandra haematocephala*, sometimes called C. inaequilatera, is a small South American tree with large puffy flower heads, dark green fernlike leaves and flat pods. It is called the powder puff and looks very much like an acacia. It makes an attractive greenhouse tub plant.
BELOW: *Calla palustris* is the diminutive wild calla native to North America bogs and swamps. Although it is a delightful plant for a spot at the edge of a natural pool, it is protected in many states, and so may not be moved from its natural setting.

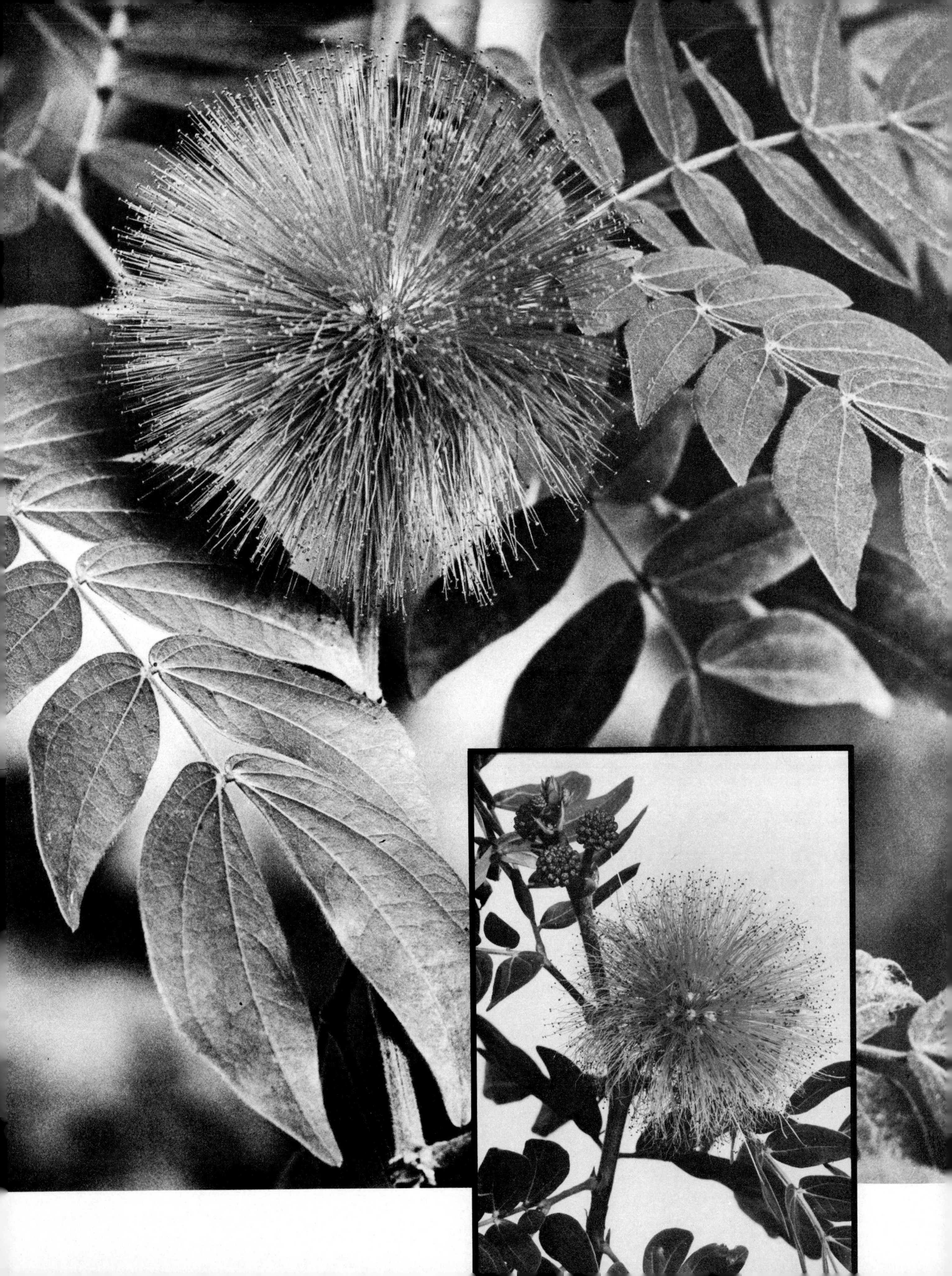

CALLIANDRA

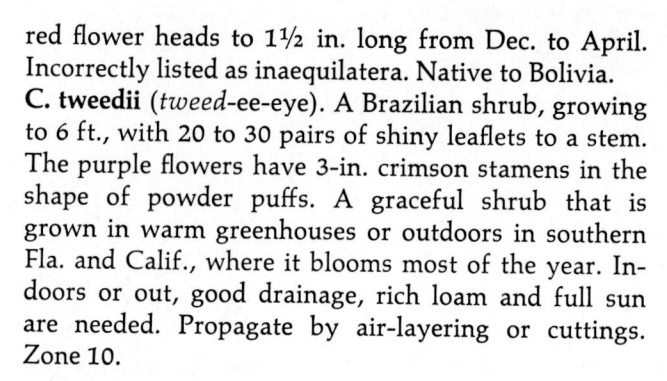

red flower heads to 1½ in. long from Dec. to April. Incorrectly listed as inaequilatera. Native to Bolivia.

C. tweedii (*tweed*-ee-eye). A Brazilian shrub, growing to 6 ft., with 20 to 30 pairs of shiny leaflets to a stem. The purple flowers have 3-in. crimson stamens in the shape of powder puffs. A graceful shrub that is grown in warm greenhouses or outdoors in southern Fla. and Calif., where it blooms most of the year. Indoors or out, good drainage, rich loam and full sun are needed. Propagate by air-layering or cuttings. Zone 10.

CALLICARPA (kal-lik-*karp*-uh). BEAUTY-BERRY. Verbena Family (*Verbenaceae*). Deciduous shrubs or small trees of tropical and temperate regions of N. and S. America, Asia and Australia. Opposite leaves and small pink, blue or white flowers in clusters.

UPPER LEFT: A close-up of the "powder puffs" of *Calliandra tweedii*, a small purple variety that blooms most of the year.
LOWER LEFT: Another unusual tree suitable for growing as a tub plant in the cool greenhouse or outdoors in southern Florida and California is *Callistemon*, the bottle-brush tree.
BELOW: The bottle-brush flower of *C. lanceolatus*.
OPPOSITE: *Callicarpa bodinieri*, variety *giraldii*, beauty-berry.

These plants are grown chiefly for the uniquely colorful berries that appear in the fall and last after the leaves have fallen. Stems may sometimes be winter-killed in the North, but new growth from the base will flower and fruit the same year. Sun and rich soil are needed. Propagate by seeds, layers or cuttings. May be grown also in airy, bright greenhouse.

C. americana (am-eh-rik-*kay*-nuh). To about 6 ft. tall, with leaves 4 to 6 in. long. It has small bluish flowers and a profusion of bright purple berries in fall. There is also a white form, *lactea* (lak-tee-uh), which is especially effective when planted with the purple.

C. bodinieri (bod-i-*neer*-eye). Shrub 6 to 10 ft. high, with toothed leaves 5 in. long. It has dense clusters of pale pink flowers in summer and violet fruit. Native of China. *Giraldii* (jir-*ald*-ee-eye) is the variety usually encountered in cultivation. Zone 7.

● **C. dichotoma** (dye-*kot*-oh-muh). This is the most attractive and the hardiest species, growing to 4 ft., leaves to 3 in. long, toothed in the upper half. Pink flowers are followed by clusters of lilac-violet fruits, for which the species has considerable garden merit in late summer. Zone 6.

C. japonica (jap-*pon*-ik-uh). Grows to 4 ft., leaves to 5 in. long and finely toothed, with pink to white flowers in Aug., followed by violet berries. Zone 7.

Calliopsis. See *Coreopsis tinctoria*.

CALLIRHOE (kal-*lihr*-oh-ee). Poppy-mallow. Mallow Family (*Malvaceae*). A native N. American genus of herbaceous annual and perennial plants that thrive in dry, sunny positions and give a long season of bright bloom. Propagate by seeds sown in ordinary soil as soon as the ground is warm; also by root division in spring or fall. Seeds of the perennial kinds should be planted where plants are to remain.

C. digitata (dij-it-*tay*-tuh). A perennial, growing 1 to 1½ ft. high, with alternate leaves that are irregularly and deeply lobed, mostly from the base. Red to purple flowers, 1½ to 2 in. across, bloom from May to July. Native to Ark. and Tex., this makes an attractive plant for the border. Zone 6.

C. involucrata (in-vol-yew-*kray*-tuh). A sprawling perennial, native from Minn. southward. Grows about 1 ft. high, with rounded, lobed leaves and crimson flowers that remain in bloom for three months. Good for rock gardens if the drainage is adequate, and also good in the open wild garden. Best raised from seeds where plants are to remain, since depth of rootstalk makes transplanting or dividing of mature plants difficult. Zone 4.

C. papaver (pap-*av*-er). A perennial, 3 ft. high, with violet-red flowers 2 in. across. Native from Fla. to Tex.

C. pedata (ped-*day*-tuh). An annual, to 3 ft. high, leaves lobed and parted. The flowers, in panicles, vary in color from reddish purple to lavender. Native from Mo. to Tex.

C. triangulata (trye-an-gew-*lay*-tuh). Perennial, to 3 ft. or more. Leaves are lobed, 2 in. long. Flowers are a dark purple. Native from N.C. to Tex. and north to Minn.

CALLISTEMON (kal-liss-*steem*-on). Bottle-brush. Myrtle Family (*Myrtaceae*). Showy, fast-growing evergreen shrubs or small trees of Australia, with narrow, alternate leaves and handsome flowers. Grown indoors and in cool greenhouses, and outdoors in Fla. and southern Calif., where they bloom in spring and summer. They are not particular as to soil (indoors, use Basic Potting Mixture), and are tolerant of dry conditions. Propagate by seeds or cuttings. Zone 9.

C. citrinus: *C. lanceolatus.*

C. lanceolatus (lan-see-oh-*lay*-tus). Lemon bottle-brush. Often listed in catalogs as *C. citrinus*. Grows to 30 ft. high, with lance-shaped leaves 3 in. long. The flowers have tufted, bright red stamens in rather loose clusters to 4 in. long.

C. rigidus (*rij*-id-us). The narrow, lanceolate leaves grow to 5 in. long. Flowers, with red stamens, in dense spikes.

C. speciosus (spee-see-*oh*-sus). Sometimes reaches 40

The Massagno strain of cactus-flowered annual asters, a hybrid form of *Callistephus chinensis*, was bred in Germany. 'Rose Star,' ABOVE, is brilliant pure rose-pink. Other named cultivars with the same needlelike petals, all splendid for cutting as well as garden display, include 'Capriole,' spotless pure white; 'Firebird,' intense ruby red; 'Starry Sky,' glowing golden-yellow; and 'Silver Lining,' azure-blue.

ft., leaves to 4 in. long. This is the showiest species when in bloom; the dark red stamens are tipped with golden anthers, in dense spikes to 5 in. long.
C. viminalis (vim-in-*ay*-liss). A tree of pendulous form, with oblong leaves and flowers with red stamens in dense spikes. To 40 ft.

CALLISTEPHUS (kal-*liss*-tef-us). CHINA ASTER. Composite Family (Compositae). The only species is a popular annual from Asia, with a great range of color, style and size. The varying shades of the flowers—from white through pink and red to violet-blue and purple—combined with its long blooming season and lasting qualities when cut, make it a universal favorite. For early bloom, start seeds indoors in early March and plant out as soon as possible. Outdoors, when the ground has warmed up, sow seeds in well-drained garden loam dug to a spade's depth and enriched with humus and artificial fertilizer, as well as lime. Full sun is necessary. Very appealing in borders of annuals, to fill in bare spots in perennial borders and in the cutting garden. Although not a true aster, this plant is beset by the same diseases: mosaic and stem rot, which cause wilt and rust. However, seedsmen have bred wilt-resistant varieties, which the gardener should try to buy. Avoid planting in successive years in the same soil. Keep the ground clean of weeds and the plants well watered and sprayed against pests.
● **C. chinensis** (chin-*nen*-siss). Grows 1 to 2½ ft., with alternate leaves. The blossoms vary from showy, flat-rayed types with golden-yellow centers to every form of double, stiff or fluffy, with flat or quilled petals (with tubular rays), and in almost all shades. There is also much variety in the growing habit, from upright through branching and spreading forms. Literally scores of named varieties are offered in catalogs. Often blooms from summer to frost, but "stars" among the annuals for flowers in late summer. The more you cut, the more they'll bloom.

Space Saver

Any pot plant will bloom sooner and more abundantly if it is crowded a little. And given a little fertilizer (preferably in liquid form), almost any pot plant will grow successfully in a quarter as much earth as it might have in a pot of its own. *R.B.*

CALLITRIS (kal-*lye*-triss). CYPRESS-PINE. Cypress Family (*Cupressaceae*). Evergreen trees of Australia, hardy only in warm, dry regions. They are rapid-growing and are planted extensively for their fine foliage in southern Calif. and, less commonly, in Fla. Propagate by seeds.
C. preissii (*price*-ee-eye). Pyramidal tree to 70 ft., but often much less when trained for use as a hedge. Of dense habit, with dark green, scalelike foliage and cones about 1 in. across. It is reminiscent of the red cedar. Zone 10.
C. robusta: *C. preissii.*

callosus (kal-*loh*-sus), **-a, -um.** Thick-skinned; having callosities or calluses.

CALLUNA (kal-*lew*-nuh). HEATHER. Heath Family (*Ericaceae*). There is only one species, from Europe, a popular and attractive evergreen shrub. Effective in mass plantings on sandy, sunny slopes. May be sheared in spring. Propagate by cuttings. Zone 5.
● **C. vulgaris** (vul-*gay*-riss). Widely grown, hardy shrub to 3 ft., of spreading habit, with tiny, overlapping scalelike leaves. A profusion of small, nodding

CALLUNA

UPPER LEFT: Annual aster—*Callistephus*—variety 'Waldersee' produces small single flowers with intense yellow centers and is one of the best for cutting. The annual asters are superb flowers for the late summer and early fall garden, as they will go on blooming when most other flowers in the border have died down. Although modern disease-resistant strains have eliminated most problems formerly associated with these annuals, it is a good idea to avoid planting them in the same spot on successive years.
LOWER LEFT: 'Ostrich Plume' china aster, which grows to 18 inches, has graceful well-branched growth. Asters will succeed in the cool greenhouse. From sowings made from September to February, flowers can be provided through most of the winter months.
ABOVE: A group of dwarf chrysanthemum-flowered china asters shows a wide range of good colors. Plants may be raised from seed sown out of doors. They may also be sown indoors and transplanted to their place in the border when they are a few inches tall.

Calluna vulgaris is the species from which all the heathers pictured on this page were developed. All of them make long-lasting cut flowers and some dry nicely.
Upper left: 'H. E. Beale' is a double pink variety lavishly endowed with tiny bells. Above: 'C. W. Nix,' a vibrant rosy purple. Lower left: *Alba plena* is a double white variety. Below: 'J. H. Hamilton' is dwarf and rose-pink.

rose-pink to purplish flowers, in dense clusters 10 in. long, bloom in late summer. Numerous varieties, some with English, some with Latinized names, are available, with white to crimson flowers. They do best in lean, porous, acid soil.

From this species many forms have been developed, including *alba*, white-flowered; *hammondii*, with white flowers and bright green leaves; *searlei*, feathery foliage and white flowers; *alportii*, pinkish-red flowers; *coccinea*, a small form with red flowers; *carnea*, pink; *cuprea*, bronzy foliage; and *hirsuta*, which forms a grayish spreading plant.

CALLUNA VARIETIES IN CULTIVATION

VARIETY	COLOR	IN BLOOM	SIZE
'Aurea'	Purple	Aug.–Oct.	18 in.
'County Wicklow'	Pink	"	"
'Cuprea'	Purple	"	12 in.
'Dainty Bess'	Lavender	Aug.–Sept.	4 in.
'J. H. Hamilton'	Rose-pink	Aug.–Oct.	12 in.
'Mair's White'	White	July–Sept.	24 in.
'Mrs. Pat'	Light purple	"	8 in.
'Mrs. Ronald Gray'	Red	"	3 in.
'Nana Compacta'	Pink	"	5 in.
'Plena Multiplex'	Pink	Aug.–Oct.	18 in.
'Roma'	Dark Pink	"	9 in.
'Searlei Aurea'	White	"	12 in.
'Tomentosa'	Light purple	July–Sept.	10 in.

callus. The repair tissue that forms over a plant stem or root that has been cut. In the rooting of most forms of cuttings, it is from the callus tissue that new roots emerge. See *propagation*.

CALOCEDRUS (kal-oh-*seed*-rus). Pine Family (*Pinaceae*). *Calocedrus decurrens* (dee-*ker*-renz), formerly listed as Libocedrus decurrens, is a tree of columnar or narrow, pyramidal form to 130 ft. or more. Cinnamon-red, scaly bark. Shiny, dark green leaves, closely pressed to the stem. Light reddish-brown cones to 1 in. long. A tree of remarkably stately appearance where it can be given room; hardy in southern New England. Zone 6.

CALOCEPHALUS (kal-oh-*seff*-al-us). Composite Family (*Compositae*). Annuals from Australia or small shrubs with woolly alternate leaves and silvery inflorescence.
C. brownii (*brown*-ee-eye). This is the only species grown in this country. It is used as a low border plant in Calif. A 1-ft.-high plant, the small leaves have white woolly hairs. Propagate by cuttings in late summer. Zone 9.

CALOCHORTUS (kal-oh-*kort*-us). Mariposa-lily. Globe tulip. Fairy lantern. Lily Family (*Liliaceae*).

Cormous plants from the western U.S. Each corm sends up, in early spring, a stem with slender leaves somewhat like those of a trout-lily, but more slender. The showy yellow, white, pink, lavender or purple flowers, usually with a streak of darker coloring at the center, may be borne singly or in clusters at the top of the stem or in the leaf axils. These plants thrive in poor, light, sandy soil, in full sun or light shade and with a good supply of moisture during the period of growth, but must be completely dry during the summer rest period. Outside its native range, it does best if planted in the fall just before frost; and then, after its spring growth and bloom, it should be dug and the bulbs stored in a dry place through the summer. Occasionally these bulbs are grown in pots in a cool greenhouse. Propagate by bulb offsets or by seeds. If alternate freezing and thawing can be prevented by appropriate mulching, these plants are hardy to Zone 6. All native species of *Calochortus* (Mariposa-tulip of Calif. and Mariposa-lily of N. Mex.), are on the preservation lists and are protected, that is, not to be picked or dug up. Sego Lily, *Calochortus nuttallii*, was declared the official flower of Utah in 1911.

Calocephalus brownii is a silvery, woolly low-growing shrub, generally known as Leucophyta brownii, that is used in California and related climates as a border plant. A native of Australia, it grows in most soils and is about one foot tall.

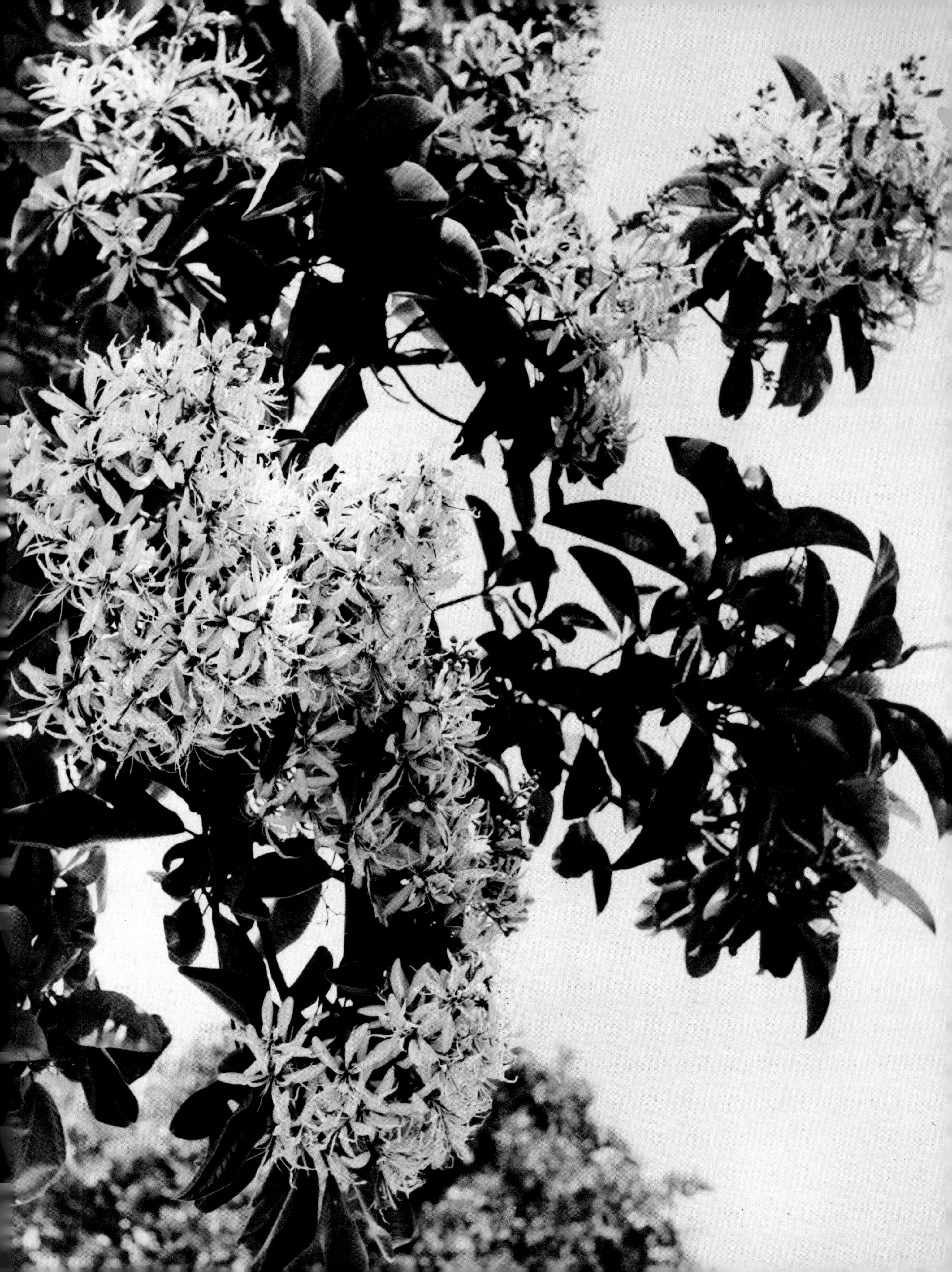

● **C. albus** (*al*-bus). Grows 1 to 2 ft. high, with bluish-green leaves. The pearly white flowers, about 1¼ in. across, with a slight purple tint at the base of the petals, are borne in the leaf axils, with two or three forming a cluster at the top of each stem. Since the petals do not open out, the flowers give the charming effect of gracefully nodding globes.

C. amabilis (am-*mab*-il-iss). GOLDEN GLOBE TULIP. Similar to *A. albus*, except that the nodding flowers are bright yellow.

C. apiculatus (ap-pik-yew-*lay*-tus). GIANT STAR GLOBE TULIP. Grows 12 to 18 in. high, with narrow leaves up to 1 ft. long. Wide-open, white or pale yellow flowers, several from each bulb.

C. caeruleus (see-*rew*-lee-us). CAT'S EARS. Narrow leaves, about 6 in. long, and wide-open, blue flowers, hairy inside, held upright on slender stalks up to 6 in. high.

● **C. clavatus** (klav-*vay*-tus). Large, tulip-shaped yellow flowers with reddish veins on branching 3-ft. stems. One of the most attractive of all.

C. gunnisonii (gun-nis-*soh*-nee-eye). Grasslike foliage and flower stems up to 1½ ft. high, bearing upright, white or pale blue flowers, about 2 in. across, banded toward the center with yellow-green and purple.

C. kennedyi (ken-*ned*-ee-eye). A desert species growing from a small oval bulb with long, narrow leaves. The flowers grow in umbels and may be red-orange to vermilion, purple-spotted at the center. Beautiful natives of southern Calif., Nev. and Ariz. but difficult to grow.

C. macrocarpus (mak-roh-*karp*-us). GREEN-BANDED MARIPOSA-LILY. Narrow, pointed leaves and a flower stalk up to 2 ft. high. Light purple flowers, up to 2 in. across, with narrow, pointed petals, with a green streak down the midrib of each.

C. maweanus (maw-wee-*ay*-nus). Grasslike leaves with flower stems 6 to 8 in. high, sometimes branched but usually bearing a single white flower with a purple center, hairy inside. The variety *purpurascens* (pur-pew-*rass*-senz) is larger with a dark purple center, and *roseus* (roh-*zee*-us) is pink-centered.

● **C. venustus** (ven-*nuss*-tus). WHITE MARIPOSA-LILY. WHITE MARIPOSA-TULIP. White or pale bluish 4-in. flowers with a reddish "eye" at the top of each petal and a brown band at the center, on stems 10 in. or more high. Varieties include *citrinus* (sit-*rye*-nus), dark yellow with black "eye" and *oculatus* (ok-yew-*lay*-tus) cream-white with purple tint and dark "eye."

CALODENDRUM (kal-oh-*den*-drum). CAPE-CHESTNUT. Rue Family (*Rutaceae*). There is only one species, an evergreen tree from S. Africa, grown in warm regions such as southern Fla. for its dark green foliage and colorful bloom. It needs good drainage. Water thoroughly and allow to dry out before the next watering. Propagate by seeds or cuttings. Zone 10.

C. capense (kap-*pen*-see). Grows 30 to 60 ft. high, with opposite or whorled leaves 5 in. long. It has showy, rose-lilac flowers 1½ in. long, in large clusters. The nearly round, warty fruits have shiny black seeds.

CALONYCTION (kal-oh-*nik*-tee-on). MOONFLOWER. Morning-glory Family (*Convolvulaceae*). These night-blooming relatives of the morning-glory perfume the garden as they bloom after dark. Tender, perennial, twining vines from tropical America, they are usually treated as annuals in all but the warmest regions of the U.S. The seeds are slow to germinate and should be notched or soaked overnight in water of room temperature. Seeds started indoors in March, two or three in a 5-in. clay pot, can be set outdoors when all danger of frost is past. Full sun, light, rich, porous soil, a sheltered spot and plenty of water are needed. The closed flowers, if cut late in the day, will open in

OPPOSITE: Calodendrum, the cape-chestnut comes from South Africa. It will grow only in the warmest sections of southern Florida and California, where it produces breathtaking balls of rosy-lilac blossoms.

RIGHT: *Calochortus kennedyi* is the modest desert mariposa-lily, its dark-centered vermilion flowers here entwined with the fairylike ones of a clump of *Eriophyllum wallacei*.

the evening and are effective for decoration. They also make a pleasant choice for the cool greenhouse, lending shade in the daytime, if trained along the roof.

C. aculeatum (ak-kew-lee-*ay*-tum). Large-leaved, somewhat prickly vine, with beautiful large white morning-glorylike flowers, 5 to 6 in. across and as long. These fragrant and decorative blossoms open while you watch at dusk. Very abundant in bloom and fast-growing, covering as much as 20 ft. in a few months. The large, heart-shaped leaves make a substantial screen on trellises. Zone 9.

CALOPOGON (kal-oh-*poh*-gon). Orchid Family (*Orchidaceae*). Delicate, dainty orchids found in marshes and bogs of N. America. They have long, grasslike leaves and clusters of flowers in late spring. Like all orchids, they are difficult to transplant, but they may be transferred to bog or wild garden if given rich, moist, acid soil and shade. Propagate by division.
C. pulchellus (pul-*kell*-us). GRASS-PINK ORCHID. Tuberous-rooted plant to about 15 in., with a slender stem that bears a single bright green leaf to 8 in. long. The delicately fragrant, rose or purplish flowers, with fringed lip, appear in June. Also called *C. tuberosa*, the grass-pink orchid is on the preservation list of Conn., Me., Md., Mass., Mich., N.H., N.J., Vt. and W. Va. and is protected, that is, not to be picked or dug up. Zone 5.

CALTHA (*kalth*-uh). Buttercup Family (*Ranunculaceae*). Low-growing, moisture-loving, hardy plants found through the North Temperate Zone. Clusters of smooth, round or heart-shaped leaves spring directly from the root, which grows submerged in a swamp, but will succeed in rich garden soil with plenty of moisture, in sun or partial shade. The flowers, which may be white, yellow or pink, appear in clusters in spring and early summer on stems from 5 to 18 in. high. Propagate by root division or seeds in early spring. Marsh-marigold, *Caltha palustris*, is on the preservation list of Conn., Washington, D.C., Iowa, Md., Mich., N.J., Ohio, R.I. and S. Car. and is protected, that is, not to be picked or dug up.

LEFT: *Calopogon pulchellus*, the grass-pink orchid, is one of the aristocratic wildlings native to our North America bogs and marshes. Growing from a tuber, it sends up erect stems with two or three lovely fragrant rose-purple flowers A native treasure, it has been thoughtlessly picked and dug up so often that it is in danger of becoming extinct.
OPPOSITE: *Calonyction aculeatum* is the fragrant night-blooming climber appropriately called moonflower. Not surprisingly it is related to the morning glory and is sometimes called Ipomoea bona-nox. To protect its large white blossoms, the vine has cleverly armed itself with prickles.

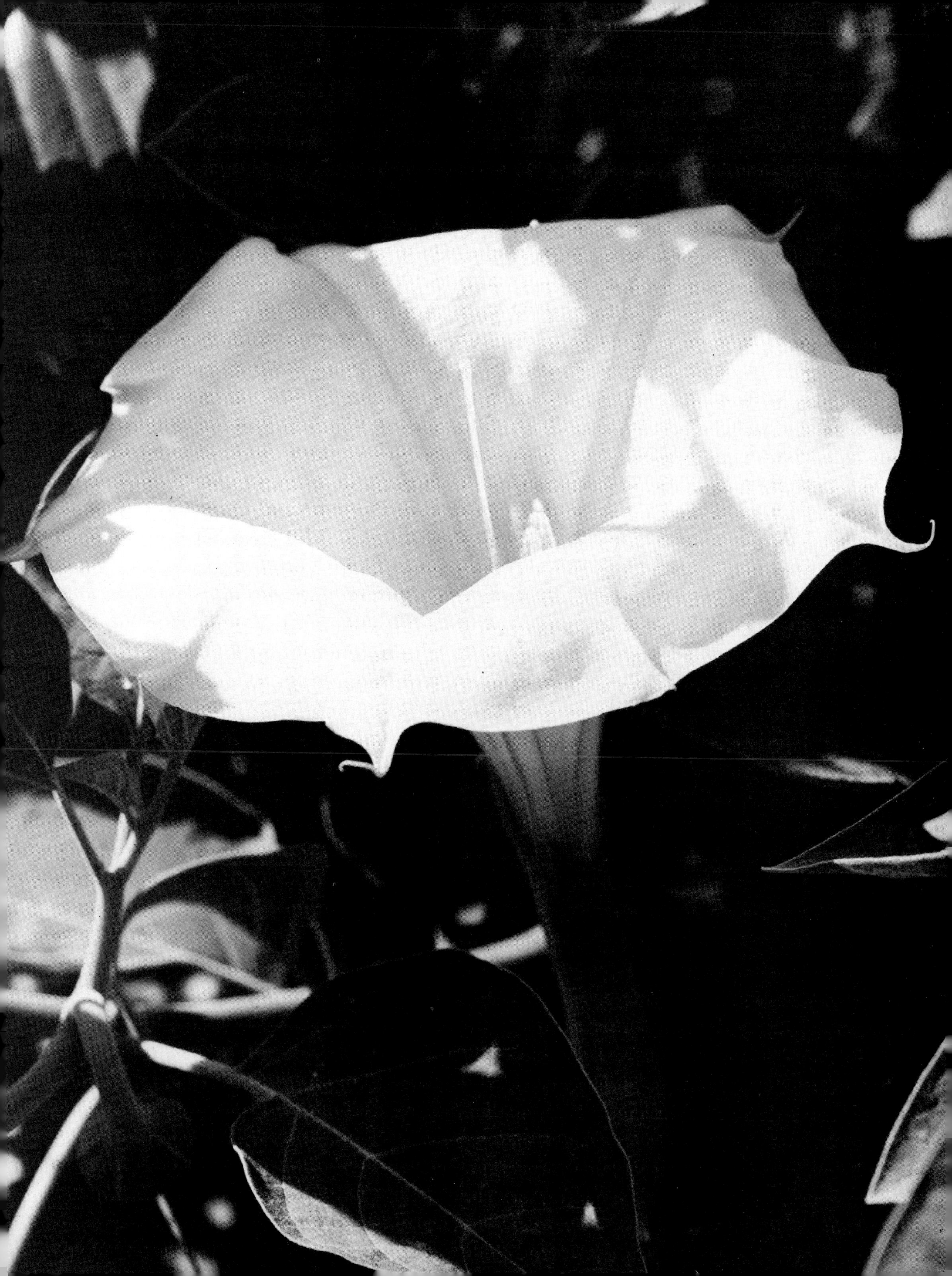

ABOVE: *Caltha palustris* is the marsh-marigold whose sunny golden-yellow flowers grow in plentiful profusion throughout North America. The cheerful blooms appear in April and May, nodding above heart-shaped glossy green leaves. Don't move it to your bog garden before checking a protection list.

C. biflora (bye-*floh*-ruh). The white flowers on this foot-high plant are up to 2 in. across. They bloom from June to Aug. and are fine for the bog garden.

C. leptosepala (lep-toh-*see*-pal-uh). The 6-in.-long oval-shaped leaves grow in clumps. Flowers are white tinged with blue, an inch across. It blooms all summer.

● **C. palustris** (pal-*lust*-riss). MARSH-MARIGOLD. COW-SLIP. This perennial, the most commonly grown species, is a native wild flower of early spring, the "golden Marybud" of Shakespeare's sonnet, and the delight of all who watch for its golden display in late April and early May along brooks and in swampy, wet places. It grows from 1 to 3 ft. high, and has large, heart-shaped leaves of dark, shining green, 3 to 3½ in. across. Successful in the border if there is plenty of water, especially in spring and early summer. The leaves disappear by late June. *C. monstrosa-pleno* (mon-*stroh*-suh-*plee*-noh) is a double variety. Zone 3.

calyc-. Prefix meaning calyx-bearing.

Calycanthaceae. See Calycanthus Family.

CALYCANTHUS (kal-ik-*kanth*-us). SWEETSHRUB. Calycanthus Family (*Calycanthaceae*). Fragrant, deciduous shrubs of N. America, with opposite, glossy but rather coarse leaves, turning yellow in autumn. These plants will grow in ordinary garden soil in sun or shade, but do best in rich, well-drained soil. Of chief interest for aromatic leaves and spicy flowers in spring. The fruits are dark brown capsules 2 in. or more long. Propagate by seeds, layers or division. Zone 6.

C. fertilis (*fer*-til-iss). PALE SWEETSHRUB. A bushy shrub 4 to 10 ft. high, with oblong leaves to 6 in. long, whitish beneath. Large, reddish-brown flowers to 2 in. across. Zone 5.

C. floridus (*flor*-id-us). CAROLINA ALLSPICE. A densely hairy shrub, 4 to 8 ft. high, with dark green elliptic leaves to 5 in. long, pale beneath. Reddish-brown flowers to 2 in. across; this is the most fragrant and therefore the most commonly grown species—and also the hardiest. Zone 4.

C. occidentalis (ok-sid-en-*tay*-liss). This species is a more open form and grows to 12 ft. tall. Leaves are 8 in. long; flowers are brownish. Native to Calif. Called sweetshrub in that state, it is on the preservation list there and is protected, that is, not to be picked or dug up.

Calycanthus Family (*Calycanthaceae*). *Calycanthus* and *Chimonanthus*, the two genera in cultivation, include ornamental, deciduous, aromatic shrubs native to N. America (*Calycanthus*) and Asia (*Chimonanthus*).

CALYPSO (kal-*lips*-oh). Orchid Family (*Orchidaceae*). The only species is a terrestrial bog orchid, native not only in America but Europe and Asia as well. It is strictly a wild-flower fancier's plant. Very difficult to transport or establish, it requires shade, cool temperatures and moist, acid soil. *Calypso bulbosa* is on the preservation list of Ore. and is protected, that is, not to be picked or dug up. The plant is protected in Calif., Maine, Mass., N.H. and Vt.; *bulbosa* is called fairy-slipper in Colo., and is on that state's protected list. Zone 4.

C. bulbosa (bulb-*oh*-suh). A single leaf, oval in shape, to 2½ in. wide, emerges at the base of a naked stalk, 6 to 9 in. high, bearing a solitary, variegated purple, pink and yellow flower with a pouchlike lip.

calyx. The small petal-like or leaflike sepal that surrounds the true petals of a flower. The calyx is commonly green, but in some flowers such as the lily or the anemone, it assumes the same color as the flower. It may consist of either separate or united segments. For further information on the component parts of flowers, see *flower*.

Camass. See CAMASSIA.

CAMASSIA (kam-*mass*-ee-uh). Camass. Lily Family (*Liliaceae*). Graceful, bulbous plants from the northwestern U.S. A cluster of long, narrow, tapering leaves grows directly from the bulb, with the flower stalk rising from the center in late spring. The showy

UPPER RIGHT: *Camassia leichtlinii*, or camass, is a hardy plant of the Lily Family native to western North America. Its fragile creamy-white flowers and gray-green leaves make it a prime garden selection.
LOWER RIGHT: *C. cusickii* stages a prodigious display, each three-foot spike having as many as 300 pale blue, long-lasting flowers. The bulb was a source of food for Indians.

ABOVE: *Camassia scilloides* raises its dainty blue and white stars on stalks 2 feet tall. Excellent for the wild garden.

flowers, with long, narrow, widely separated petals, are mostly blue or lavender, but are white or pale yellow in some varieties. Camassias are excellent plants for late spring bloom in the border or wild garden and are particularly effective at the edge of a pond or bog. Plant bulbs in the fall 4 in. deep and 9 in. apart in any good garden soil (sandy loam is best). Ample moisture is necessary during the growing season, but they should be dry during the summer dormancy period. Being flooded in winter seems to be the best protection for the bulbs. They do best in full sun, but will tolerate partial shade. Most are extremely poisonous. Propagate by division or seeds. Hardy to Zone 5.

C. cusickii (koo-*sik*-ee-eye). The large bulb sends up a heavy cluster of bluish-green leaves up to 16 in. long and 1½ in. wide. The flower spike grows as high as 3 ft., with from 50 to 300 pale blue flowers, each about 1 in. long, which remain open over a long period of time.

C. esculenta: *C. scilloides*.

C. howellii (how-*wel*-ee-eye). Sparse, narrow leaves about 1 ft. long. The flower spike grows up to 2 ft. tall, with a large number of small, pale blue flowers opening late in the day.

● **C. leichtlinii** (lykt-*lin*-ee-eye). Grows up to 2 ft. with narrow leaves up to 3 ft. long. Many large flowers in shades of dark purple through pale blue to white and cream. Perhaps the most satisfactory species for the open border. Native from British Columbia to Calif.

C. quamash (*kwah*-mash). The Indians used to eat the bulbs of this species. It grows up to 3 ft., with broad leaves ¾ in. across. Dark to pale blue flowers, about 2 in. across, on stalks 1 ft. long.

C. scilloides (sil-*loy*-deez). WILD HYACINTH. Often listed in catalogs as C. esculenta. Grows to 2 ft., with narrow, grasslike leaves and a flower stalk that has eight to ten pale blue or white flowers. It blooms in May and June. The bulbs can be transplanted to well-drained soil in late summer or fall. Excellent for the wild-flower garden. This species is on the preservation lists of Ky., Va. and Tex.

cambium. The soft, formative, embryonic tissue between the bark of a tree and the inner wood. The cambium forms a new layer of wood and bark each year. The phloem (bark) and xylem (wood) cells, by means of which a woody plant lives and grows, are formed in the cambium layer. With certain exceptions, any complete horizontal severance of the cambium layer will result in the death of the tree or member affected. Damage that does not prevent the vertical flow within the cambium layer is seldom fatal, however grievous it may seem.

Photographers, Volume 3

MOST COLOR ILLUSTRATIONS FROM I. G. A.

MORLEY BAER
RALPH BAILEY
PAT BRINDLEY
COLONIAL WILLIAMSBURG
RALPH D. CORNELL
GEORGE DE GENNARO STUDIO
MARJORIE J. DIETZ
J. E. DOWNWARD
T. H. EVERETT
CHARLES MARDEN FITCH
FLOWER AND GARDEN

PAUL E. GENEREUX
GOTTSCHO-SCHLEISNER
HAL HARRISON
GRANT HEILMAN
HORT-PIX
HOWLAND ASSOCIATES
EMIL JAVORSKY
WARD LINTON
JOHN A. LYNCH
ELVIN MCDONALD
FRANK LOTZ MILLER

J. FRANCIS MICHAJLUK
MARY NOBLE
MAYNARD PARKER
ROCHE
H. SMITH
GEORGE TALOUMIS
C. G. TRIBERGEN
U.S. DEPT. OF AGRICULTURE
TOM WIER
THOMAS L. WILLIAMS

GARDENER'S READY REFERENCE CHART

BASIC POTTING MIXTURE

4 parts coarse builder's sand
2 parts sedge peat pr peatmoss
1 part dried cattle manure
1 part vermiculite

add to each bushel:
8 level tb. superphosphate
8 level tb. cottonseed meal
4 level tb. sulfate of potash
4 level tb. ground limestone

To increase drainage:
double the sand

To increase moisture retention:
double the peat

PLANTING DEPTH FOR SEEDS

Small seeds
broadcast over soil surface and tamp

Large seeds
plant at 3 times depth of seed diameter

Bloom in Early Spring

Bloom in Spring

SNOWDROPS — CROCUS — PUSCHKINIA — GLORY OF THE SNOW — SQUILL — SNOWFLAKE — IRIS RETICULATA — SPECIES TULIP — ANEMONE BLANDA